CHAMPIONSHIP TENNIS

Frank Giampaolo

with Jon Levey

Human Kinetics

Library of Congress Cataloging-in-Publication Data

Giampaolo, Frank.
  Championship tennis / Frank Giampaolo with Jon Levey.
    p. cm.
  Includes index.
  1. Tennis--Training. I. Levey, Jon. II. Title.
  GV1002.9.T7G53 2013
  796.342--dc23

                              2012038830

ISBN-10: 1-4504-2453-8 (print)
ISBN-13: 978-1-4504-2453-0 (print)

The web addresses cited in this text were current as of January 2013, unless otherwise noted.

Acquisitions Editor: Justin Klug; **Developmental Editor:** Laura E. Podeschi; **Assistant Editor:** Tyler M. Wolpert; **Copyeditor:** Patrick Connolly; **Indexer:** Alisha Jeddeloh; **Permissions Manager:** Martha Gullo; **Graphic Designer:** Joe Buck; **Graphic Artist:** Kim McFarland; **Cover Designer:** Keith Blomberg; **Photograph (cover):** JC Salas/Icon SMI; **Photographs (interior):** © Human Kinetics, unless otherwise noted; **Photo Asset Manager:** Laura Fitch; **Visual Production Assistant:** Joyce Brumfield; **Photo Production Manager:** Jason Allen; **Art Manager:** Kelly Hendren; **Associate Art Manager:** Alan L. Wilborn; **Illustrations:** © Human Kinetics, unless otherwise noted; **Printer:** United Graphics

We thank the Lake Forest Beach and Tennis Club in Lake Forest, California, for assistance in providing the location for the photo shoot for this book.

Human Kinetics books are available at special discounts for bulk purchase. Special editions or book excerpts can also be created to specification. For details, contact the Special Sales Manager at Human Kinetics.

Printed in the United States of America   10 9 8 7 6 5 4 3 2 1

The paper in this book is certified under a sustainable forestry program.

Human Kinetics
Website: www.HumanKinetics.com

United States: Human Kinetics
P.O. Box 5076
Champaign, IL 61825-5076
800-747-4457
e-mail: humank@hkusa.com

Canada: Human Kinetics
475 Devonshire Road Unit 100
Windsor, ON N8Y 2L5
800-465-7301 (in Canada only)
e-mail: info@hkcanada.com

Europe: Human Kinetics
107 Bradford Road
Stanningley
Leeds LS28 6AT, United Kingdom
+44 (0) 113 255 5665
e-mail: hk@hkeurope.com

Australia: Human Kinetics
57A Price Avenue
Lower Mitcham, South Australia 5062
08 8372 0999
e-mail: info@hkaustralia.com

New Zealand: Human Kinetics
P.O. Box 80
Torrens Park, South Australia 5062
0800 222 062
e-mail: info@hknewzealand.com

E5669

This book is dedicated to Lisa.

Contents

Preface

Like every sport, tennis is constantly evolving. The level of play on the pro tours continually sets new standards which trickle down to the mere mortals littering the adult leagues and junior ranks. Because the competition has gotten bigger, faster, and stronger, a new training methodology has been created. What Andre Agassi did well, Rafael Nadal does better. And as the game continues to evolve, one of you will surely be the next innovator. Shake hands with the racket to learn a forehand? That has gone the way of the Walkman. Tennis has long since entered its digital age.

The purpose of this book is to assist players and coaches in developing every aspect of the modern game at an accelerated rate. It starts by evaluating a player's current skills and organizing a personalized blueprint for development. After that comes laying down a solid foundation of fundamentals to build upon. Then each pillar of the game is enhanced using revolutionary stroke principles, teaching concepts, and state-of-the-art drills. Insights into mental and emotional training are covered in great detail. Components such as strategy, tactics, conditioning (physical and mental), and proper practice regimens are all presented to help the player advance through the different levels of competition.

For players wishing to accelerate the learning curve at the quickest rate, customization is the key. Too many players and coaches use a one-size-fits-all approach. No two players are exactly alike and neither should their training methods. Accelerated learning demands strong consideration of a player's brain and body types (genetic predisposition), as well as previous athletic and tennis achievement. In this book, readers will quickly understand how to tailor a developmental program to their individual needs rather than adapt to a fixed, singular model of teaching. Even though two players can be of similar ability, their development and training may be polar opposite.

Anyone with the desire to pick up the sport for the first time will find this book an excellent reference providing both information and inspiration. And for those who have played tennis, but want guidance toward significant improvement, this book will offer a wealth of invaluable new insights. Regardless of ability or experience, all players looking to enhance their games using the latest teaching concepts can use *Championship Tennis* as their ultimate tennis resource.

Acknowledgments

To Linda, I am honored to have you as my wife.

To my tennis mentor, true visionary, and dear friend, Vic Braden. Vic changed the entire world of professional tennis coaching.

To Chuck Cannon. Chuck's soulful dedication to the craft of writing prepared me to take each subject and go deeper, then deeper again.

To Jonathan P. Niednagel. John's brilliant system of brain typing engrosses me on a daily basis.

To Brian Antecki. Brian's superior knowledge of tennis-specific, off-court training helped me fill in the blanks in chapter 12.

A special thank-you goes to my partners in this project:

Jon Levey (cowriter). Jon's expert attention to detail polished the rough edges and made this book shine.

Bob Silverstein (literary agent). Thanks again, Bob, for putting this whole crew together. Without you, it would not have happened.

Lastly, the great staff at Human Kinetics publishing, including Justin Klug, Laura Podeschi, and Laurel Plotzke. You made this two-year project painless.

—Frank Giampaolo

To Frank for letting me tag along on his book. You put your heart and soul into developing players. Your students are lucky to call you their coach.

Bob Silverstein for setting up this partnership and getting the project off the ground. It's heartbreaking that we have to cross the finish line without you. I will miss our talks about Grand Slams and bestsellers.

Laura Podeschi, Laurel Plotzke, Justin Klug, Tyler Wolpert, and everyone at Human Kinetics who made this book possible.

Martin Barnard, Nick Saviano, and Paul Roetert for sharing their advice and experience.

All the great coaches and players I've collaborated with and learned from over the years. I hope some of that wisdom found its way into this book.

To all those hackers and hopefuls who are addicted to smacking a fuzzy yellow ball over a three-foot-high net. You're the lifeblood of the sport. Keep searching for that perfect forehand.

My parents, Julie and Mark, for putting a racket in my hand, getting me hooked, and feeding my addiction.

And to Allison, my doubles partner in life. You cover so much more than your half of the court. I couldn't play this game without you.

—Jon Levey

Key to Diagrams

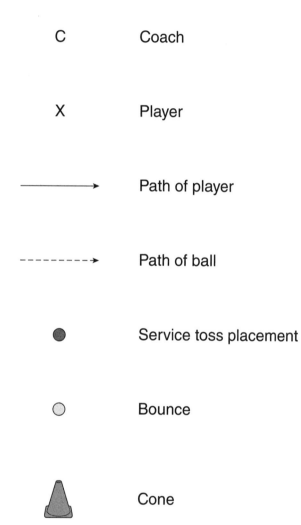

C   Coach

X   Player

⟶   Path of player

-------➤   Path of ball

●   Service toss placement

○   Bounce

      Cone

Athlete Assessment

chapter 1

Player Profiles

Nature versus nurture is one of the oldest debates in sports: Are great athletes born or made? Are innate physical qualities—size, speed, and coordination—more important than learned behaviors? Scientists and coaches have rallied back and forth over the issue. Most agree that it would be foolish to boil it down to an either–or conclusion. Plenty of evidence supports the belief that both factors play an integral part in an athlete's development. The influence of either factor generally depends on the athlete. From this perspective, every player's profile is unique. To maximize the player's potential, the player and coach must understand the player's genetic predisposition along with personal life experiences.

BRAIN TYPING

When establishing a player profile, the best place to start is between the ears. For something that seems so physical, playing sports, especially tennis, is truly a mental endeavor. The root of brain typing dates to the 1920s and the pioneering work of Carl Jung, a renowned Swiss psychologist. His 1921 book, *Psychological Types,* theorized that people generally fall into specific mental categories that define behavior. During World War II, the mother–daughter team of Katharine Briggs and Isabel Myers used Jung's teachings to design a personality type questionnaire in order to help women find suitable jobs as they were entering the industrial workforce. That questionnaire eventually evolved into the Myers-Briggs Type Indicator, first published in 1962. Although neither Briggs nor Myers was formally educated in psychology, their psychometric questionnaire has become the world's most widely used personality assessment tool.

In the past two decades, sport scientists have been using brain typing to assist in athletic profiling. In my own experience, I have seen my students achieve remarkable improvements when we have redesigned their developmental plans to fit their brain types. It starts with players discovering and embracing a playing style that suits their personality. Tennis is a difficult sport, and it becomes even more difficult when players struggle to find their playing identity. Improvement takes time, and it won't occur if the process seems boring and laborious to the player. This cuts to the heart of the "nature" dynamic of development: A player must choose a style that comes organically.

For example, 11-year-old Sarah and her mother came to one of my tennis workshops that focused on the mental and emotional aspects of the game. At the time, Sarah was struggling with an inflated ranking in the 12-and-under division of Southern California. After I gained her trust, Sarah confided to me that she didn't like tennis—she found it horribly boring. Then I asked Sarah several questions in an effort to discover her genetic predisposition (in other words, her nature). I followed those with questions about her training (or how she was being nurtured on and off the court).

Sarah was being taught by a South American clay-court specialist. He had fitted Sarah with a Western forehand grip and systematically began to develop Sarah's game in the model of his own defensive, patient style of play. Sarah complained, "He makes me hit 300 groundstrokes in every lesson. Nothing else! I never get to serve or volley. I just hit the same boring groundstrokes from 15 feet behind the baseline. I hate it. I want to quit!"

Sarah shared a similar brain type with all-court offensive players such as Roger Federer, Andy Roddick, and Pete Sampras. After explaining the importance of brain and body types (described next) to Sarah and her mother, I suggested that she give tennis three more months using a redesigned developmental plan. After one year of training with the style and patterns that develop an all-court player, Sarah found herself ranked number 1 in her age group in Southern California. The following year, she was ranked number 1 in both the girls' 14 and 16 age divisions simultaneously. Sarah would go on to earn a top 300 WTA ranking and play in the U.S. Open by age 15, and end up with 10 U.S. national junior titles.

Sarah is far from the only example. Hundreds of my students have improved exponentially once they adopted a developmental plan that fit their brain design. This is not to say that a player with a certain brain type can't be nurtured to play a style that is not intuitive for that player. Both Roddick and Sampras had success early in their junior careers using a counterpunching, defensive style of play. Who knows what would have happened if their developmental advisors had insisted that they continue in that style? My guess is that their professional careers would have turned out much different. We may have never even heard of them.

Let's peek into the tennis world and see how a player's brain type, or preferred intelligence, may affect the player's performance style, strengths, and weaknesses on the court:

Extroversion Because extroverts draw energy from action, they generally prefer to make things happen with a proactive style of play. They often enjoy the socialization and harmony of good doubles.

Introversion Introverts draw their energy through quiet reflection. In many cases, they feel comfortable behind the baseline in a counterpuncher role (refer to the Playing Styles section later in this chapter). Introverts often hesitate when they have the opponent in a vulnerable position; thus, they often miss opportunities to gain an on-court positioning advantage. Introverts commonly prefer the solitude of singles over doubles.

Sensing Sensates make on-court decisions based on concrete evidence. They enjoy details and facts. Sensates only rush the net after they have digested all the necessary data and have determined that attacking is an acceptable behavior. For a sensate, playing it safe is the logical protocol on the court.

Intuition Intuitive players have a deeper level of trust in their hunches. They rely on their sixth sense or their gut instinct. An intuitive player might say, "I had a feeling he was choking, so I attacked!" Intuitive players would be wise to apply intelligent between-point rituals instead of winging it.

Thinking Thinkers are more detached from the emotional climate of the match. They use systematic logic rather than random choices for shot selection. Thinkers prefer being truthful over being tactful, so they generally have no problem dealing with on-court confrontations.

Feeling Feelers express emotions easily on the tennis court. They are frequently heard verbalizing their feelings during match play. Feelers express empathy toward an opponent who is performing badly, and in many cases, they are easy prey to the drama of a crafty opponent's gamesmanship.

Judging Judgers enjoy predictability, routines, and rituals. They take satisfaction in running the same old boring—but winning—patterns over and over again. They rely on percentage play to gain the upper hand.

Perceiving Perceivers habitually enjoy the freedom to be spontaneous. On the doubles court, perceivers unknowingly surprise their partner as much as the opponents. Perceivers are comfortable adapting to and applying a wide range of secondary shots and patterns. Because a perceiver's mind is often focused on the future rather than the present, this type of player commonly has a difficult time closing out leads.

To learn more about brain typing, visit www.braintypes.com.

BODY TYPING

Besides matching a playing style to their personality, players must also recognize their body type. The two predominant body types are classified as gross motor skills and fine motor skills. Being a sport of both power and finesse, tennis demands proficiency in each:

Gross Motor Skills Gross motor skills require the use of large muscle groups—the legs, core, and shoulders. This is where a player derives most of the power for a shot. Resistance training, swimming, biking, and yoga are good cross-training exercises for developing gross motor skills.

Fine Motor Skills Fine motor skills require the use of smaller muscle groups—the forearms, wrists, and fingers. Players with well-developed fine motor skills are said to have "good hands" and generally thrive hitting touch shots. Arts and crafts, drawing, playing a musical instrument, and carpentry are a few cross-training techniques for enhancing fine motor skills.

ATHLETIC HISTORY

Another important consideration in the player profile is a player's previous athletic history. Although two players may be at a similar ability level, their sports backgrounds may necessitate vastly different developmental models. For instance, a few months ago, Kaitlin and Laura signed up for the free Tennis Across America clinic offered at my club. This was a beginners' clinic that would be run by my assistant pro, Jay. Before the clinic, I offered Jay one quick piece of advice: "Make sure you ask the players about their backgrounds in sports." Jay responded that the players were all beginners. What difference would it make?

Five minutes into the clinic, Jay was nervous and confused. It turned out that Kaitlin was an Olympic gold medalist in volleyball. She had spent thousands of hours developing the physical, mental, and emotional tools of a world-class competitor. Before long, she started whipping topspin forehands over the net that had her fellow beginners backing up to the fence. Laura, on the other hand, failed to make contact with any of the three balls that Jay fed her. She had spent thousands of hours developing her accounting skills at a major law firm. She had never played sports before or even owned a pair of decent athletic shoes. Although these two women fell into the beginner category, their skills were worlds apart.

This is an extreme example, but it underscores the importance of recognizing differences in players. Someone with a background in dance may have wonderful balance, footwork, and cardiovascular endurance but may struggle mightily with eye–hand coordination. Working on making clean contact with the ball should be this player's primary order of business. Conversely, someone with many years of baseball experience may strike the ball beautifully but may stumble around the court and rarely be in position to do so. These two players may be of similar ability, but what they bring to the court greatly influences how they should play and develop.

PLAYING STYLES

Once players are fully attuned to their personality, body type, and athletic foundation, they can more effectively adapt their playing style. Having an innate stylistic preference leads to numerous advantages. The player

- has the knowledge to hire coaches and trainers who possess personalities best suited to accelerate her learning curve;
- has the confidence that comes with knowing exactly how she performs best;
- has the ability to lure opponents out of their preferred style and force them to play out of their comfort zones;
- is able to impose her best style, strategies, and tactics on the most important points;
- improves her ability to reach the goal of mastering a minimum of three playing styles—called A, B, and C game plans—which adds depth and variation to the player's game; and
- can select a stylistically complementary doubles partner to help form a winning team.

Though there are subtle variations, six basic playing styles are seen in tennis. Let's review each of these styles and how the styles match with a player's personality.

Net-Rusher   Given the shift toward baseline play in the modern game, the true net-rusher is becoming more difficult to find. Usually possessing a strong serve and volleys to back it up, a net-rusher loves to apply relentless pressure and keep the points short. Groundstrokes are viewed as a means for advancing forward so that the point can be determined at the net. Patience can be a liability to the net-rusher, because this type of player prefers 2- or 3-ball rallies. Net-rushers rely on quick feet and reflexes to cover the net and pick off passing shots. With such weapons, net-rushers generally thrive on the doubles court.

All-Court Player   All-courters have well-rounded, fully developed games. They can be flexible in their style of play depending on the conditions, the surface, and the opponent. They feel at home in offensive, neutral, and defensive situations and can quickly adapt to any of the three. Medium-length rallies of 8 to 10 balls don't faze them, but eventually they will go for a bold winner from any court position. Having a deep repertoire of shots and styles is advantageous most of the time, but it can also be a curse. The all-courter can sometimes lose focus, become too experimental, and wander from a winning game plan.

Baseline Counterpuncher   Some players thrive on using their opponents' strengths against them. When playing against a net-rusher, these players execute their passing shots and lobs. If they're up against a big hitter, they enjoy taking the ball early, changing the direction, and taking away the opponent's recovery time. Counterpunchers possess solid groundstrokes, good court coverage, and excellent stamina. They don't mind long rallies, and they relish the idea of wearing down opponents. Because counterpunchers retaliate rather than initiate, they can fall victim to opponents who successfully take pace off the ball by using height, depth, and patience. Many counterpunchers don't possess the weapons to hurt opponents who play a retrieving style of tennis.

Aggressive Baseliner   This has become the most prevalent style on the professional tennis tours. Aggressive baseliners try to dictate play from the center of the court, usually with a powerful forehand. They are usually physically strong, and they hit with lots of pace and spin, trying to elicit a short ball that they can crack for a winner. This is a macho style of play in which the player looks to end points within 4 to 6 shots with a winner rather than wait for an opponent's mistake. When playing well, aggressive baseliners can blow people off the court. On the other hand, if they're misfiring or playing a talented counterpuncher, they can implode in a hail of ill-advised shots and unforced errors.

Retriever   Although hitting winners feels very satisfying, most points end courtesy of a player's miscue. Retrievers understand this, and nothing pleases them more than allowing their opponents to self-destruct. At the club level, where unforced errors greatly outnumber winners, the retriever is still the most challenging opponent. Retrievers have ample patience, determination, speed, and endurance. They have steady groundstrokes, and 20-ball rallies are standard operating procedure for them. Grit, more than any stroke, is the retriever's primary asset. But that also means that retrievers are usually reactive and at the mercy of their opponent's tactics.

Finesse Player   Finesse players possess excellent fine motor skills and enjoy hitting with angles and touch. They like using all the dimensions of the court by executing delicate drop shots or well-placed lobs. Manipulating the ball trajectory with high, looping topspin or low slice is also a staple of the finesse game. With the changes in speeds and the use of deception, these players are sometimes even referred to as "junk ballers." Because they are rather creative, they tend to not have a very high shot tolerance, and big hitters can overpower them. But their soft hands and inventiveness make them rather effective on the doubles court.

MOTIVATION

A few years ago, after winning Wimbledon, a famous WTA tour veteran said that her desire to win came from the fact that her boyfriend had recently broken up with her. She used this setback as added incentive to work toward another title. In essence, she was proving to him that she's a winner. Extrinsic forces—such as pleasing a parent or coach or proving a naysayer wrong—can be powerful motivators, as can intrinsic forces such as enjoyment, the gratification of mastering a sport, the need for exercise, and wanting to be part of a group.

For players to get the most out of tennis, they must know what they are hoping to accomplish. Is it making the club team? Receiving a college scholarship? Finding an activity to enjoy with friends? Motivations can change throughout the course of a player's career, but most experts agree that self-motivation is imperative for long-term success. Once players familiarize themselves with what they hope to accomplish, designing a proper developmental plan becomes much easier.

FINDING THE RIGHT COACH

The surest way for a player to get the greatest fulfillment and enjoyment out of tennis is to find a coach who is best suited to the player's needs. This can take some effort. There's nothing wrong with testing out a coach and moving on if that coach isn't the right fit. (Remember Sarah's problem earlier in the chapter?) There's also nothing wrong with using multiple coaches for different parts of the game as long as there's no overlap. Using two different teachers to fix the serve can result in conflicting information and battling egos. But using one for the serve and another who specializes in groundstrokes can be an effective combination. In the early stages of development, however, most players choose their coaches based on cost, proximity, and availability. Once players move into more competitive stages of the game, they should identify those who possess the coaching styles and personalities that are most effective for furthering their development.

There are eight primary types of coaches, although some fit into multiple categories. Different styles may be appropriate at different stages of an athlete's career.

Detailed Analyzers   These are strong technical coaches who like to break down a player's strokes to the core elements, often employing the use of video replay.

Off-Court Fitness Experts   Although these coaches know tennis, they specialize in the conditioning aspect of it. Players with established games or those primarily looking for a workout will be attracted to this type of coach.

Fun Lovers   Such coaches are kind-hearted and easygoing. They appeal to players who see the court simply as a place to enjoy themselves.

Hitters   These coaches may not be great technical instructors, but they are highly skilled players. This is a good coach for players who are looking for someone to compete against. The forte of these coaches is the "playing lesson."

Psychoanalysts   Many of these coaches have studied sport psychology and can help students who struggle with the mental or emotional challenges of tennis.

Strategizers   Such coaches prefer to discuss the Xs and Os of a match and the characteristics of an opponent rather than the nuances of personal technique, movement, or focus control.

Academy Recruiters   This type of coach works in tandem with other like-minded coaches who believe that competition between students fosters the greatest success.

Drill Sergeants   These coaches employ a no-nonsense, demanding approach that works well with students who respond to tough love.

Coach's Corner

Here are some tips to consider when selecting a coach:

- **Realize that only a handful of coaches actually teach the top players.** What should be of interest is not whom the coach says he has coached, but whom the coach has trained under.

- **Look for coaches who love what they do.** This kind of attitude is contagious. Players can't help but be further drawn into the sport when they train with coaches who are passionate.

- **Seek out pros who are so busy that they don't need more business.** As the old saying goes, there's safety in numbers. These coaches must be doing something right if their court time is continually booked.

- **Remember that being a master coach is a learned experience.** Just as it takes thousands of hours of practice for athletes to hone their skills, the same is true for teachers.

- **Seek out a pro who understands genetic predisposition.** A one-size-fits-all approach should be unacceptable. A coach has to embrace the unique brain and body type of each individual in order to customize the lessons.

- **Contact tournament directors in your area.** These people know which coaches are producing champions. Contacting these people is an important step for players who have the goal of winning tournaments and achieving a high ranking.

- **Observe the coach.** Ask coaches if you can see them in action. This provides a much better way to understand their style. A player could also pay coaches to watch and chart one of his matches and then devise a game plan for improvement. This helps the player evaluate how much knowledge the coaches have and their eye for the game, as well as determine if the player's and coaches' developmental plans match.

- **Realize that being a great player doesn't always translate into being a great coach.** Just because someone enjoyed success as a player at a top college, in the challenger circuit, or even on the pro tours doesn't mean that the person knows how to coach. Some of the game's most accomplished coaches were marginal players.

- **Avoid coaches who discourage working with other coaches, hitters, or trainers.** This shows a lack of confidence and a lack of interest in the growth of their students. Coaches should encourage independent, not dependent, thinking from their students.

From *The Tennis Parent's Bible* (www.thetennisparentsbible.com). © Frank Giampaolo.

FINDING THE RIGHT SUPPORT TEAM

At every level of tennis, an entourage means something a little different. For top pros, this may include agents, public relations specialists, personal trainers, and even fashion stylists and celebrity friends. These are obviously not part of the equation for average players. For them, the entourage is more of a support team, and most of the members of this team don't travel to or see the player's matches. In addition to a coach, the average player's entourage may include a physical trainer, racket stringer, and playing partner.

Physical Trainer   Besides finding the right coach, serious competitive players often seek out physical trainers who specialize in sport performance. These experts can advise players on the types of exercises and routines they should be doing to improve performance and prevent injury.

Racket Stringer   Another member of the player's support team should be an experienced racket technician. A string job done at a big box store can be adequate, but it will not be exceptional. A player should do research and find a person who knows how to skillfully string a racket and customize the frame (add weight and alter the grip). This person should also know all the latest equipment offerings.

Playing Partner   Whether to take in a regular practice match, improve a specific stroke or strategy, or team up for a doubles tournament, a dependable and like-minded playing partner is a valuable asset. In fact, it doesn't hurt for a player to have several playing partners at his disposal. Besides giving the player options if one playing partner is unavailable, it also offers him varying playing styles to practice against.

chapter 2

Stroke and Tactical Evaluations

Let's say that we are sitting in my hometown of Laguna Beach, California. "Meet me at Tennis West Sports and Racquet Club in El Paso, Texas," I say as I toss you the keys to my car. You have no maps and no instructions—just a car and a full tank of gas. The ride would take longer than it should, and the process would at times be maddening, but eventually you would probably still find the club. Now if the car has a navigation system with the address already plugged in, the trip would certainly be easier. And if the navigation system also reroutes for traffic jams and construction delays, the trip would be even faster, less stressful, and a more pleasurable experience. Well, think of this book's evaluation chapters as a customized navigation system that maximizes potential at the quickest rate. Whatever the goal, having a detailed road map is the most efficient and effective way for a player to achieve it.

The evaluations that follow will uncover each player's confidence and ability levels in performing strokes as well as in executing tactics. These components are the foundations of competitive tennis.

To make these evaluations meaningful and effective, the components should be evaluated based on how they hold up under match conditions. In other words, hitting second serves from a hopper of balls on a relaxed practice court is not a good indicator of the dependability of the player's second serve. The true barometer is whether the player's second serve is reliable when the score is 5-6 in a tiebreaker.

The player may also want to consult a coach, parent, or playing partner to gain another perspective on his game. This second opinion can often be eye opening. Many players aren't completely honest with themselves or don't recognize their shortcomings. For instance, consider the three versions of a forehand: offensive, neutral, and defensive. A player may have a terrific offensive forehand, capable of crushing any ball bouncing short in the court. He may consider this his money shot. Yet a coach may reveal that the neutral and defensive characteristics of the player's stroke are underdeveloped and unreliable under stress. In the player's opinion, the forehand doesn't need improvement, but in reality, it could use a lot of work.

STROKES

The sample self-evaluation in table 2.1 addresses inadequacies related to strokes. A blank version of this form is available for download at www.humankinetics.com/products/all-products/championship-tennis. To complete the self-evaluation, rate your confidence level in each listed skill, using a scale of 1 to 5 (very low to very high). Feel free to include any related notes. Don't worry if some of the topics listed are unfamiliar. This simply means that you're leaving a comfort zone and entering a learning zone. Each component in the evaluation will be touched on in later chapters of the book. Be sure to give enough time and careful scrutiny to each element. Speeding through the evaluation will only hurt the process. If done properly, the evaluation will provide you with a list of strengths to build on and weaknesses to strengthen.

Table 2.1 Stroke Evaluation

Skill	Rating	Notes
FOREHAND		
Topspin drive	4	This is my bread and butter.
Topspin loop	2	If I'm hitting high, I'm usually hitting long, too.
Short angle or side door	1	I'm not sure what this is.
Slice	5	I'm like a Ginsu on the court.
BACKHAND		
Topspin drive	2	Backhands are my downfall.
Topspin loop	1	I'm completely hopeless on this shot.
Short angle or side door	1	I'm not sure what this is.
Slice	4	I can bring opponents in with my slice.
VOLLEY		
Traditional punch	3	This is the only one we practice.
Swing volley	1	What's this?
Drop volley	2	I've got hands of stone on these shots.
Half volley	1	I'm not sure what this is.
Lob volley	1	It never even occurred to me to try one.
SERVE		
Flat	5	I've got a bomb first serve.
Slice	3	I'm not bad at taking my opponents out wide.
Kick	1	This concept escapes me.
RETURN OF SERVE (POSITION)		
Behind the baseline	1	I refuse to give up ground when I'm returning.
On the baseline	4	This is where I stand.
Inside the baseline	3	If the opponent has a weak serve, I'll move in.

Skill	Rating	Notes
APPROACH SHOT		
Traditional approach	3	This is my best ticket to the net.
Moonball approach	1	What's that?
Swing volley approach	1	I don't know what this is, either.
Slice approach	3	My backhand is effective, but I don't even bother on my forehand.
OVERHEAD		
Stationary	4	I can nail short overheads.
Moving	2	My footwork is borderline laughable on these.
LOB		
Topspin lob	2	I'm OK off the forehand, but it's not even worth trying off the backhand.
Slice lob	4	I'm much more comfortable hitting this type of lob off both sides.
Relob	1	What's that?

From *The Tennis Parent's Bible* (www.thetennisparentsbible.com). © Frank Giampaolo.

TACTICS

The sample self-evaluation in table 2.2 addresses inadequacies related to tactics—one's ability to strategize on the tennis court. Again, a blank version of this form is available for download at www.humankinetics.com/products/all-products/championship-tennis. As in the previous evaluation for strokes, when completing this self-evaluation, you should rate yourself on a scale of 1 to 5 (very low to very high) for each strategy. Feel free to include any related notes. Again, it's OK if some of the components included are unfamiliar to you. Each one will be touched on later in the book. Be sure to review every element thoroughly. That way, at the end of the process, you will have a list of strengths to build on and weaknesses to improve.

Table 2.2 Tactical Evaluation

Skill	Rating	Notes
Implementing game plan A	1	My plan is always to attack and play offensively.
Implementing game plan B	1	It's one way or no way.
Implementing game plan C	1	A third option? Let's work on B first.
Stroke consistency	3	I can keep four balls in most of the time.
Stroke placement	3	I don't have radar, but I'm pretty decent at hitting my spots.
Using zonal tennis (air zones and court zones)	1	What's this?
Playing offensively	4	I love to attack.
Playing defensively	1	If I'm on my heels, I'm in serious trouble.
Sustaining neutral rallies	3	This is not my best, but clearly not my worst, skill.
Use of percentage shot selection	1	What's this?
Playing the elements	2	We play indoors because I hate the wind.
Exposing your strengths	4	I like my forehand, so I run around the backhand.
Hiding your weaknesses	3	I don't give away too much.
Self-charting (awareness during the match)	1	I don't know how to do this.
Dissecting the opponent	2	I play every opponent pretty much the same way.
Controlling playing speeds	2	I'm stuck in fifth gear.
Elongating points	1	How do I do this?
Beating hard-hitting baseliners	3	I've had success going toe-to-toe with these players.
Beating moonballers and pushers	1	It's a total train wreck when I play against these guys.
Beating all-court players and net-rushers	3	I like a target, so their pressure games don't bother me too much.

From *The Tennis Parent's Bible* (www.thetennisparentsbible.com). © Frank Giampaolo.

Once you have completed these evaluations and have read through the contributing chapters, you will have a fully customized road map that leads to rapid improvement in strokes and tactics. This blueprint is clearly laid out for accelerated success; all that's left to do is to turn this plan into action.

chapter 3

Physical Fitness and Emotional Stability Evaluations

Most people would agree that champions train like champions well before they win their first titles. They understand the importance of developing the four components of winning: stroke mechanics, tactics, physical fitness, and emotional stability. The evaluations in chapter 2 focused on the first two components, strokes and tactics. The evaluations in this chapter focus on the other two components, fitness and emotional stability. Although all four components are essential in developing a champion, the physical and emotional aspects of the game are those most likely to be neglected when developing players.

Tennis players around the world spend countless hours on the practice courts diligently perfecting their strokes, yet the ability to win tournaments ultimately depends on physical fitness and emotional control. Solid strokes will get you in a tournament and strong tactics will lead you to early-round wins, but fitness will catapult you deep into the draw and emotional stability will secure you the trophy.

PHYSICAL FITNESS

The sample self-evaluation in table 3.1 addresses inadequacies related to physical fitness. A blank version of this form is available for download at www.humankinetics.com/products/all-products/championship-tennis. To complete the self-evaluation, rate your confidence level in each listed skill area, using a scale of 1 to 5 (very low to very high). In the heat of competition, how dependable is this aspect of your game? Once again, be diligent and deliberate in these assessments. Give each category real thought and don't be afraid to seek second opinions from a coach, parent, or playing partner. Just as with the evaluations in chapter 2, you shouldn't worry if some of the categories are unfamiliar to you. All the topics will be covered later in the book.

Table 3.1 Physical Fitness Evaluation

Skill	Rating	Notes
Up and back movement	4	I'm in my element moving north and south.
Lateral movement	1	My feet are practically stuck moving from side to side.
Aerobic fitness	3	I don't feel that this costs me any matches.
Ability to accelerate	2	I'm quick once I start moving, but it takes me a while to get going.
Ability to decelerate	3	I am good on indoor hard courts, but a klutz outside on clay.
Speed and agility	3	These could be better, but are certainly not a weakness.
Stamina	2	I would like more in the tank come the third set.
Recovery time (between points)	2	I spend too much time bent over and not enough time strategizing.
Recovery time (between matches)	2	The same goes for matches.
Strength (upper body, core, and lower body)	3	My upper body is strong, but my core and lower body need some work.
Body coordination (gross motor skills)	2	All too often, my feet are going one way and the rest of my body is going the other.
Eye–hand coordination (fine motor skills)	4	I've got quick hands.
Flexibility and stretching	1	I do not stretch enough and have limited flexibility.
Anticipatory speed	1	My anticipatory speed is nonexistent.

From *The Tennis Parent's Bible* (www.thetennisparentsbible.com). © Frank Giampaolo.

EMOTIONAL STABILITY

The sample self-evaluation in table 3.2 addresses inadequacies related to emotional stability—one's ability to handle frustration, tension, and anxiety while on the tennis court. A blank version of this form is available for download at www.humankinetics.com/products/all-products/championship-tennis. On a scale of 1 to 5 (very low to very high), rate your confidence level in each listed area. During competitive play, how dependable are these aspects of your game? Again, be thorough in these assessments. Give careful thought to each component, and don't be afraid to seek out second opinions. As with the previous evaluations, if any of the categories are unfamiliar, do not worry. All topics will be covered in the following chapters.

Table 3.2 Emotional Stability Evaluation

Skill	Rating	Notes
Between-point rituals	4	I look at my strings like the pros.
Changeover rituals	2	I don't really have these.
Managing adversity and stress	2	I don't think about doing this during games.
Controlling heart rate	1	How can I do that?
Designing proactive patterns	1	Nah, I just react to whatever happens.
Understanding frustration tolerance levels	1	What are frustration tolerance levels?
Temperament (controlling your emotions)	2	It's good if I'm winning . . .
Distraction control	1	Like what?
Quieting the mind	2	My mind wanders when I get a solid lead.
Adapting and problem solving	1	If my game is off, I'm toast.
Ego and arrogance control	2	I hate to lose.
Controlling lapses in concentration	2	I usually can't go a few games without thinking about off-court stuff.
Controlling nervousness	3	My nerves are rarely too much for me to handle.
Controlling self-condemnation (negative self-talk)	3	I generally don't beat myself up.
Controlling "bad" anger	1	Isn't all anger bad?
Handling cheaters and gamesmanship	4	I'm pretty good at this.
Remaining in the present	1	I'm either looking forward or looking back. It's tough for me to stay in the moment.
Recognizing important points	2	Is this like score management?

From *The Tennis Parent's Bible* (www.thetennisparentsbible.com). © Frank Giampaolo.

Recognizing strengths and limitations in each of the four major components of winning is the critical first step toward improvement. Strokes and tactics generally receive more attention, but the fitness and emotional components are equally important. At the higher levels of the sport, choosing to develop *all* four components can truly decide the outcome match after match.

Skill Development

chapter 4

Groundstrokes

The most glaring example of the game's evolution is found in groundstrokes. It can be argued that the serve is still the most important shot and the greatest potential weapon, but the serve has not seen the metamorphosis that forehands and backhands have undergone over the past generation. Consistency and precision from the baseline are still rewarded, but the modern game demands that players pay greater attention to power and aggression. This becomes even more evident at the higher levels of play. Still, for any shot to be effective, it must be rooted in certain fundamental principles.

GRIP

Every stroke starts from the same essential element: the grip. How a player holds the racket has an enormous impact on the resulting shot. At contact, the angle of the racket face, the ball's distance from a player's body, and the potential spin and pace are all directly affected by the grip. Before any discussion of stroke technique, we need to review the various types of grips and what they offer.

But first, let's look at some basics. The grip has an octagonal shape with four longer and four smaller sides, generally referred to as bevels. The most common reference point in determining the placement of the hand for a particular grip is the base knuckle of the index finger; which bevel this knuckle is placed against establishes the grip. A simple, illustrative way to find different grips is for a player to hold the racket by the throat with his nondominant hand so that the face is perpendicular to the ground. In this position, the player looks at the bottom of the handle, or butt cap, and imagines it as a compass (figure 4.1). If a right-handed player places the base knuckle of the index finger of his dominant hand against the bevel that is directly east (west for a left-hander), this will be an Eastern forehand grip. Shifting the knuckle to the

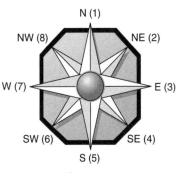

Figure 4.1 The grip as a compass.

bevel directly south would result in a full Western forehand grip. For a Continental grip, the base knuckle should be on the northeast bevel for a righty or the northwest bevel for a lefty. Keep this compass analogy in mind when grips are discussed throughout the book.

Forehand Grip

As discussed in chapter 1, nature and nurture play a tremendous role in an individual's preferred style of play. As the style of play is customized to fit the individual's tendencies, so are the basic stroke components. In other words, what's best for a backcourt counterpuncher may not be what's best for a net-rusher. This applies to grip selection as well.

This book aims to make obsolete the one-size-fits-all approach to tennis development. Although there is no perfect grip system, the most popular and effective on the forehand side at this point is the semi-Western grip (figure 4.2), which has the base knuckle on the southeast bevel for a righty or the southwest bevel for a lefty. Can a player get by with an Eastern grip? Lindsay Davenport racked up some Grand Slams using one. Is it possible to play at a high level with a full Western? Rafael Nadal can speak to that. But at this stage in the evolution of the game, the semi-Western offers the best compromise.

Figure 4.2 The semi-Western forehand grip.

The closed racket face gives a player the ability to impart topspin, yet it's not so extreme that it's difficult for a player to quickly switch to a backhand grip or a volley grip when transitioning forward. Also, because so many players in today's game use some form of a Western grip, balls generally bounce higher, resulting in higher strike zones. A generation ago, the strike zone was predominantly at waist level; now it's more common for players to hit incoming balls closer to shoulder height. The semi-Western grip also allows players to defend and remain offensive on balls hit in this elevated strike zone.

The reason for this is the principle known as incident and reflected angle. Simply put, when a rising ball with heavy topspin hits a vertical wall (or racket face), the ball will travel upward. If a player swings with a vertical racket face—a prominent feature of traditional grips—to return a shot with those characteristics, the resulting shot will generally sail long. It's basic geometry: The incoming upward angle of the ball is matched by the outgoing rising angle (figure 4.3). Tennis evolution, however, found a solution. By sliding more of their palm underneath the racket handle, players were able to close the face slightly at contact. This allowed for better control when returning shoulder-level shots—thus, the popularity of Western grips.

The disadvantage of modern Western grip systems is the loss of versatility, and this comes into play when a player is stretched out and on the defensive, putting the ball well out of her strike zone. The more Western the grip, the more difficulty a player generally has in dealing with these types of shots. To combat this, modern players have learned to use an emergency Continental slice (a secondary stroke) for the occasional low or wide ball (some refer to this shot as a "squash" or "hack" shot). This stroke will be discussed in greater detail later.

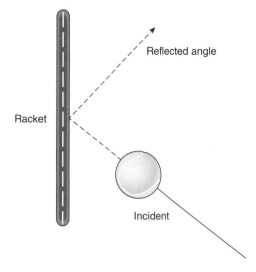

Figure 4.3   Incident and reflected angle.

Backhand Grip

When Chris Evert, Jimmy Connors, and Bjorn Borg achieved great success in the 1970s, the two-handed backhand gained immense popularity. Ever since, a debate has persisted over whether players should use a one- or two-handed backhand. From a technical standpoint, players who fall into the category of having more developed fine motor skills (such as Roger Federer) may be best served by adopting a one-handed grip, thus taking advantage of their talented upper arms and hands. Those players who have well developed gross motor skills (such as Maria Sharapova) are well designed for executing the two-handed backhand because they can generate the angular momentum used in the uncoiling of the larger links of the kinetic chain.

From a practical standpoint, although the one-handed backhand is alive and well, the dominant backhand in today's game is by far the two-handed stroke. The most popular and effective variety has the dominant hand (on bottom) applying the Continental grip, with the nondominant hand (on top) applying the Eastern forehand grip (figure 4.4). To use the compass analogy, the base knuckle on the bottom (dominant) hand would be on the northeast bevel, and the one on the top (nondominant) hand would be on the west bevel.

As with the forehand, players can be successful with subtle variations, or even completely unorthodox grips or styles of play. It would be foolish to demand absolute conformity to what is considered the norm. Every player and every swing is different, and a slight shift on the grip in either direction can have a positive impact. If something works, don't mess with success.

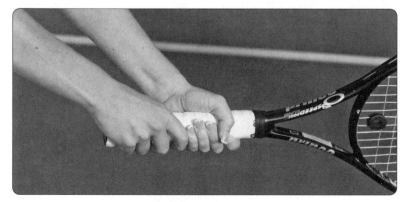

Figure 4.4   The two-handed backhand grip.

Grip Changing

A crucial aspect of the grip is the level of pressure applied by the hands. Many players squeeze the grip too tightly, which tenses the hands and forearms. Although this firm grip gives the feeling of strength and power, it ultimately results in a muscled swing that lacks acceleration.

This is a simple at-home drill that helps players get comfortable holding the racket and making quick, seamless grip changes. Start the drill without holding a racket. Place both hands in front of the chest, facing one another. Position 1 is pointing both thumbs up (figure 4.5a). Quickly rotate to position 2 by turning both thumbs downward until they are pointing at each other (figure 4.5b). Repeat this sequence until the feeling of both hands making a quarter of a turn down feels effortless.

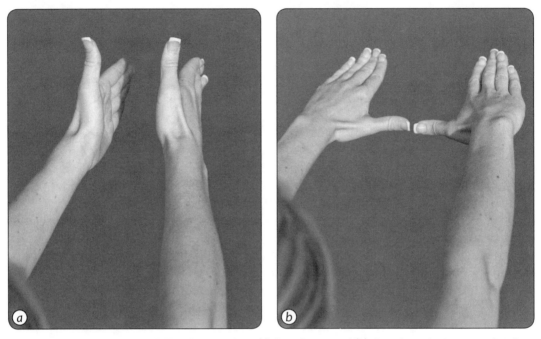

Figure 4.5 Grip-changing drill without racket: (a) thumbs up and (b) thumbs pointing at each other.

Now with the racket, place the left hand on the top portion of the racket handle using the Eastern forehand grip (west), and place the right hand on the bottom of the handle using the semi-Western forehand grip (southeast); see figure 4.6a. Simultaneously, turn both palms down a quarter of a turn just as you did without the racket (figure 4.6b). The left hand continually holds the racket throughout the grip change as the palm of the right hand effortlessly slides from the semi-Western grip to the Continental grip.

Players should repeat this quick drill (the movement takes just milliseconds) off court until they can reproduce the movement subconsciously. This drill is especially good for helping players with two-handed backhands get comfortable switching from forehands to backhands (particularly for returns of serves, when time can be so limited).

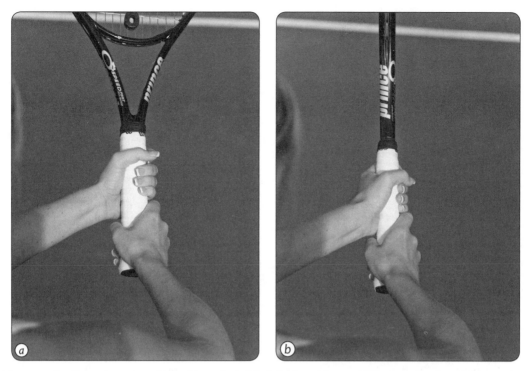

Figure 4.6 Grip-changing drill with racket: (*a*) right hand in semi-Western forehand grip and (*b*) right hand in Continental grip.

STANCE

Once the grip is established, the next part of the hitting sequence for a player to get familiar with is the stance. The debate over open- versus closed-stance groundstrokes has raged for over a decade. Now that the dust has settled, experts agree that players have an advantage when they are able to use all variations and stances depending on the situation.

Closed Stance

A player's ability to develop both an open and closed stance begins with footwork. The traditional closed-stance forehand is struck after a player's nondominant, or lead, foot has stepped toward the net. If the player were standing on a clock face, the back foot would be at 6 o'clock, and the front foot would be positioned at nearly 12 o'clock. The player's feet are almost perpendicular to the net (figure 4.7*a*). For a closed-stance backhand, the feet are reversed (figure 4.7*b*).

The closed-stance forehand should not be confused with a crossover-step forehand, an emergency stance in which the front foot crosses completely in front of the body and points toward the side fence. This footwork locks the hips which inhibits core rotation and can cause balance issues. The stance should only be used in extreme defensive situations when the player is on a dead run and has zero time to apply a more desirable setup.

Figure 4.7 The closed-stance (a) forehand and (b) backhand.

Open Stance

The open-stance forehand is struck after the player steps to the side to line up the incoming ball with the dominant leg. To use the clock analogy again, for a right-hander, the dominant foot is standing on 3 o'clock, and the nondominant foot is around 9 o'clock (reverse the positions for a lefty). In this stance, the player's feet are nearly parallel to the net (figure 4.8a). For an open-stance backhand, a player will line up the incoming ball with the nondominant leg (figure 4.8b).

Uses

The traditional closed-stance, or square-stance, groundstroke is most effective when a player gets a short ball and is moving forward on the offense. Use of the closed stance enables the player to flatten out an offensive stroke, gain forward momentum, and decrease the opponent's recovery time. These benefits are particularly important when coming to the net. When players transition to net using a traditional closed-stance groundstroke, their center of gravity is moving into the court. This gets them closer to the net for the first volley. (Benefits of closing in tighter at the net will be covered in chapter 5.)

On the other hand, open- and semiopen-stance groundstrokes are more often used in neutral and defensive situations. Because of the prevalence of Western forehands and two-handed backhands, the primary contact point for many players is just to the side of the body. This later contact point aids in preparation time and helps disguise a player's intentions, making an open stance very appealing. Plus, with this type of stance, it takes less time for the player to decelerate, set up, and then recover for the next shot than with a traditional closed stance, making it more effective for court coverage.

Figure 4.8 The open-stance (*a*) forehand and (*b*) backhand.

BACKSWING

As a player is moving into close proximity to the strike zone, the backswing begins. Early preparation is, of course, still required to ensure proper stroke mechanics. Proponents of old-school methodology are adamant about taking the racket straight back in preparation for the incoming ball. Although this isn't necessarily bad advice, it's not the optimal way to set up for a swing. Biomechanical studies show that when players take their rackets back—approximately 3 feet (91 cm) behind their body—it is actually only the first half of the process. Once the kinetic chain begins to uncoil forward into the court, the racket is forced back another 3 feet. When the racket finally starts forward toward contact, it has to travel back 3 extra feet just to return to the original take-back position. That's 6 unnecessary feet added to the backswing. This results in a longer, horizontal swing path that leads to a loss of depth and topspin.

Instead of a *backswing,* a more efficient approach is to take a side swing: The player starts with the racket head out to the side of the body, somewhere between waist and shoulder height (whatever feels most comfortable); see figure 4.9*a*. Then, once the kinetic chain begins, the racket naturally moves back 3 feet directly behind the strike zone (figure 4.9*b*). This makes for a much smoother and more fluid swing, resulting in more consistency and power.

Figure 4.9 Moving the racket to the side on the backswing results in a smooth, fluid swing.

STRIKE ZONE

Although the most critical element of any groundstroke is the strike zone, it seems to attract the least amount of attention. Let's start with a basic definition: The hitting zone, or strike zone, is the 3-foot (91 cm) racket path window in which the strings may contact the ball.

The preferred contact point of most players is waist level about a foot in front of the body. This is commonly referred to as the power zone. The racket passes through the strike zone faster than our eyes can register, but that hasn't prevented many well-intentioned people from inaccurately speculating on what happens during this critical moment. Common myths such as "the windshield wiper" movement and "rolling over the ball for topspin" have played havoc with countless forehands.

The truth is that the strike zones of world-class players are remarkably similar. In fact, analyzing strike zones of tour players is quite boring. A professional's motor program fires the same way time after time. His racket face is smooth and quiet throughout the hitting zone. On the other hand, an amateur's racket face often wavers, dips, and rolls, resulting in inconsistent shot placement. Andre Agassi can be late or early on any swing, and his shots still go in. Why? Because he maintains a quiet racket face entering and exiting the hitting zone. Those recreational players who have been instructed to roll over the ball for topspin are fighting a losing battle. If they roll a millisecond too early, the ball winds up in the net; a millisecond late and it's 10 feet long.

Traditional methods of development focus on the tunnel-vision approach or singular development of the waist-level strike zone. That's fine, but it's incomplete. Although every player would love to hit every shot around waist level, this will never happen.

Adjustments in footwork and stroke mechanics have to be made. The backswing, strike zone, and follow-through of a groundstroke are greatly influenced by the incoming ball's trajectory, speed, and path. Sticking with this book's theme of maximizing potential at the quickest rate possible, players must practice in the manner in which they are expected to perform. Let's take a deeper look at the three primary hitting zones.

Waist-Level Strike Zone

In the waist-level strike zone, or primary strike zone, the ball is hit when it reaches the height of the player's waist (figure 4.10). When hitting the ball in this strike zone, the player should use a compact loop backswing, along with a closed racket face that drops about a foot (about 30 cm) below the contact point before accelerating up to the strike zone. At impact, the racket face should be quiet and vertical.

Figure 4.10 Hitting the ball at waist level.

Coach's Corner

Players often ask, "If contact occurs in a few milliseconds, how can I analyze it?" Modern technology offers a wonderful solution that's absolutely free and always available: YouTube. Yes, the website that's home to videos of cats napping and bad karaoke also has a vast reservoir of high-speed films of top tennis professionals. Simply go to the site and search for your favorite player and the desired stroke. You'll likely be able to watch a slow-motion replay of a perfect hitting zone.

Below-the-Waist Strike Zone

In this modification, the ball is struck below waist level (figure 4.11). When using the below-the-waist strike zone, a player may need to use an abbreviated loop backswing or no loop at all, depending on the severity of the incoming ball. The lower the ball or the more rushed a player is, the less of a backswing that is needed. The player should accelerate forearm speed to quickly lift the ball over the net and should apply additional topspin to bring the ball back down into the court. If the ball is too low or too far away from the strike zone, the player may need to switch to a Continental grip (especially on the forehand). This grip promotes a more open racket face, making it easier to get underneath the ball and return it over the net.

Figure 4.11 Hitting the ball below the waist.

High Strike Zone

In this modification, the player hits the ball above waist level (figure 4.12). When using a high strike zone, the player uses a compact loop backswing and a vertical racket face at shoulder height, about a foot below the contact point. The player decelerates on the follow-through over and down, and the racket finishes around the opposite hip.

Note that a player who contacts a still rising ball with a vertical racket face will see his shot travel well beyond the baseline. This is because of the cause and effect of incident and reflected angles. The solution for keeping a head-level, rising ball from sailing long is to meet it with a slightly closed racket face. This will lower the trajectory of the reflected angle.

Figure 4.12   Hitting the ball above the waist.

Coach's Corner

Here's a common scenario: John takes a lesson on Friday with his local teaching pro. The pro feeds every ball right to John's primary strike zone. After a half hour of hitting these perfectly placed balls, John thinks, *Forget the club tournament tomorrow—I'm going pro!* John leaves the lesson feeling great about his game. The next day, he draws a moonball pusher in the first round of the tournament. The opponent plays at two speeds: slow and slower. He also hits with a higher trajectory than John is accustomed to, forcing John to hit at head level all match long. Not surprisingly, John goes down in flames. After the match, he thinks, *I don't get it. I was on fire yesterday. I'm great in practice, but I stink in a real match.*

The moral of this story? Players must practice in the manner in which they are expected to perform. This is why some players feel good about themselves during lessons but seldom improve. Accelerated learning means practicing shots in those pesky secondary strike zones so that they're second nature during competition.

FOLLOW-THROUGH

After the player makes contact, there should be a relaxed deceleration as the upper arm and racket flow over the opposite shoulder. As mentioned earlier, because of differing ball heights and grips, players may also occasionally finish the stroke by the opposite hip. That's perfectly acceptable. What's most important is that the racket slows down in a controlled manner so that the player maintains good balance and can properly recover for the next shot. The ball is long gone at this point, and a violent follow-through garners no extra power.

On the forehand topspin drive, the trigger (index) finger of the dominant hand remains underneath the grip through the hitting zone until the dominant shoulder touches the chin. Then the racket can release, and the wrist can turn over (figure 4.13). For the two-handed backhand, the trigger finger would remain until the back, or nondominant, shoulder rotates around and touches the chin (figure 4.14). The one-handed backhand requires a full extension forward of the hitting arm before the player rotates the wrist over (figure 4.15).

Figure 4.13   The forehand follow-through.

Figure 4.14   The two-handed backhand follow-through.

Figure 4.15 The one-handed backhand follow-through.

CONNECTING THE SEQUENCE

Now that we've established the core elements of the groundstroke, let's put them all together into one fluid motion. The key to mastering fundamentally sound strokes lies in the art of removing all the unnecessary additions that will rob the player of potential power and control—and potentially even cause injury. Players often believe that they need to add to their game in order to improve. This is not always the case. The secret to improving a groundstroke often lies in trimming the fat off the existing stroke rather than adding more to the stroke. The body parts that are traveling toward unwanted directions are the flaws in a player's strokes.

To begin to trim the unwanted fat off their strokes, players can use the following guidelines for the positions of fundamentally sound groundstrokes.

Forehand

When it comes to the forehand, remember that less is more. A compact, relaxed, and fluid swing that results in a steady racket face at contact will pack more consistent punch than a longer, wilder swing that is more difficult to control. A famous former player once said that if it looks like you're trying, you're probably not very good.

The six positions of a fundamentally sound forehand are as follows:

1. Begin in the ready position, with the elbows away from the body and with the knees bent and slightly more than shoulder-width apart (figure 4.16a).

2. As the ball approaches, coil the upper body to the right and stop with the racket hand at head level; the right elbow is up and away from the body (figure 4.16b). As stated earlier, the modern backswing is essentially a side swing.

3. Drop the racket head to knee level and close the face by angling it toward the ground (figure 4.16c).

4. Begin a 30-degree lift, imparting a gradual low-to-high flight pattern, stopping with the racket head as close to vertical as possible at the point of impact (figure 4.16d).

5. Extend the racket toward the target for an additional 2 feet (61 cm) until the right shoulder meets the chin (figure 4.16*e*).

6. Relax the tension in the arms as the racket decelerates across the left shoulder (figure 4.16*f*).

Figure 4.16 Fundamentally sound forehand sequence.

Spacing

In the early 1990s, I did high-speed video analysis of players' strokes and discovered that a large majority of mis-hits occurred because of the player being too close to the ball at impact. Mis-hits also resulted from the player being too far away from the ball, but being jammed was clearly more prevalent. This is why proper spacing plays such a large role in clean stroke production. Hitting effectively on the move is a requirement for high-level play, and it's something that must be practiced repeatedly.

This is a great drill for developing the footwork required for proper spacing. An experienced feeder is mandatory for this quick-paced drill. The feeder customizes the ball's speed, spin, and trajectory to suit the player's ability level.

Begin with the coach standing with a basket of balls, positioned behind the ad-side doubles alley. The coach will deliver a rapid-fire two-ball sequence to the player's forehand wing at three different stations on the court.

1. The player begins by standing behind the baseline on the opposing ad-side corner. The coach feeds a high deep ball directly at the player. The player has to run around to the side of the ball and space herself to hit an aggressive inside-out forehand. As the ball is struck, the coach feeds another ball, this time short and inside the service box. The player has to move into the court, properly space herself away from the ball, and once again hit an inside-out forehand (figure 4.17a).

2. The player quickly slides back to the baseline, this time at the center hash mark, and the coach repeats the sequence—deep ball followed by short ball (figure 4.17b). The player continues to direct her shots toward the coach's corner.

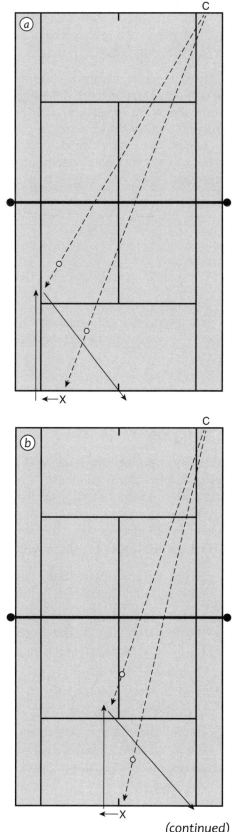

Figure 4.17 Spacing drill: beginning from (a) the ad side and (b) the center hash mark.

(continued)

3. The player quickly slides back to the baseline, this time to the deuce-side corner. The coach again repeats the sequence of deep ball followed by short ball (figure 4.17c). The player's target remains the coach's corner of the court.

After the player hits from all stations, repeat the stations with the coach drilling to the backhand wing. Next, repeat the drill for both the forehand and backhand with the coach standing behind the deuce-side doubles alley. This corner of the court now becomes the player's target area.

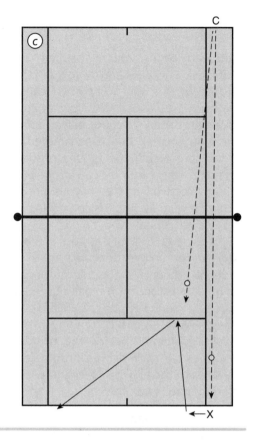

Figure 4.17 (continued) Spacing drill: beginning from (c) the deuce side.

Backhand

Attitudes regarding the backhand have evolved a great deal since the game of tennis was first introduced. At one time, the backhand was seen as the weaker sibling to the forehand, serving as a bridge until a player could use that weapon. Now, however, when players have the right technique and mentality, the backhand can be the more dependable and even more destructive wing.

The six positions of a fundamentally sound backhand are as follows:

1. Begin in the ready position, with the elbows away from the body and with the knees bent and slightly more than shoulder-width apart (figure 4.18a).
2. Coil the upper body to the left while simultaneously changing to the backhand grip (figure 4.18b). Again, the modern backswing is essentially a "side" swing.
3. Drop the racket head to knee level and close the face by angling it toward the ground (figure 4.18c).
4. Begin a 30-degree lift, imparting a gradual low-to-high flight pattern, stopping with the racket head vertical at the impact point (figure 4.18d).
5. Extend the racket toward the target for an additional two feet until the left shoulder meets the chin (figure 4.18e).
6. Relax the tension in the arms as the racket decelerates across the right shoulder (figure 4.18f).

Figure 4.18 Fundamentally sound backhand sequence.

Turning on the Off Hand

The challenge of the two-handed backhand lies in the player's use of the off hand. Electromyography studies (studies used to analyze electrical signals created during muscle contractions) show that professionals and club players differ greatly in this area. Professionals most often use greater muscle contractions in their off arm. In other words, right-handed players hit left-handed dominant forehands on their two-handed backhands. At the club level, it's much more common for players to have the uncoordinated nondominant arm act as a drag.

Here's a very simple way to learn a two-handed topspin backhand: The right-handed player grips the racket handle firmly with her left, or nondominant, hand in a full Eastern forehand grip (left-handers would grip the racket with their right hand). The player gently holds the racket handle with only the thumb, index, and middle fingertips of the right (left for lefties), or dominant, hand (see figure 4.19). By getting players to hit what are essentially lefty forehands (or, as is the case for lefties, righty forehands), this accelerated learning drill teaches the players the most effective way to use their off hand on a two-handed topspin backhand.

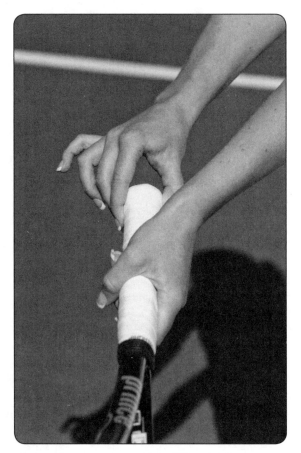

Figure 4.19   Turning on the off-hand drill.

PRIMARY AND SECONDARY GROUNDSTROKES

The beginning and intermediate stages of stroke development often resemble a game of catch. Players are content to simply hit the ball back and forth. At the advanced levels, training starts to look more like a game of keep-away.

To maximize potential and accelerate the learning curve, players should begin by understanding the components of winning groundstrokes. To the untrained eye, perfect primary strokes are the main reason for players reaching the advanced levels of tennis, just as being tall is a prerequisite for playing top-flight basketball. But if just being tall was all it took to play in the NBA, my cousin, Big Vinnie, wouldn't be driving a limo at Kennedy Airport.

Owning only primary strokes in tennis—or unusual height in basketball—is usually not enough. For players to experience accelerated learning, they need to develop additional tools and skills, or what are known as secondary strokes.

A good comparison that can be used to help players understand the importance of these strokes is to look at the differences between amateur and professional painting. Anyone looking to get started in painting generally begins at the same place: a prepackaged painting set that comes with a canvas or paper, brushes, and a strip of colored paint containing basic colors. As the person dabbles more in painting, though, one thing becomes evident: Using only basic colors makes the painting look amateurish. Advanced artists and professionals have learned that to make a painting jump off the canvas—to make it become lifelike—they need to use secondary colors as well. Instead of applying 1 shade of green, they may use up to 12 different versions.

The process of developing groundstrokes into weapons follows a similar principle: A player should start with a base version and then enhance it with three secondary options.

Primary Groundstrokes

This bread-and-butter shot is often the sole weapon of intermediate players: a hard-driving net skimmer that lands in the center of the court. Although this shot looks terrific, it's actually the easiest shot for opponents to handle, generally landing near the service line and bouncing up to waist level right into their primary strike zone. Getting adequate net clearance and depth is essential; otherwise, the shot becomes a batting-practice fastball that's ready to be tagged.

Secondary Groundstrokes

Versatility is the hallmark of any successful competitor. Repeatedly hitting the same type of stroke in terms of pace and height is a predictable and beatable formula. To become well-rounded players and, more important, tougher opponents, players must add the following types of shots to their arsenal.

High-Looping Groundstrokes

High-looping groundstrokes are used to push the opponent back behind the baseline to create gaps on the court. They're also effective for buying time when players are scrambling or in defensive positions. When a high-looping shot lands deep, this also forces an opponent to hit from an elevated strike zone. This can cause havoc, often producing errors or return shots that land short in the court. Because of the geometry of the court, the latter result provides a positional advantage, giving the player an opportunity to move up inside the baseline to hit offensive shots into the gaps created by the high-looping strokes.

Figure 4.20 High-looping groundstroke sequence.

The player should focus on ball height over the net, rather than pace, as the barometer for this shot. The elevated arc will achieve the requisite depth and a higher ball bounce. A slightly exaggerated low-to-high brushing motion will also help add height and topspin (figure 4.20); the topspin provides safety by bringing the ball down in the court and also enhances the resulting bounce.

Short-Angle (Side-Door) Groundstrokes

In a tennis match, most players prefer hitting hard to running hard. A short-angle, or side-door, shot is a terrific short-ball option that forces opponents to produce shots from an uncomfortable position. Instead of crushing the ball back, a player creates a short angle and demands movement, fitness, and agility from the opponent. Like any undeveloped tool, this is a risky option if attempted without training and repetition. When executed properly, however, it results in taking opponents' legs out from under them (wearing them out), putting opponents on the extreme defensive, or even giving the player an outright winner.

Unlike the high looper, the target window over the net for this shot is typically lower than on a standard drive. Because this is a crosscourt shot, the ball travels mostly over the middle, or lowest part, of the net. Adding extra spin, especially topspin (figure 4.21), helps bring the ball down quickly into the court, and the resulting bounce can drag the opponent even farther outside the court.

Figure 4.21 Short-angle groundstroke sequence.

Slice Groundstrokes

A slice shot imparts underspin to the ball, making it skid and stay low after the bounce. This exposes the weakest strike zone for opponents who use a Western or semi-Western grip. A low slice will land short and force opponents off the baseline into no-man's land, challenging them to either continue forward to the net or retreat to the baseline. Slice is also the spin used on drop shots, an important weapon versus skilled retrievers or players with limited movement. Keep in mind that the best slice strokes usually result in limited ball rotation. When players try to exaggerate the spin, this produces a ball that floats over the net and sits up after the bounce.

For this shot, the optimal technique is for the player to change to a Continental grip (though on the forehand, the player might be able to get away with an Eastern forehand grip). Rather than using a severe high-to-low swing path, the player employs a moderate high-to-low trajectory (almost level, similar to the shape of a stretched-out letter *U*) in order to cut the ball and apply the spin (figure 4.22). Envision driving the ball versus imparting an overabundance of backspin.

Figure 4.22 Slice groundstroke sequence.

Shot Sequencing

This shot-sequencing drill helps players develop consistent strokes while increasing their decision-making skills. This exercise is easily adapted to a player's forehand or backhand side. Advanced players may even combine both strokes in a random fashion.

A ball machine or feeding coach is required for this drill. Begin with the player standing on the baseline on the center hash mark. Balls are fed to the player, who returns them in a sequence of the four types of forehands (or backhands): primary drive, high-looping topspin, short-angle topspin shot, and slice shot. Once the player is comfortable with the sequence, begin to incorporate flexible skills training. This is done by having the player call out his intended shot before hitting the ball. For instance, shouting "angle" would mean hitting a short-angle stroke. The sequence is entirely up to the player.

This quick decision-making drill helps a player reduce hesitation because it speeds up the motor program (the signal transferred from the brain to the muscle groups). Quicker decisions equate to smoother strokes and fewer unforced errors.

GROUNDSTROKE MYTHS

Unfortunately, tennis is full of stock teaching methodology that should be banished—well-intentioned, catchy phrases that have become dated or, worse yet, were never even correct to begin with. Here are a few of the bigger culprits concerning groundstrokes.

Roll over the ball for topspin. This is a favorite among TV commentators. Sadly, countless teaching pros are still using this phrase, too. Players try to time the racket roll at contact, resulting in shots that spray all over the court.

Here are the facts: Depending on the type of shot, the ball is on the strings for about 2 to 4 milliseconds. It takes another 150 to 200 milliseconds for an electrical signal to travel from a player's hand back to the brain. The brain then sends a new motor program back to the muscle group to begin the wrist roll. This takes an additional 150 to 200 milliseconds, by which time the ball is now 8 to 10 feet off the racket face toward the opponent's side of the court. In other words, it's impossible to roll over the ball for topspin. The spin comes from the brushing motion of a low-to-high swing path.

Watch the ball hit the strings.   As mentioned earlier, the human eye cannot register a two-millisecond event. No one has ever seen a ball hit the strings. It's simply a blur. Keeping the head down and still through contact is the best recipe for a steady racket path through the strike zone. Watch film of the best baseliners, and it's easy to see how quiet they keep their head during their groundstrokes.

Skim the net.   On television, it appears that professionals barely clear the net on their groundstrokes. This is rarely the case. The deception occurs because the television cameras at pro tour events are often placed high in the stadium. This angle offers a clear view of match play, but it distorts the trajectory of the ball flight.

In actuality, players use a variety of heights, generally dictated by their court positioning. This is often the result of managing the time between hits. When players are on the defensive, they generally hit higher to buy more time for recovery. Conversely, they move forward and hit harder and lower to take time away from a vulnerable opponent.

At the club level, a ball that barely clears the net lands midcourt and bounces perfectly into an opponent's primary strike zone; this is not recommended unless losing is the main objective. The net skimmer only becomes a smart choice when the opponent is transitioning to or established at the net and a passing shot is in order, or when an opponent is well behind the baseline and the player wants to bring her in, specifically if the opponent is weak at the net.

Stay down on groundstrokes.   A player's center of gravity plays an important role in generating power and depth on groundstrokes. Three critical elements lift up on world-class strokes: the knees, the backside, and the racket face. Even on slice backhands, all three critical elements rise at completion of the stroke. If not, the resulting shot will lack pace and penetration. Players who prematurely lift their head before contact do indeed need to "keep their head down" through the shot. But it's a fallacy to apply the principle to the entire body.

Keep your eye on the ball.   This is correct . . . half the time. Vision control plays various functions over the course of a point that are critical for consistent ball striking and court coverage. Narrow vision is applied on an incoming ball: watching it leave the opponent's racket, cross the net, and bounce up and into the strike zone. In this regard, a player should absolutely be keeping an eye on the ball.

Broad vision, on the other hand, is used to spot the dozens of visual clues after the ball leaves the racket toward the opponent's side of the court. Such clues include an opponent's court position, body language, strike zones, swing speed, and swing length. Broad vision is a crucial component of anticipatory speed. The best movers know how to assimilate the information from their broad vision and instinctively adjust their positioning accordingly.

chapter 5

Volleys

If groundstrokes have evolved and moved to the forefront of the modern game, especially at the higher levels, then volleys have been the component retreating to the background. It's not that the skill is no longer important or worth developing; approaching the net is still an effective tactic and a core ingredient for successful tennis. But given the prevalence of aggressive baseline play, it has become increasingly difficult for players to find opportunities to transition forward. Plus, once a player does take a position in the forecourt, the pace and heavy spins applied to passing shots make it that much more challenging to volley effectively. But by using an assortment of primary and secondary approaches, along with gaining a better understanding of when to attack (which will both be further explored in subsequent chapters), a player can make volleying a trusted asset.

BRAIN TYPES AND VOLLEYS

Why do some players rush the net with abandon while others stay glued to the baseline? Some players are so allergic to the net that after moving inside the baseline with an offensive opportunity, they will slam on the brakes and retreat. Others can't wait to get off the baseline and make something happen.

Eduardo Rodriguez is a student of mine. He's known around Newport Beach, California, as "Steady Eddie." Eddie has never gone to the net, and he never will (though that hasn't prevented him from winning most 4.5 NTRP tournaments in Orange County). Before a match, Eddie will run two miles around the track at the local high school just to loosen up and get his game plan in order, so obviously a lack of fitness or the unwillingness to move are not reasons for his reluctance to approach the net. Why do players such as Eddie despise moving forward, then? Conversely, why do other less mobile players enjoy the thrill of attacking the net?

In chapter 1, we discussed the importance of preferred intelligence and its influence over a player's style of play. Such inborn personality traits show themselves in all their glory when an individual makes the split-second decision on whether or not to attack the net. Therefore, understanding a player's comfort level at the net and how he can achieve success there begins with understanding personalities within styles of play. As an example, let's break down how a counterpuncher's perspective on match play would differ from that of a net-rusher:

Counterpuncher	Net-rusher
Patient	Impatient
Wants opponent to self-destruct	Wants to hit bold winners
Energy conserving	Energy expending
Responds after reasoning	Responds before reasoning
Inspired by the real or practical	Inspired by the imaginative
Thinks in the present	Thinks in the future
Concerned with the task	Concerned with the outcome and the perception of it
Organized in thoughts and plans	Improvisational
Avoids surprises	Enjoys surprises

As demonstrated, understanding the psychological profile of a player, an opponent, or even a doubles partner can be quite revealing. Simply instructing a player (such as the counterpuncher in the previous example) to play more aggressively and attack the net is a foolish directive if that player is not wired to do so. Frustration is guaranteed when a player is asked to perform under stress in a manner that is outside her comfort zone or unique design. With that said, even devout baseliners can become accomplished volleyers with practice. For these players, success at the net will build confidence and eliminate their fear of moving forward. Rushing the net will never be the focal point of their game plan A, but it can develop to the point of being a component of game plans B and C.

Rafael Nadal rose through the rankings thanks to his punishing groundstrokes and superior court coverage. Along his way to number 1, he continually worked on his net game and turned what was once considered a liability into a strength. So now when he is compelled forward by a short ball, or after putting his opponent in an extremely defensive position, he can confidently end the point with a volley.

READY POSITION

All strokes start from a singular universal ready position, right? Wrong. In the modern era of tennis, a large majority of tour players, as well as recreational players, use two-handed backhands. So while positioned on the baseline—and not knowing which side the next ball is coming to—they stand with both hands on the racket handle. But if they move forward into a traditional volley situation, their left (or nondominant) hand slides up to the throat of the racket, while the right (dominant) hand adjusts to a volley grip. Those who employ a two-handed backhand volley, which is not normally recommended, would simply keep both hands on the grip.

Depending on the types of groundstrokes and grips used, a player's ready positions on the baseline and for the volley can vary greatly. That's why many professionals take advantage of having two very different starting positions. A player with a one-handed backhand will only need to address the grip change. Ideally, players should set their net ready position as though they are going to hit a backhand volley, with the feet slightly more than shoulder-width apart, the knees flexed, the weight on the balls of the feet, and the racket out in front (figure 5.1).

Figure 5.1 Ready position at the net.

GRIP

The classic methodology is to use one universal grip to hit all volleys. Because time is at a premium at the net, it makes sense for players to hold the racket in a way that allows them to seamlessly hit either a forehand or backhand from down around the feet up to eye level. And the grip of choice for this has generally been the Continental grip (northeast on the grip compass for righties and northwest on the grip compass for lefties; figure 5.2). This grip is still the best option on the backhand volley and is not a bad choice for the forehand volley.

However, if there's time for a player to step toward the ball before contact, there's also enough time to switch grips. A slight adjustment toward a modified Continental to Eastern forehand grip gives the player a better foundation on the forehand wing. Pete Sampras was a master at this.

Here are three important reasons why switching grips at the net is so helpful:

1. When using the Continental grip, players often have consistency issues on both the down-the-line and high forehand volleys.

Figure 5.2 The Continental grip.

Applying the added strength and dexterity it takes to displace the wrist in order to properly position the racket face in the optimal strike zone is more difficult than making a subtle grip adjustment in the preparatory phase.

2. High-speed video of tour players hitting volleys shows clearly that they adapt their grips to accommodate the desired racket face angle at impact.

3. If there are primary and secondary types of volleys, it stands to reason that the grips for these should reflect the differences. Although the traditional punch and drop volleys may benefit from the Continental grip, players can incorporate their groundstroke grips for the swinging and half volleys. The one-size-fits-all volley grip is becoming obsolete.

Throughout the backswing and follow-through phases of strokes, players should apply light, relaxed hand pressure on the grip. This promotes relaxed, fluid strokes because it prevents mechanical and rigid movements. Extensive grip pressure often leads to unnecessary stress, which causes early fatigue and injury. Grip pressure is applied through the brief strike zone of a volley (or any other stroke). The player can simply squeeze the bottom three fingers of the hitting hand at contact. Instability in the wrist at contact, which can result from too little grip pressure, leads to a lack of power and direction.

THREE STAGES OF A WORLD-CLASS VOLLEY

Once the ready position and grip are established, the rest of the volley sequence falls into three main parts: advancement, preparation, and impact. As with any stroke, each segment connects to the next. The proper execution of one makes the subsequent part that much easier and more effective.

Advancement

Players move forward after they have identified—and decided to exploit—a vulnerable opponent. Developing the desire to take advantage of these situations is a prerequisite to mastering this part of the volley sequence.

By advancing forward, the player profits from simple geometry: The closer the player is to the net, the more angles there are available, and the better the player's chances of hitting an effective volley (figure 5.3). The advance forward could be a result of offense (a heavy forehand or big first serve), defense (a lob pushing the opponent way behind the baseline), or a miscue (an opponent hitting a poor shot that lands short in the court).

Recognizing cues from an opponent that indicate an opening has been created is a learned behavior. This is called an anticipatory skill. The success of the player's advancement can often be determined by how quickly the player spots a wounded opponent and transitions to the net, thereby limiting the opponent's recovery time and ability to regain equal footing in the rally.

Preparation

After the player advances forward, there is a brief moment when the player gathers himself with a split step (figure 5.4)—a little hop onto the balls of the feet performed right around the time that the opponent is about to start the backswing. The split step puts a player into the ready position and allows him to spring in any direction with equal ease to better intercept the passing shot or cover the lob. Advanced players will sometimes recognize a completely vulnerable opponent and wisely skip the approach shot and split step. In this situation, the player charges straight to the net and steals a volley.

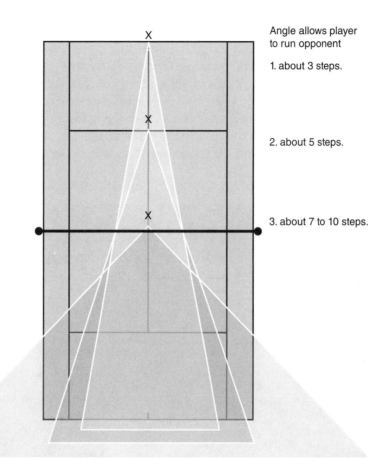

Angle allows player to run opponent

1. about 3 steps.

2. about 5 steps.

3. about 7 to 10 steps.

Figure 5.3 The closer the player gets to the net, the more angles open up to run the opponent.

Figure 5.4 The split step.

If the player does need to perform a split step, he is now ready to spot the intended location of the incoming ball. Once this occurs, the preparation part of the swing begins. This is the synchronization of the upper-body coil (figure 5.5)—or shoulder turn—with the desired placement of the backswing for the optimal strike zone. Ideally, the length of the backswing is the distance the racket travels while the player is turning the shoulders; the racket face should be lined up at the level of the incoming ball. This is true on both the forehand and backhand volleys. On the backhand volley, added assistance is provided by the nondominant hand on the racket's throat, which can help position the racket.

Figure 5.5 Upper-body coil.

However, the backswing and strike zone can be modified depending on the quality and location of the opponent's shot. The five basic modifications of the volley's strike zone are low (figure 5.6*a*), medium (figure 5.6*b*), high (figure 5.6*c*), stretched wide (figure 5.6*d*), and body (figure 5.6*e*).

At this stage, the player also starts to lay the groundwork for volley choices. When hitting a knee-level volley from around the service line, a player may choose to hit a "building" volley that is deep in the opponent's court and allows for more progress toward the net and a more offensive position. If the opponent's shot is floating softly, this may be an opportunity to close quickly and finish the point with a high-volley winner. Adjusting to the situation is a critical factor at the preparation stage.

Figure 5.6 The five modified strike zones for the volley: (a) low, (b) medium, (c) high, (d) stretched wide, and (e) body.

Impact

Hitting a successful volley begins with the transfer of energy through the kinetic chain into the ball. This movement starts from the feet and culminates with the racket. There's an old saying that good volleying is done from the legs. The best volleyers understand the importance of moving their body forward and into the shot. The general rule is to step forward with the nondominant foot on a forehand and with the dominant foot on a backhand. The only swinging motion on a standard volley is the uncoiling of the shoulders to bring the racket to the contact point.

World-class volley technique applies the art of acceleration–deceleration. A compact, violent acceleration through contact is needed, followed by an abrupt deceleration of the racket head. Using a large swing causes issues related to control and consistency.

The player should time the impact so that the racket meets the ball just in front of the hitting shoulder with a square racket face, as though catching the ball on the strings (figure 5.7). The player should drive the racket through impact with a short, controlled follow-through. This is often referred to as a "punching" motion, but think of it as a jab rather than a roundhouse hook. A compact volley motion uses the pace of the opponent's passing shot and redirects it back to the desired location.

Figure 5.7 At impact, the player catches the ball on the strings and then follows through.

Transitioning or moving through the volley can often be advantageous. Advanced volleyers will accelerate through a volley, but they will almost never stop. They smartly keep their center of gravity moving forward into the court. An old-school tip that people sometimes give to volleyers is that they should stop and volley. This tip is outdated. Think of an automobile stopping abruptly. The inertia pulls the front end of the car violently downward. If a volleyer abruptly stops, the same laws of physics apply. This violent, downward acceleration most often pulls the ball directly into the net.

Running through the volley benefits the net-rusher in three distinct ways:

1. It puts the rusher in a tighter net position, which translates into hitting more volleys higher in the strike zones.

2. It limits the opponent's passing shot angles.

3. It offers greater angles to finish the point with a winning volley.

Transition Volleys

Remember this book's motto: "Practice in the manner in which you are expected to perform." To accelerate the learning curve at the net, try this fun, multitasking drill. It assists in improving fitness, movement, spacing, and agility. The drill also helps players learn to spot when they should attack—finding the first, second, and even third volley in a sequence.

Ask a friend or a coach to feed a vulnerable ball from the baseline, followed by two randomly placed strokes. The mission of the volleyer is to start at the baseline, run through a midcourt transition volley off the first feed, and systematically track down and put away the remaining two feeds with volleys. The volleyer then backpedals to the baseline and repeats.

SECONDARY VOLLEYS

The previous section describes the technique for the traditional punch volley, which is one of the four fundamental shots of the game and is the stroke used most often at the net. But several other types of volleys are also useful weapons in the forecourt, and these shots round out a potent net game. Following are the four main variations.

Swing Volley

Although it's within the volley genre, the swing volley is essentially a groundstroke struck out of the air. A player generally uses the swing volley while transitioning forward to the net and intercepting a soft floating ball that can be driven. The grips used are the same as those for the player's groundstrokes. Because the shot is usually executed from well inside the baseline, the player should contact the ball above net level, around shoulder height (figure 5.8). A low-to-high brushing motion is required; this brushing motion applies topspin to help bring the ball down into the court quickly. The player should avoid the temptation to hit down on a dropping ball.

Figure 5.8 Swing volley.

Drop Volley

The drop volley is a volley that bounces two or more times before reaching an opponent's service line. The value of this shot is that it forces an opponent to defend inside the court. Two of the evolutionary elements of the modern game are the backcourt position of baseliners as well as their grip systems. Most often, opponents are found 5 to 10 feet (1.5 to 3.0 m) behind the baseline. This defensive court position makes it difficult to track down a drop volley. Also, the most common grip systems are the Western or semi-Western grip. These grips are custom made to handle deep, high strike zones but are extremely vulnerable on short, low balls.

Hitting drop volleys requires touch. Instead of punching the volley, the player practically catches the ball on the strings (figure 5.9). The idea is to take all of the pace out of the passing shot and delicately drop it over the net. Players who are adept at hitting these shots are often said to have "soft" hands.

Figure 5.9 Drop volley.

Tap–Catch

Although some players seem to be naturals at the drop volley, fostering this kind of finesse is a learned behavior. The tap–catch drill helps players develop such finesse. In this exercise, a player stands inside the service line in the ready position. A ball is fed to the forehand, and the player gently taps the ball with a high-to-low brushing motion to apply mild backspin (figure 5.10a). The ball should only travel about a foot (about 30 cm) up in the air. The player then catches the ball with the nondominant hand (figure 5.10b) and repeats. After a set amount of attempts, switch to the backhand side.

Once the player establishes the proper feel, the player should progress to applying the same technique while feathering the drop volley over the net.

Figure 5.10 Tap–catch drill.

Half Volley

A half volley is struck immediately after the bounce. This secondary volley may be executed by using abbreviated groundstroke grips and techniques or by applying volley grips and techniques, depending on the player's position on the court. If the player is in between the service and base lines, she can return the shot using a modified groundstroke. Because of the condensed timing of the shot, modifications include an abbreviated backswing, a lower center of gravity, a deeper knee bend, a slight low-to-high swing path through the strike zone, and an abbreviated follow-through (figure 5.11).

Figure 5.11 Half volley using a modified volley technique.

If the player is positioned inside the service line, then the volley grips and techniques will likely be applied. Modifications include a lower center of gravity, a deep knee bend, an open racket face, and a slight low-to-high swing path through the contact zone, which allows for a higher degree of lift (figure 5.12). Often, because of the low, vulnerable strike zone, half volleys struck from inside the service box should be performed using the drop volley technique.

Figure 5.12 Half volley.

Lob Volley

This is another touch volley that is used to lift the ball over an opposing net player's head. The lob volley is a delicate shot because it needs enough arc to successfully get over the opponent's head without sailing past the baseline. The technique is similar to the standard volley except the racket face is more open in order to promote the higher shot (figure 5.13). Also, instead of punching through the shot to drive the volley, the player uses a swing path that is more of a gentle incline. There's no need for pace on this shot because placement is the key result.

Figure 5.13   Lob volley.

BROAD VISION

Once stroke fundamentals are solidified, the next step in achieving volley success is incorporating vision control—more specifically, shifting from narrow vision to broad vision. Narrow vision is applied when the incoming ball is approaching a player's racket. At this stage, a player should just be focusing on the ball. Broad vision comes into play once the ball leaves a player's strings and travels across the net to the opponent's side of the court. At this stage, a player can recognize a host of cues that can affect strategy, such as the following:

- Where in the court the ball is landing
- The opponent's court positioning
- The opponent's body language
- The opponent's contact point or strike zone

- The opponent's swing speed, path, and length
- The opponent's recent history in similar situations

Being able to see the big picture on a tennis court enhances the art of educated guessing. Developing the ability to read passing shots is just as important as developing proper volley form. Why? Because a player must find the ball before hitting it. No matter how good the stroke mechanics, if a player is not in position to use them, it won't matter. Developing this ability will turn an average net player into a net master. For instance, the volleyer should understand these points:

- The best option off a ball landing close to the sideline is usually a down-the-line pass.
- The best option off a deep ball landing close to the baseline is the defensive lob.
- The best option off a short ball landing in the center of the court is usually a cross-court short-angle pass.

By understanding the high-percentage passing options, a player has a greater chance of establishing a winning position against them. An educated net-rusher shuts down the preferred play and makes the opponent go for the riskier pass.

VOLLEY MYTHS

Just as with groundstrokes, volleys have a number of faulty teaching concepts that shadow them. These directives aren't necessarily completely wrong, but they don't give players the opportunity to maximize their volleying techniques. Here are a few of the prime culprits:

Stand close to the net to practice volleying. Instead of practicing stationary volleys, players should focus on practicing midcourt or transition volleys. These are the volleys that players hit more frequently in matches and that ultimately determine how well the players perform at the net.

Stop moving before volleying. Moving through the volley is much better than stopping, volleying, and then starting to move again. When the feet of a player in motion abruptly stop, the upper body often continues forward and collapses over. Consequently, this pulls the volley in a downward path into the net.

Volley with one grip. Players can volley with one grip, and if they are content and effective with that setup, then there's no need to change. But if a player is struggling with mediocrity for the sake of conformity, that's a huge mistake. Making subtle changes to the grip, especially on the forehand volley, can pay huge dividends.

chapter 6

Serves

There's an old saying in golf: "Drive for show, putt for dough." The tennis version should be "Rally for show, serve for dough." The most important shot in tennis has always been the serve. What's second? In my opinion, it's the second serve! Having a service weapon enables a player to win cheap points, to control the court, and to dictate play with patterns. A smooth, reliable missile saves the player's physical, mental, and emotional batteries for breaking the opponent's serve. At the same time, players who own such an essential tool will tax their opponents' emotions. Any loss of serve means the set is in dire jeopardy. Confidence plays a major role in winning matches, and a big serve can help rob it from opponents. A good question for a player to ask himself is, "Does my serve make me or my opponent pay?" If the player wants to play at the highest levels of tennis, there can be only one answer.

PRE-SERVE ROUTINE

Biofeedback studies show that relaxing all muscle groups (even facial expressions) when preparing to serve decreases muscular contractions and assists in executing a rhythmic motion. When it comes to serving, relaxed rhythm is paramount in achieving elastic, fluid power. This relaxed rhythm begins with the pre-serve ritual. A pre-serve routine, along with a well-rehearsed plan for the subsequent point's pattern (envisioning how the first few strokes of the point will play out), carries great weight. Although different players have different idiosyncrasies, such as bouncing the ball six times before each serve, effective servers all share one thing in common: the proper use of their pre-serve rituals.

Some examples of pre-serve routines include taking several deep, relaxing breaths; singing a happy song to yourself; relaxing grip pressure; rocking or shifting your body weight back and forth; taking practice swings; adjusting articles of clothing; or adjusting your strings. A tennis player will adjust her relaxation routines hundreds of times throughout her playing career. What the pre-serve routine entails is not as important as establishing the ritual itself. Routines and rituals assist a player in staying relaxed and focused. Both internal and external rituals will be discussed in detail in chapter 11.

GRIP

Top servers come in a wide array of shapes and sizes, and their motions can often be just as unique. However, at the higher echelons of the game, players use one exclusive technique: the Continental grip. The Continental grip is found by placing the base knuckle of the index finger on the northeast (northwest for lefties) bevel of the racket handle (figure 6.1). This grip provides numerous benefits for the server, including amplified service speed, increased spin, variations of serves, and sharper service angles into the service box. Perhaps most important, the Continental grip decreases the chance of arm trauma or injury due to poor technique.

Figure 6.1   The Continental grip.

Beginners and intermediates often start serving with an Eastern forehand grip, and they have a difficult time switching to the more advanced Continental grip. This is primarily because of the pronation of the forearm needed to square the racket face with the ball at contact. The Eastern forehand grip—also known as the "frying pan" grip—promotes a squared racket face but limits the arm and wrist action needed to apply added pace and spin on the ball. The two forces that help bring a serve down into the opposing service box are gravity and spin. Players who use the Eastern forehand grip to serve must rely on gravity. As a result, their second-serve strategy is often to decrease arm speed and push the serve into the box. This type of serve is unreliable under pressure and easy prey for solid opponents.

Once players are ready to take the necessary steps to develop a spin serve using a Continental grip, they must also accept the possibility of setbacks. Coaches may need to choose their battles and be sensitive to the fact that a player may not be ready to tackle such a big change. If a player is in jeopardy of leaving the game, it may be in the coach's and the player's best interest to allow the player to temporarily remain with the Eastern forehand grip.

STANCE

The two predominant service stances are the platform and pinpoint stances. The one that is best for an individual player depends on the player's comfort level, personal preference, core stability, flexibility, and body type.

Platform Stance

The platform stance provides a more stable base. In this stance, the feet of the server remain shoulder-width apart throughout all serving stages (figure 6.2). Players with fine motor skills but less core stability may enjoy the benefits of a platform service stance. Research shows that the platform stance promotes a balanced uncoiling of power sources and a full weight transfer. This stance generally provides stability and consistency within the ball toss and contact phases of the stroke. In essence, fewer things can go wrong.

Pinpoint Stance

The pinpoint stance provides enhanced lifting acceleration into contact. As the uncoiling stage (described later in this chapter) of the serve begins, the back foot slides up together with the front foot into a singular "launch" movement (figure 6.3). Players who have solid core stability and favor their gross motor skills may enjoy the benefits of the pinpoint service stance. Research shows that the pinpoint service stance accelerates the vertical "up and out" forces, which aid in acceleration up and into the court. Although both styles provide unique advantages, the pinpoint stance is the most common at this time on both the ATP and WTA tours.

Figure 6.2 The platform stance.

Figure 6.3 The pinpoint stance.

Other Stance Considerations

Other stance considerations include the variations of weight distribution through the coiling phase as well as the server's position and alignment along the baseline. Studies show that weight distribution varies with personal tendencies. Some very successful servers begin their weight transfer in the coiling stage, beginning on their back foot and then rocking to the front foot only to reshift to the back foot. Other world-class servers simply begin with their weight forward, shifting it back during the ball toss stage and then forward once again through the contact stage.

Establishing personal comfort through the service stance trumps copying a teaching pro's or an idol's personal stance. Alignment and position are determined by a few important factors:

1. Mentally tough competitors try to feature their strengths and hide their weaknesses. This particularly applies to the server's first groundstroke after the serve. For example, while serving on the deuce side, players seeking to feature a forehand weapon may choose to position themselves close to the center hash mark. On the ad side, these players would benefit from standing 5 feet (152 cm) toward the doubles alley in order to strike a larger percentage of forehands.

2. Exposing the opponent's weaknesses is another critical factor in mentally tough tennis. For example, a player's backhand is usually weaker than her forehand; therefore, while serving to the ad side of the court, the server can align the feet, upper body, and racket edge toward the ad-side net post in order to help ensure that a larger percentage of serves reach the backhand corner of the box (versus right-handers).

3. In doubles, tactically savvy competitors apply a variety of formations and tactics. World-class doubles players emphasize strengths and hide weaknesses by positioning the server anywhere from the center hash mark to the doubles alley. This helps the team construct points in their favor.

SEVEN STAGES OF A WORLD-CLASS SERVE

There's perhaps no stroke that fosters more unusual techniques than the serve. Sky-high ball tosses, dancing feet, pliés (knee bends), and staccato racket swings are a few of the common pitfalls that beset the average server. Maybe such quirks come about because the serve is the only shot in the game that's not reactive. And although a little idiosyncrasy won't undermine the entire stroke, a smooth, sequential integration of the seven steps described here is the surest way to develop a dependable and destructive serve.

Coiling

As the service motion begins, the server must be sure to rotate the upper body first before tossing the ball. This is defined as the coiling stage. Although this rotation does involve a slight knee and hip turn, the essential rotation of a tennis serve involves the shoulders (figure 6.4). Envision the upper body of an effective baseball pitcher rotating enough to show the batter his back. Many club players fail to coil because they fall into the trap of attempting to toss first; this inhibits their ability to facilitate the sequential coiling stage.

In the initial coiling stage, a crucial thing for the server to remember is to avoid contracting muscles. Tight muscle contractions work against the relaxed transfer of weight. Remaining loose promotes a fluid yet powerful delivery.

Figure 6.4 Coiling.

Once again, the one-style-fits-all approach is obsolete. Extremely successful servers such as Roger Federer, Pete Sampras, and Andy Roddick chose different approaches to the coiling stage, yet all three deliver devastating bombs. In the development of a world-class serve, backswings may vary, but coiling is king.

Ball Toss

After coiling, the player must start his ball toss. To establish the foundation of a dependable service toss, the player begins by softly holding the ball in the fingertips of the nondominant hand (figure 6.5a). A common blunder is to cradle the ball firmly in the palm of the hand. When the ball rolls down the palm, unwanted spin is applied, usually resulting in an inconsistent toss. Once the ball is in the fingertips, the player uses a slow, deliberate lift of the shoulder hinge to raise the ball up. This hinge is preferred over using the wrist or forearm to locate the toss. Involving the wrist or forearm usually results in a flicking motion, and more moving parts mean less accuracy. For the player to avoid unwanted muscle contractions, the toss should rise with the forearm relaxed in a sideways position (figure 6.5b). Then, as the toss approaches the release stage, the palm turns upward to the sky as it releases the ball (figure 6.5c). Research shows that these factors contribute to a player's ability to limit the spin of the toss, which in turn adds to the control and consistency of the toss.

Other performance factors that contribute to an ideal toss would be the angle and height of the toss in relation to the type of serve and contact point. For instance, an ideal toss for a flat serve would be a few feet in front of the body and slightly to the right of

Figure 6.5 Ball toss.

the hitting shoulder (for a right-hander; refer to figure 6.14 later in this chapter); a slice service toss should again be slightly to the right (for a right-hander; refer to figure 6.15 later in this chapter); and a kick service toss should be directly overhead (refer to figure 6.17 later in this chapter).

The most common and costly mistake that servers commit is chasing an errant toss. Vic Braden repeatedly said, "Toss to the perfect swing rather than ruining a perfect swing to accommodate a lousy toss."

There's no shame in or rule against catching a poor toss. Yet it's amazing how often players want to accommodate a lousy toss. Pursuing a bad toss often leads to the following:

1. Aborting the primary power source, which is the natural service rotation
2. Service inconsistency
3. Loss of natural rhythm and timing
4. Increased chance of injuries to the wrist, elbow, rotator cuff, lower back, hips, and knees

Shadow Swings

In this practice exercise, the player first performs a few loose shadow swings and takes notice of the actual flight path of a natural service swing. Ideally, the racket should extend high above the right ear of a right-handed server. Once the player achieves a fluid service motion, he should switch between a shadow swing and an actual serve with a ball toss. The swing should be identical with and without a ball toss.

Backswing

As the ball is leaving the nondominant hand, the backswing stage begins. The nondominant hand, the body, and the racket arm turn away from the net toward the back fence (figure 6.6*a*) as the body weight transfers from front foot to back, loading the energy. The important checkpoint at this stage is when the racket slowly lifts as the dominant hand and elbow reach shoulder height. In this critical position, the dominant hand or palm should be facing downward (figure 6.6*b*). The fingertips point toward the side fence as the hitting elbow points toward the back fence. The palm facing down in the backswing limits unwanted and unnecessary muscle contractions because it facilitates the 450 degrees of racket rotation throughout the loop. This greatly enhances racket head speed.

Figure 6.6 Backswing.

A great tip is to freeze at this palm-down position and gradually let go of the grip pressure with the top four fingers. The racket should rest comfortably between the thumb and palm of the hand (figure 6.7). If a player's backswing has contorted into a palm-up position, the racket will instantly fall out of the outstretched hand. Once again, a loose arm is essential as the uncoiling process is about to begin.

Figure 6.7 Palm-down test.

Uncoiling

As the uncoiling process is set in motion, leg drive and trunk rotation back toward the net begin the uninterrupted rhythm of the server's loop. At its full upward extension (figure 6.8*a*), the nondominant hand starts its path down toward the front side of the body (figure 6.8*b*), tucking into the belly just before impact.

A rhythmic serve is a thing of beauty. Unfortunately, some players add creative but undesirable muscle contractions and spoil the party. Here are some other common flaws during this phase:

1. *The hitch.* A stop and start in the motion commonly caused by a poorly executed ball toss.
2. *The pull-down.* The dominant arm's elbow dramatically drags downward into the body, disrupting energy flow.
3. *The windmill.* An overly exaggerated loop that draws the grip over the head as the racket face passes in front of the server's vision.

Figure 6.8 Uncoiling.

Open Stance

The evolution of open-stance footwork has been the primary cause of the evolution of the modern ground game. Players can essentially coil and uncoil to a larger degree, facilitating additional power and spin. This service drill incorporates the same principles. It will be a great help to players looking to integrate the kinetic chain and synchronize the uncoiling of the larger muscle groups.

To perform this drill, stand along the baseline with both toes facing the net (figure 6.9a). Coil to the right (left for lefties). Delay the ball toss until the coil brings the tossing hand directly over the baseline (figure 6.9b). Toss the ball exaggeratedly to the right (figure 6.9c). Uncoil and abruptly stop the third link (the shoulders), catapulting the fourth link (the hitting arm) into a whiplike frenzy (figure 6.9d).

Figure 6.9 Open-stance drill.

Long Bomb

This drill promotes a powerful serve and assists players who are dramatically falling to the side or dropping their head before impact. Engineers call this "opposing force vectors." Energy being pulled in opposing directions robs players of any real possible power.

To execute this drill, simply stand at the back fence and hit line-drive serves directly into the opponent's back fence. The only way to do this effectively and consistently is to keep the head and chest up through contact. If court availability permits, walk four courts over and bomb the serve into the side fence four courts away.

Strike Zone

As the uncoiling process ends and the hitting process begins, the synchronization of the pivot, leg drive, and core rotation churns the forces upward toward contact. Exercise researchers refer to this transfer of energy as the kinetic chain.

The racket head passes between the racket hand and the player's head. The dominant elbow is now practically pointing at the net, the arm is bent, and the hitting hand is right by the ear, as though the player is talking on a telephone. The nondominant hand now tucks into the belly as the upward forearm rotation begins. The abrupt tuck of the left hand delivers a critical function: slowing the shoulder rotation, or the third link on the kinetic chain. As we know from physics, as one link abruptly stops, the next link accelerates faster. This human whip is now activated, and the violent pronation of the forearm turns outward and upward into the contact zone (figure 6.10).

The three types of serves—flat, slice, and kick—all have different strike zones and racket face angles at impact. When a player is delivering a flat serve, the ball is struck at the top of the full pronation stage (refer to figure 6.14 later in this chapter). On a slice serve, the ball is struck slightly to the right side of the ball with the racket face at an angle before the pronation phase (refer to figure 6.15 later in this chapter). On a kick serve, the racket face contacts the ball much lower through a low-to-high brushing motion, well before the pronation stage (refer to figure 6.17 later in this chapter). Players should keep their head and chest up throughout the critical contact zone. If a server's head pulls down early, this can dramatically change the racket face angle, which in turn can severely alter the placement of the serve.

Figure 6.10 Strike zone.

Tennis researchers have uncovered some interesting data: 70 percent of a serve's ball speed is produced by the internal rotation and hand speed of the arm. To have a monstrous serve, a player should focus on these elements. Sometimes, though, in an effort to accentuate forearm pronation, players mistakenly try to hit down on the ball. After all, this feels natural; almost all players are contacting their serves from well above the net. However, back in the early 1980s at the Vic Braden Tennis College, we did an interesting serve study. One of our students was Artis Gilmore, the 7-foot-2 former star center for the Chicago Bulls. Even at his extreme height, Artis was still too short to hit down on his serve. Even though ATP players will probably soon reach the 7-foot mark, it's safe to say that they, along with the rest of us, still need to hit up and out on the serve to incorporate critical spin.

Crackdown

Some players contract the muscles in the hitting arm in the hopes of serving bigger. But the real key to hitting massive serves is having a loose arm that whips the racket through the hitting zone. This is a great exercise for developing that skill.

Begin with a normal service stance but choke up to the top of the handle with the appropriate Continental service grip (figure 6.11a). Next, toss the ball 2 feet (61 cm) in front of the baseline but only slightly above eye level (figure 6.11b). Accelerate the hand speed and hammer down on the ball (figure 6.11c), causing it to bounce inside the backcourt and over the net as high as possible. This violent forearm pronation equates to achieving tremendous hand speed and racket head speed.

Figure 6.11 Crackdown drill.

Follow-Through

As forearm pronation is achieved, the follow-through stage begins. A millisecond after the ball leaves the racket face, the server's hitting thumb begins to point downward as though she is looking at her wristwatch (figure 6.12). At this stage, the off hand has abruptly tucked into the belly as the inertia of the kinetic chain has pulled the server off the ground.

Notice how the player becomes airborne during the service motion in figure 6.12; this is a natural by-product of tapping all the power sources to create swing speed. In other words, a player should never make a conscious effort to jump when hitting the serve. This doesn't increase power, and it commonly causes timing issues. In fact, knee bend, though it can be important to the rhythm of the motion, really doesn't add much in the way of pace.

Figure 6.12 Follow-through.

Fall-In

Another wonderful example of evolution is found in the fall-in stage of the serve. Old-school technique dictated that a server swivel into the tennis court—the front foot remains stationary, and the back foot (right foot for a right-handed player) swings around to land first inside the court; "Like a gate" was the commonly used analogy. As I conduct my mental and emotional tennis workshops across the country, I still find coaches teaching this method.

However, modern serving technique requires the player to land inside the court with the front foot first (figure 6.13*a*), followed quickly by the back foot (figure 6.13*b*). At the fall-in stage, the nondominant hand (left hand for a right-hander) swings away from the body to the left as the deceleration process begins. The player should allow the hitting arm to gradually slow down and come across the body, almost replacing the departed nondominant arm. Maintaining a relaxed and controlled fall-in is critical to being balanced after completing the serve and being ready to contend with the return.

Figure 6.13 Fall-in.

THREE KINDS OF SERVES

Most instructional books on tennis do a wonderful job of describing how to hit strokes, but they often neglect the topic of when and why a shot is chosen. These hidden gems are the key to accelerated learning. For instance, most players are consumed with the goal of hitting their serves harder. But sheer pace is rarely the answer to a better serve. Holding serve more regularly—and consequently winning more matches—requires the maturity to switch the focus from power to variation and consistency. The statement "I broke 110 mph today!" should be replaced with "I served 65 percent of my first serves in today!" The common serving strategy found at every club is to kill the first serve and then, depending on the level, dink or kick the second serve. This routine has no variation, and the code is easy to crack.

First, if a player enjoys achieving a numerical goal, he should switch the focus from increasing the number on the radar gun to bettering his first-serve percentage. Second, applying variations of first and second serves is crucial for keeping an opponent uncomfortable. An intelligent server mixes the speed and spin of the serve so that the returner is reactive and constantly guessing. However, once a weakness is found, a savvy server mines that vein until the gold runs dry. The following sections contain information on three serves that players should master in order to keep opponents on their toes, along with descriptions of when to use them.

Flat

There's no such thing as an entirely flat serve. Video analysis that I did back in the mid-1980s at the Vic Braden Tennis College clearly showed that some ball rotation is always present. But the secret to a well-struck flat serve is contacting the ball during midpronation. Contacting the back of the ball limits the spin, which promotes a straighter ball flight and enhanced pace (figure 6.14). The downside is that there's less margin for error.

Because it's a low-percentage shot, a flat serve is almost exclusively used as a first serve. Still, score management is a key factor in knowing when to deliver the lethal bomb. Pulling this trigger with a 40-0 lead makes more tactical sense than using it when down 0-40. But the pace of a well-developed flat serve is worth the occasional risk because of the intimidation factor and free points that it can provide.

Figure 6.14   The flat serve.

Slice

In the modern game, the slice serve has undeservingly taken a backseat to its sibling, the kick serve. On a slice serve, the racket face must hit the upper right side of the ball (left side for a lefty) in an 8-to-2 o'clock swing path (4-to-10 o'clock for lefties). The slice serve is contacted during the up and out phase of the swing before the forearm pronation begins its accelerated turnover phase (figure 6.15).

Figure 6.15 The slice serve.

Slice serves should be used as both first- and second-serve deliveries. Wicked slice serves stay low and have a right-to-left ball flight (opposite for lefties), which is usually accentuated after the bounce. These serves play havoc with opponents who use a Western forehand grip (because they struggle with low balls) and opponents who have difficulty spacing away from a body serve. The slice is also a great choice after a long, grueling point when an opponent is winded and lacks the energy to move out of the way of his own swing, resulting in a defensive, short return.

Kick

In the advanced levels of the game, the development of an effective kick serve is vital. To deliver the massive kick serve, a player must make three key adjustments to the standard serving motion. First, the player should supersize his Continental grip. While leaving the base knuckle of the index finger on the northeast bevel (northwest for lefties), the player slides the heel of the hand up to the north bevel, moving from a Continental to an Eastern backhand grip (figure 6.16). This advanced grip system closes the racket face slightly to help promote more ball rotation.

Next, the player places the ball toss slightly back over the head or even over the hitting shoulder. This is where the service motion's natural upward velocity lives. The player should avoid tossing the ball in front and to the left; this is a leading cause of rotator cuff tears. Finally, the player must reroute the actual swing path. The momentum of the swing of the racket head shifts from accelerating toward the net to accelerating toward the right-side fence (opposite for lefties). The ball is struck with a vertical racket face at a 7-to-1 o'clock face angle (5-to-11 o'clock for lefties). Ball contact is made in the upward drive phase, well before the forearm pronation begins its turnover phase (figure 6.17).

Figure 6.16   Supersizing the Continental grip.

Figure 6.17   The kick serve.

As with the slice, kick serves should be used as both first and second serves. Although the kick serve doesn't have the pace of a flat serve, the trickiness of its spin makes the kick challenging to return. After the bounce, the ball tends to jump up and to the right (left for lefty servers). Old-school opponents who use Continental or Eastern forehand grips are extremely vulnerable to a massive kick serve because of the weakness of their grip system's high strike zone. Opponents who use one-handed backhands are also vulnerable because they are forced to employ their defensive slice backhand. Because of the inherent safety supplied by the added topspin, the kick has become the dominant second serve, but players should remember that a solid kick serve is also an intelligent percentage play to use as a first-serve option.

ANALYZING THE SERVICE RETURN

In chapter 9, we'll discuss the evolution of the return of serve. Paying attention to the returner's position will provide extremely important information to the server. Some returners vary their positions, while others remain fairly stationary. The server's tactical choice should be dictated by the returner's tendencies. Unfortunately, the majority of players don't bother to consider this information, and they lose a precious tactical advantage. In fact, monitoring the opponent's return position should be part of the relaxation rituals used before each serve (more information on between-point rituals is provided in chapter 11).

For instance, if a server notices that an opponent prefers to return from right on top of the baseline, a hard body serve could draw a weak reply. On the other hand, if an opponent stands well behind the baseline to allow more time for the return, a wide slice or kick serve could push the returner outside the doubles alley, opening up the court for the next shot.

A returner may also take positions that highlight a strength or protect a weakness. An opponent with a big forehand may take a step to the left (right for a lefty) in order to create a better opportunity to hit his preferred stroke on the return. A smart server recognizes this tactic and makes the opponent pay for leaving a significant portion of the service box uncovered. This forces the returner to respect a well-placed serve to the forehand, which opens up the serve to the weaker backhand side.

Paying attention to proven shot sequences for the return of serve is another example of mental training. Does the opponent like to hit an inside-out forehand from the ad court? Does a kick serve to the backhand illicit a low chip crosscourt? Being observant is a critical learned behavior. Identifying an opponent's return tendencies enables a seasoned competitor to control the important "mega" points—essentially the game points—found in every match. Experienced opponents choose to run their best shot sequences on these crucial points. Wouldn't it be smart to identify and eliminate their favorite successful patterns beforehand and force them to attempt something less proven?

SERVING MYTHS

In addition to involving the most varied technique, the serve also invites the most interpretations on how it should be performed. Although certain parts of the motion can be debated (e.g., pinpoint versus platform stance), there are some popular teaching points that time has proven to be dated or inaccurate. Here are a few:

Toss high and you'll have more time.   Studies using slow-motion cameras have determined that a ball tossed 6 feet (183 cm) higher than the top of an outstretched racket head passes through the hitting zone of the service swing 20 times faster than a ball tossed around the peak of a server's reach. If the player tosses lower, the ball sits in the hitting zone longer.

Scratch your back on the backswing.   As the racket head passes between the dominant hitting hand and the server's head, the uncoiling inertia of the body's kinetic chain actually throws the racket away from the back, or the center of the axis. This desired centrifugal force doesn't allow for a muscle contraction, which would pull the racket head down to accommodate a back-scratching position.

Hit down on a serve.   Remember Artis Gilmore from earlier in the chapter? He was 7-foot-2 and still too short to hit down on a serve. So unless the player is about 8 feet tall (according to our serve study at the Vic Braden Tennis College), it is in his best interest to hit up and out while serving.

Bend your knees for great power.   Though it can be important to the rhythm of the server's motion, knee bend supplies the least amount of racket head speed for the serve. Instead, the player should focus on fluid, liquid power and hand speed.

There's an ideal service motion.   One of the most talked about myths in this book is that there is one best way to hit a tennis ball. In fact, customization and personal preferences play a critical role in a player's ability to advance to the highest levels of play.

chapter 7

Returns of Serve

From years of charting and coaching more than my fair share of matches, I've learned that one thing is very clear: The most missed shot in the game is the return of serve. Why? Players seldom if ever practice this critical skill set.

Let's review this book's mantra: "There is no one-size-fits-all approach." That statement applies to the return of serve as well. To begin developing options for the return of serve, the player must first understand her brain and body type. She must also have a strategic knowledge of her own style of play. The first question a player should ask is, "How do I win matches?"

Certain personalities, such as Caroline Wozniacki in the women's game, choose patience and consistency as their primary weapons. Their elevated frustration tolerance level invites longer rallies. If a player's strengths include a calm demeanor and consistent groundstrokes, the player should take a position 5 to 10 feet (1.5 to 3.0 m) behind the baseline while returning serve. This will promote the patience contest that suits a defensive counterpuncher style of play.

Other more offensive players, such as Novak Djokovic, may enjoy torturing their opponents with groundstroke aggression. These players excel at changing the direction of the ball. They are constantly on the lookout for a short reply from their opponent so that they can deliver a devastating blow. It makes sense for this type of player to take a neutralizing return position by standing a little closer to the baseline and moving forward as the ball leaves his opponent's tossing hand.

A third personality and body type favors the all-out forward attack. Ivo Karlovic is an example of this type of player. These players prefer short points and volley warfare instead of backcourt grinding. The logical strategy for these players is to take an offensive return position inside the baseline in order to intimidate and showcase their quick reactions. This is especially daunting on the opponent's second-serve delivery.

By starting points on their terms, players can gain a decisive tactical and psychological advantage. Advanced returners practice anticipation, movement, and mechanics as they work to improve their returns. Following are some of the key components of a good return of serve.

PRE-SERVE ROUTINE

Highly advanced players begin their return points with personalized routines that are well developed and rehearsed. As mentioned in chapter 6, pre-serve components include exhaling, relaxing, deciding on the most advantageous position in which to stand, and reviewing a strategic plan based on awareness of score management and point management. Routines and rituals will be covered in depth in chapter 11.

GRIP

One of the most talked about stats on the professional level is service speed. Today, pros on the ATP tour serve consistently in the 130 mph range. Yet their opponents still have plenty of time to change grips in order to accommodate their stroke. So at the mere mortal level, where serves don't frequent triple digits, there's plenty of time to perform a grip change while returning. In the ready position, two-handed players have their dominant hand in a semi-Western forehand grip, and their nondominant hand is in an Eastern grip (figure 7.1a). If they detect that an incoming serve is going to the forehand wing, they simply release the top hand as the coil process begins (figure 7.1b). However, if a serve is coming to the backhand, the top hand anchors the racket while the bottom hand slides upward two bevels to the desired Continental grip (figure 7.1c). This change of grip happens simultaneously with the coil stage. Because the grip change takes only milliseconds to perform, it is seldom detected by the naked eye.

Figure 7.1 Two-handed return-of-serve grip: (a) at the ready position; (b) against a serve to the forehand; (c) against a serve to the backhand.

Coach's Corner

Players who have a weaker backhand can give it a little head start. To do this, they stand in the ready position with a preset backhand grip. This eliminates the "find the grip" link in the return process.

POSITIONING

On the return of serve, the player should begin in a low, crouched position (figure 7.2*a*), with knees bent and elbows up. As soon as the server's ball toss leaves the fingertips, the returner should lift straight up (figure 7.2*b*). The returner's momentum must then be forward toward the court. This movement begins with a split step (figure 7.2*c*). The split step should be timed to occur right before the service is struck (figure 7.2*d*). This helps the returner quickly detect the intended location of the incoming serve and leads to better execution of the return stroke (for instruction on the stroke itself, see the Swing Execution section).

Figure 7.2 Return-of-serve positioning: The returner (*a*) begins low, (*b*) rises straight up, (*c*) performs a split step into the court, and (*d*) prepares to make contact.

To achieve an effective return-of-serve position, the player needs to detect the range of angles in which the opponent can successfully hit; the player then stands in the mid-point of that range of attack. A secondary consideration is to identify which incoming serve is causing problems and to "stop the bleeding." If an opponent is receiving cheap points off slice serves out wide in the deuce court, the returner should stand well inside the doubles alley. This essentially shuts down that successful pattern of play, forcing the opponent to try the less favored serve down the center service line. This is an example of tactical and psychological warfare.

Figure 7.3 Open stance on the return of serve.

STANCE

One key evolutionary factor in the return of serve is the development of the open stance (figure 7.3). This is the preferred return-of-serve platform on the professional tours. Essentially, the feet remain parallel to the net while the upper body coils and uncoils in order to provide power on the shot.

The importance of the development of this additional stance can't be emphasized enough. By using an open stance, the player can generate additional power, spin, and angle because of the larger degree of upper-body rotation and dynamic balance through the weight transfer. An additional advantage of the open-stance return is the added core rotation, which increases the player's ability to hit an offensive ball even when making contact farther back or wider in the strike zone; this extended offensive strike zone is a great benefit when the player is stretched wide by a serve, for example.

The most important benefit of the open-stance return, however, is greater recovery. Because there's no step forward—and subsequently back—as in a closed stance, the open stance provides a significant amount of additional recovery time.

SWING EXECUTION

The stroke technique for a return of serve is essentially the same as a groundstroke (see chapter 4). This includes fundamental characteristics as well as strike zone variations. Any stroke modifications are dictated by the returner's chosen position and shot selection.

When a player is returning an offensive first serve, flexibility and reactionary speed are paramount. The mind-set in such a situation tends to be more defensive: *Dear God, if I can just get this back, I promise I'll go to church every Sunday.* Yes, it's a little dramatic, but trying to handle a formidable first serve can give one a hopeless feeling. On the other hand, returning a predictable second serve can elicit decidedly more upbeat thoughts: *OK, I'm up break point; she's going to hit that kick serve out to my backhand. I'm going to move inside the court, run around it, and crush my killer forehand.*

A current trend in the pro game is to take a position 8 to 10 feet (2.4 to 3.0 m) behind the baseline when returning a first serve. This strategy gives the player a few more milli-

Figure 7.4 Swing execution from (*a*) behind the baseline, (*b*) the baseline, and (*c*) inside the baseline.

seconds to react to the incoming ball while maintaining a full 12-foot (3.6 m) swing length (figure 7.4*a*). Players standing on the baseline won't have that extra time and may need to shorten the length of their backswing (figure 7.4*b*). Those who choose to set up in an offensive position farther inside the court may adopt an even more compact swing (figure 7.4*c*), or they may go for broke and uncoil a full offensive attack (once more demonstrating that the one-size-fits-all approach is defunct).

Simple Stroke Technique

The secret to hitting bigger, better, and faster returns lies in trimming the fat. Less is more. The reason for this is the reduced time available on returns (the speed of the serve shortens the amount of time that the player has to react on the return).

One of the leading causes of errors on the return of serve is excess—extreme swing length, racket speed overkill, a rolling racket head through the strike zone, an overabundance of core rotation, or unnecessary head movement.

Andre Agassi credits his impeccable and efficient return-of-serve skills to one thing: a simple hip rotation. Players can practice this trait by having a coach or friend stand 15 feet (4.5 m) away and toss balls quickly in groups of four to the forehand and then to the backhand. This decreases reaction time and promotes the shorter, compact stroke that the player wants to develop.

Secondary Strike Zone

To be effective at returning serves, a player must also develop the ability to return serves in the head- and shoulder-level strike zones. At the higher levels of the game, opponents are able to kick serves above the returner's comfortable waist-level strike zone.

In this situation, players need to modify their standard low-to-high groundstroke flight path. While returning a shoulder-level ball, the player should keep the racket head above waist level in the backswing. The concept is to drop the racket head only about a foot (about 30 cm) below contact and decrease the low-to-high lift. This helps because of the incident and reflected angle of a rising serve off the returner's racket face as well as the reduced amount of time.

Shadow swinging without ever dropping the racket head below waist level (figure 7.5) is a terrific exercise for increasing the strength that a player needs for returning balls in this secondary strike zone.

Figure 7.5 Shadow swings in the secondary strike zone.

READING THE SERVER

Anticipatory skills are one of the most important elements in a player's ability to execute effective returns of serve. Knowing the intended serve location before the ball is struck is a serious advantage for the returner. How does it work? Basically, spotting and understanding those millisecond clues aid the brain's ability to send the desired motor program down the nervous system to recruit the appropriate muscles in the appropriate fashion. Again, this is a learned behavior that requires time and commitment. Exceptions shadow every rule, but the following sections describe the most frequent serving cues.

Watching the Server's Preparation

While in the ready position, the returner should study the server's eyes. Servers often unknowingly give away their intentions by staring down their target. The returner should be coy; he can give that corner of the box plenty of space—that is, until the server tosses the ball. Then he should quickly and quietly slide into position to crush the return.

In addition to watching the opponent's line of sight, the returner should pay attention to any other possible "tells." In Andre Agassi's autobiography, *Open,* he shares a story that illustrates this point. When returning Boris Becker's massive serve, Agassi noticed that if "Boom Boom" was about to serve to the left side of Agassi's service box, Becker would stick his tongue out of the left side of his mouth. If he was about to deliver a body serve, his tongue would point straight out the center of his mouth. Before each serve to the right side of the box—you guessed it—Becker would stick his tongue out of the right side of his mouth. Agassi could anticipate the intended serve and jump all over it. Now that's paying attention to a server's preparation!

Reading the Ball Toss

Certain serves come from certain ball tosses. For instance, if a right-handed server tosses the ball to his left side and arches the back to make contact, it will usually be a kick serve that goes out to the returner's left, or backhand, side (if right-handed). In this case, the returner should slide to the left and prepare for a backhand return in the high strike zone, or he should run around the serve to crush an offensive forehand (figure 7.6).

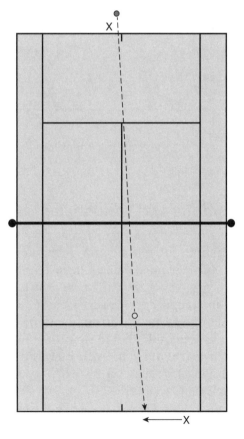

Figure 7.6 Reading a serve to the left, the returner slides to the left for a backhand or runs around the serve for a forehand return.

If a right-handed server tosses the ball out in front and slightly to his right, it will most likely be a flat or slice serve that goes to the returner's right, or forehand, wing (if right-handed). Once the returner spots this cue, he should slide to the right to prepare for a forehand return (figure 7.7). Keep in mind that the serve directions will be opposite for a lefty server.

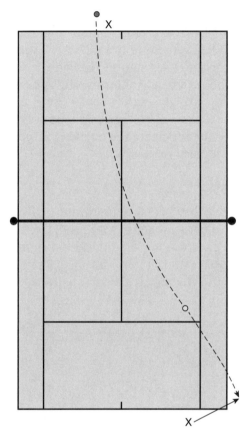

Figure 7.7 Reading a serve to the right, the returner slides to the right for a forehand return.

Reading Serving Positions and Tendencies

As mentioned in the previous chapter, taking different positions along the baseline can offer the server better angles into the service box. A right-handed server may stand a few feet over to the left while preparing to deliver an extreme kick serve out wide on the ad side. A perceptive returner will spot the shift along the baseline and then slide over toward the doubles alley to intercept the wide serve (figure 7.8).

Realizing that an opponent is repeatedly hitting the same bland slice serve down the T to the forehand on the advantage side should tip off an aware returner and instigate an offensive attack. The returner should hold a neutral position until the ball toss leaves the server's hand; then, with a fast first step, the returner should quickly slide to the right to deliver an offensive forehand blow (figure 7.9).

Reading the server often includes making educated guesses based on previous experience. Advanced opponents will choose to run the same "winning" service patterns on important points. By anticipating the serve and disrupting the pattern from the first ball, the returner will put himself in the advantage to start the point. When players practice the art of paying attention, it pays off match after match.

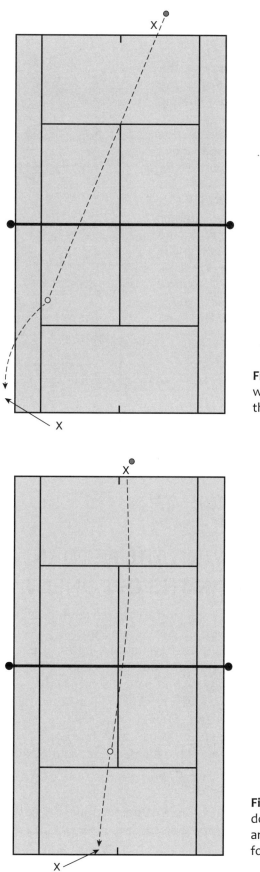

Figure 7.8 Reading a serve out wide, the returner slides toward the alley for a backhand return.

Figure 7.9 Reading a serve down the T, the returner slides around the backhand for a forehand return.

The Big X Return-of-Serve Pattern

Neutralizing an offensive first serve is a cornerstone of successful tennis. In this instance, the neutralizing factor is the craft of stealing the server's advantage in court position. The big X pattern begins with the returner positioning 8 to 10 feet back behind the baseline. His mission is to arch the return 8 to 10 feet above the net and deep crosscourt. This pushes the server back five or six steps behind his doubles alley. As the server is being forced back into a defensive court position, the crafty returner slips five or six steps into the center "home base" position. With the court-positioning shift accomplished, the returner simply drives his next groundstroke to the opponent's opposing corner. As figure 7.10 demonstrates, a big X is drawn as the server is neutralized. The shots are numbered in sequential order.

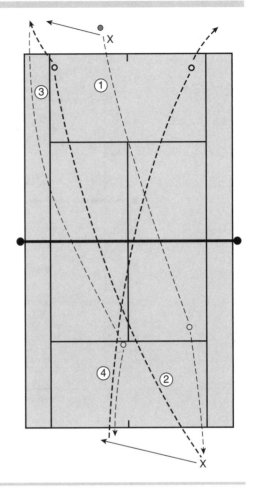

Figure 7.10   The big X return-of-serve pattern drill.

MODIFYING THE RETURN BASED ON THE OPPONENT

Earlier in the book, we discussed six playing styles: retriever, baseline counterpuncher, aggressive baseliner, all-court player, net-rusher, and finesse player (though occasionally, the drop-shot artist, or junk baller, can be found in intermediate play). Successfully breaking serve often requires the ability to pull opponents out of their comfort zone. Sometimes this means relying on shots and patterns that bother the opponent rather than falling back on what feels easy to the returner. That's the price of winning. Most players enjoy grooving the strokes they already own. Champions, however, focus on developing new skills that they have yet to master. They don't just hit the shots that feel comfortable to them; they hit the shots that feel least comfortable to the opponent.

Returning Against a Retriever

Retrievers often serve and then move back 10 feet behind the baseline to begin their slow-ball torture. They prefer that opponents hit deep returns. But a short-angle return—the side-door shot—pulls the retriever out of her comfort zone and into a vulnerable position outside the doubles alley. Imagine a goalie in soccer. Pull the goalie away from her defensive position, and there is no one left to guard the goal. The same strategic principle applies here.

Also, retrievers commonly have ordinary, even attackable, serves. A returner should think of this weak shot as an opportunity to execute an offensive short-ball option such as a drop shot—the complete opposite of the return that the server wants or expects. This pulls the retriever out of her comfort zone and forces her to use her underdeveloped volleys and overheads.

What happens if a great retriever also has forward movement skills, great touch volleys, and a killer overhead? The answer: It's going to be a long match.

Returning Against a Hard-Hitting Baseliner

Hard-hitting baseliners are continuously on the hunt for short balls to crush. For the returner, a simple yet effective strategy against this type of player is to position herself back behind the baseline and to focus on returning the serve high (8 to 10 feet above the net) and deep. The objective is to avoid delivering a low line-drive return into the server's primary strike zone, which is like handing her a winner on a silver platter.

By delivering steeper-trajectory returns up and out of aggressive players' kill zones, the returner forces these players to employ more patience, which is not usually their strong suit. Also, although these opponents enjoy hitting hard, they often don't like running hard. The returner should use the short-angle, or side-door, return pattern, essentially daring the server to strike bold winners from vulnerable positions on the run.

Returning Against a Net-Rusher

Net-rushers may be on the endangered species list in singles, but in the game of doubles, they are alive and well. To pull serve-and-volleyers out of their comfort zone, a player should use several different return-of-serve positions. This plants the seed of confusion in the net-rusher's mind.

Also, the returner should trade in the comfortable, hard high return for a slow, low ball at the feet of the onrushing server, in essence letting him volley a difficult no-pace junk ball at his shoelaces. The objective is to let go of trying to blast a winner off a 100 mph serve. Instead, a mature, educated returner can be rewarded with a much simpler shot off a short 30 mph volley.

Returning Against a Lefty

Although being a lefty is not specifically a playing style, lefties present their own unique set of challenges, the most difficult of which is on the return of serve. As stated earlier, most players seldom practice their return of serve, let alone do it against a lefty. Difficulties arise because of the opposing spin of the lefty serve, especially the slice. For lefties, this bread-and-butter weapon routinely delivers winners match after match, year after year.

The key to returning the lefty slice is footwork. Serves that appear to be heading out to a right-hander's forehand are actually going to curve directly into the body. Creating space is essential. Lefty slices that appear to be heading to the backhand wing actually slide away and continue to drag the returner out of his wheelhouse. Dissecting the angle, especially on the ad side, is paramount. Standing in the doubles alley to take away a lefty's favorite option is often an effective strategy.

These tips will help, but the best advice for a player is to befriend a lefty playing partner in order to practice and develop the return-of-serve skills.

MIND-SET

Regardless of the type of opponent or a player's style of play, the most important thing regarding the return of serve is to simply start the point. This may seem obvious, but unfortunately, most players are overly aggressive and try to end the point with their first strike. The psychological task on a return of serve is twofold. First, when returning first serves, the returner's goal is to demoralize opponents by consistently getting the ball back in play. Big servers are accustomed to receiving free points. A steady return sends this message: No free or cheap points today. Also, the return of the second serve provides the opportunity to punish the server for delivering a weak ball. As mentioned previously, offensive, short-ball options may include crushing a winner, hitting a chip and charge, placing a drop shot, or using the side-door pattern.

Coach's Corner

Players who want to improve their return-of-serve skills should consider making a shift in the organization of their practice time. The old-school approach includes rallying for 50 minutes, followed by 5 minutes of volleys and overheads, and then 5 minutes of serves. For an accelerated learning method, players should try 40 minutes of serve and return repetition, followed by 10 minutes of volleys and overheads, and then 10 minutes of groundstrokes.

RETURN-OF-SERVE MYTHS

As with all tennis strokes, some myths exist regarding the return of serve. Here are a couple of the biggest offenders:

Get your racket back early. According to old-school methodology, players should take the racket straight back early during preparation for an incoming serve. In chapter 4, we discussed how taking the racket back toward the back fence is actually only the first half of the process. Once the kinetic chain begins to uncoil forward into the court, the racket is forced back another 3 feet (91 cm). When the racket finally starts forward toward contact, it has to travel back 3 extra feet just to return to the original take-back position. That's 6 unnecessary feet added to the backswing. This results in a longer, horizontal swing path and an improper strike zone, causing a loss of depth and topspin.

Always step into the ball. Although it's true that stepping into the ball is effective when a player is returning a weak, short second serve and is moving forward offensively, players are more often in neutral and defensive situations on the return of serve. Because of the prevalence of Western forehands and two-handed backhands, the primary contact point for many players is just to the side of the body. This later contact point aids in preparation time, helps disguise the player's intentions, and most important, reduces recovery time for the next shot, making it more effective for court coverage.

Specialty Shots

When watching players exchange easy groundstrokes as they are warming up before a match, a casual observer might think that the player with cleaner primary stroke mechanics will have the advantage. But at the higher levels, everyone has mastered the fundamentals. Aesthetically pleasing strokes and clean ball striking have little to do with the art of winning when both players can do it. So what tips the scales between two evenly matched players?

This chapter starts to explore the profound depth that separates the good from the great—the winners from the thousands of merely talented players—and it begins with well-developed specialty shots. Specialty shots round out a player's game, providing her with in-depth tools of the trade. These shots—approaches, overheads, lobs, and drop shots—often provide the critical "final nail in the coffin" to put away a worthy opponent. Competitors who have put the time into cultivating specialty shots are well on their way to becoming complete players.

APPROACH SHOTS

In chapter 4, we categorized stroke mechanics into two groups: primary and secondary strokes. The approach shot is undeniably the most important secondary stroke. By definition, an approach shot is a building shot that allows a player to transition from a neutral baseline position to an offensive net position. In both singles and doubles, a dependable transition game is mandatory in nurturing a winning temperament, which is offensive in nature. Champions understand that formidable opponents won't simply cower and submit in a big match. To have a winner's mind-set, a player must focus on outplaying the opponent and *taking* the match.

Again, remember one of this book's mottos: "Practice in the manner in which you are expected to perform." Players who spend time focusing on their net skills often center their attention on a singular component: hitting their primary volleys while standing 3 feet (91 cm) from the net. This is not an entirely useless practice—it builds confidence on routine chest-level volleys—but it doesn't prepare a player for the real-match application of the stroke. The volley may occur at the net, but the genesis of the stroke occurs in the approach shot and forward move from the baseline. Skilled net players have fully developed transition games because they repeatedly practice the art of the attack.

This takes practice because the approach is not a simple dash to the net. It's an advanced tactical play used to descend on an opponent's short groundstrokes and weak second serves. For the first hundred years of the sport, the standard approach shot—deep and low—was the primary short-ball option, the "go-to" play. Those athletes from past generations chose a positioning tactic over a sheer power play. In the modern game, however, approach shots come in a wider variety. Instead of setting up a volley, it's much more common for players to go for groundstroke winners. Both tactics have their place in today's game. Regardless of a player's preferred tactic, attacking is all about the psychological warfare of multiplying the opponent's adversity and stress. There's no doubt that consistent pressure causes even the best to crack.

Perfecting the approach shot begins with learning how and when to transition properly. This chapter provides a pathway for transforming even the most ardent baseliner into an addicted "netaholic."

Knowing the Short-Ball Zone

The most opportune time to hit an approach shot is off an opponent's short ball. Players are often surprised when they receive a short ball and are subsequently late on the attack. This is a common tactical error. The truth is, at the recreational level, players shouldn't be surprised when they get a short ball; they should be surprised when the opponent can actually hit deep for three or four balls in a row. So, when is a short ball coming? In a few seconds. The player should expect it.

Players need to predetermine their short-ball range. Depending on a player's foot speed, court coverage skills, and aggression, that zone can vary. But as a general guide, the short-ball range is an imaginary line about three feet past the player's service line. Any weak ball landing before that line should be punished with an aggressive groundstroke or approach option. (Zonal tennis is discussed further in chapter 9.)

Anticipating the Attack

The most successful net-rushers at any level can sense when one of their shots will leave an opponent vulnerable. The first step in developing an effective approach sequence lies in anticipating when to attack, trusting one's instincts, and taking off to the net. Readers who have intuitive or perceiving personality types (described in chapter 1) are nodding their heads, "Yup, got that already." Those readers with sensate or judging personality types (also described in chapter 1) are not so sure. They're analyzing: "I understand, but I haven't calculated the movement requirements, wind and sun variables, or the opponent's response percentages." In other words, their analysis leads to paralysis, and they struggle to instinctively recognize a potential short-ball opportunity.

Applying informed guesswork comes from the art of paying attention to small, seemingly meaningless details. Successful net-rushers are mindful in their attacks. They base their approaches on information gathered from past experiences and informational clues gathered through broad vision.

To accelerate the process of developing anticipatory skills, players should practice spotting these seven broad vision clues:

1. **The court zone in which the ball is going to land.** This can often dictate an opponent's options and probable shot responses (it will be discussed further in chapter 9).

2. **Court positioning.** Offensive, neutral, and defensive shot selections are greatly influenced by an opponent's court position. An inverse relationship generally exists between a player's location on the court and her level of aggression. The greater the distance away from the net, the less aggressive a player tends to be.

3. **Body language.** Is the opponent balanced or unbalanced? Is she comfortably set or jammed?

4. **Incoming strike zone (knee, waist, or head level).** Where an opponent contacts the ball can make a difference in the resulting shot.

5. **Previous successful shots.** If smart tacticians receive good fortune, they repeat the process.

6. **Incoming swing length and speed.** Offensive topspin lobs are produced with a long, fast, low-to-high motion. Slice short-angle shots are produced with a short, slow, high-to-low mechanical delivery. Recognizing these types of nuances can help a player develop a better awareness of the returning ball.

7. **Opponent's arrival time.** The timing of when an opponent reaches the ball makes a great difference. Desperately lunging opponents are pressed for time and are forced out of most secondary options. By covering their highest-percentage play, a player can force them to attempt low-percentage options.

Developing anticipatory skills is a mind-set; approaching the net requires attitude as much as aptitude. By having an offensive frame of mind, a hesitant player can achieve quicker response times, which leads to proper positioning. This proactive temperament puts the player in control of the court as the aggressor (instead of reluctantly going to the net to timidly defend against the opponent's passing shots). In the modern game, spotting when an opponent is vulnerable is one of the most important aspects of storming the net.

Traditional Approach

From a stroke mechanics standpoint, traditional approach shots involve the same core elements as primary groundstrokes (see chapter 4). But because successful primary approach shots are struck from well inside the court (figure 8.1), adaptations such as compacting the backswing or flattening out a swing path are often necessary. These

Figure 8.1 Hitting a traditional approach shot.

quick modifications are based on the ball's incoming speed, spin, trajectory, and landing zone, as well as the approximate strike zone (in relation to the body).

In terms of targets for the approach shot, depth is king. A deep approach provides valuable time for the player to establish an offensive position at the net while forcing opponents to defend from behind the baseline. This positioning often causes opponents to lean back and open their shoulders. In turn, the angle of the racket face soon follows. This overrotation causes the passing shot to float well above the net, yielding a comfortable, high volley. Players have three primary options when hitting a deep approach shot.

Deep to the Backhand

When a player is picking which side of the court to direct the approach shot toward, a simple lesson in anatomy offers some useful revelations. An opponent who is coiling to hit an offensive passing shot off the forehand wing has the luxury of having the dominant hitting shoulder behind the body. This means he can hit the passing shot three feet later and still strike an offensive blow. The same player coiling to strike a backhand pass has the dominant hitting shoulder in front of the body. This means that if contact is late, he only has two options: (1) to attempt a defensive slice backhand or (2) to spend the required hours educating and coordinating his nondominant hand to hit a two-hander.

This is why hitting the approach deep to the backhand is a good tactic versus opponents who use a one-handed backhand. For a successful passing shot, a one-handed topspin backhand, such as Roger Federer's, is actually struck a foot in front of the front hip. This early contact prevents a one-hander from "holding the pass," or making contact toward the back of the strike zone (as a two-handed player like Rafa Nadal tends to do). When late, a one-hander has to abort the offensive topspin passing shot and revert to the open-face chip reply. This higher, slower return often results in an easy volley put-away. This strike zone issue is the reason why the one-handed backhand is now on tennis' endangered species list; it simply lacks the disguise and options that are available when players use a fully developed two-handed backhand stroke.

The decision on whether to attack an opponent's two-handed backhand wing depends greatly on its quality and how the opponent executes it under pressure compared to the opponent's forehand. If an opponent's backhand is her weaker shot, the deep approach shot to the backhand may still be the best option.

Deep Down the Middle

More net-rushers would be wise to take advantage of this law: Angle creates angle. When players are pushed wide, more severe down-the-line and crosscourt passing angles become available. However, attempting a passing shot off a well-struck deep approach shot down the middle is a daunting task. From the opponent's perspective, creating an angle is much more difficult. This will be the go-to approach tactic on the ATP tour in the very near future. The heights of men's professional tennis players are soon to reach the 7-foot (213 cm) mark. The next generation of incredible athletes will have the wingspan of a 747. That extended reach combined with an approach shot deep down the middle will be a million-dollar tactic.

Deep to the Forehand

With the dominance of the two-handed backhand, this shot has frequently become a player's more dependable shot. The use of both arms gives the two-handed backhand stroke a consistently quieter racket face through the strike zone, and the arm–body rotation is synchronized cleaner than on the forehand side. So, at the higher levels of the game, hitting the approach deep to the opponent's forehand is often an effective strategy.

Coach's Corner

Besides the approach shot, hitting groundstrokes deep down the middle is also a useful tactic. Here's a quick story that illustrates the effectiveness of this tactic. Before the 2011 Sony Ericsson WTA finals in Miami, I was talking with my good friend Sam Sumyk. Sam is one of the top coaches in the world and currently coaches Victoria Azarenka. Vika was set to play Maria Sharapova in the finals the next day. Sharapova is a formidable opponent, and I'm a big fan of her work ethic, perseverance, and commitment. The strategy was to have Vika focus her attack deep down the middle, thus making Maria get out of the way of her own strokes—arguably her least effective footwork pattern—and try to create winning angles where there were no angles to create. Minimizing an aggressive player's angles can pay off big-time. Maria made eight unforced errors in the first game alone as Vika went on to take the title 6-1, 6-4.

Here's another interesting insight to consider: Players often have a formidable offensive forehand groundstroke but a severely underdeveloped defensive forehand. The same player may have a backhand with an average offensive component but may be world-class when pushed into a defensive or neutralizing backhand. So, when the player is on defense, where's the weakness? Players shouldn't be afraid to attack the forehand just because it's a forehand.

Triangle

In this anticipatory drill, players work on their ability to read an opponent's highest-percentage option for a passing shot or lob. Three targets are placed on the feeder's backhand side:

1. A foot (30 cm) from the baseline toward the center of the ad side
2. A foot from the singles sideline on the ad side
3. On the service line of the ad side

These three targets should form a triangle (figure 8.2). The player's objective is to attack the imaginary opposition's backhand with the approach shot, read its landing zone, and shut down the easiest passing option.

If the approach shot is landing near the first target (A), the highest-percentage play is for the imaginary opponent to lob. The net-rusher's job is to identify this response and prepare early for an overhead smash. If the approach is headed toward the second target (B), the highest-percentage response is a down-the-line passing shot. The smart play is to cover that option. If the approach is landing close to the third target (C), the onrushing net player is in a bit of trouble.

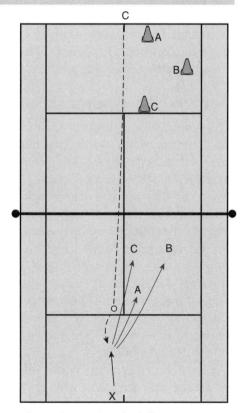

Figure 8.2 Triangle drill.

Trouble in tennis comes in the form of options: The opposition simply has too many good choices for a passing shot or lob. Still, with that said, the highest-percentage play is for the imaginary opponent to pass crosscourt. So in this case, the best move for the player is to split-step and close off that option.

The objective in rushing the net is to create doubt in the mind of an opponent and to force the opponent to attempt a lower-percentage play. The triangle drill can be performed on the feeder's forehand side as well. Once the player establishes proficiency, accelerate the drill to a live-ball exercise by adding an actual opponent who attempts to pass the net-rusher.

Moonball Approach

The arched moonball approach is a newcomer in the approach genre. To introduce this wicked secondary approach, let's start with a few questions. Is it beneficial to have the opponent backpedaling while attempting a passing shot? Is it helpful to have the opponent positioned 5 to 10 feet (1.5 to 3.0 m) behind the baseline where there are fewer angles to create an effective pass? Is it advantageous to make the opponent attempt a passing shot from a defensive, head-level strike zone? Obviously, the answers to these questions are all yes.

The technique for the moonball approach is like that of the high-looping groundstroke discussed in chapter 4. Because opponents often respond to this moonball approach with a high-arcing return of their own, it can also lead to a swing volley opportunity (which is discussed next). This secondary stroke sequence is a favorite pattern of players who beat moonball pushers on a regular basis. The moonball approach sequence is a surprise stealth attack. After a penetrating moonball approach has left the player's racket, the player's objective is to recover to the baseline and stop. This baseline "freeze" provides the disguise factor. The attacker bluffs, as if he is engaged in a backcourt moonball exchange. The opponent soon has to shift his vision from broad vision back to narrow vision and retreat back to relob. This is when the attacker quietly slides up to the service line to execute the simple swing volley winner.

Swing Volley Approach

The swing volley approach—both forehand and backhand—is taken out of the air with the same mechanics as a traditional groundstroke. This secondary approach shot is executed in response to the opponent's defensive lob. Once again, for this advanced strategic play, the player must be able to spot wounded opponents and then efficiently take away their recovery time back into the point.

Repeatedly, from the national junior ranks through the club level, I coach players who say that their favored style of play is an all-court player or net-rusher. They say, "I love being aggressive out there." Then I ask them what style of play they hate to play the most. The response? "Moonball pushers! I hate those slow, dinker rallies!" Then I proceed to chart a set versus a pusher. More often than not, I see players effectively hurting their opponents only to stop and watch lobs reset the point. Instead of moving in four steps to effectively take a swing volley, they retreat six steps toward the back fence and join the lob fest. Now, whose style of tennis are they playing, their attacking style or the moonballer's?

The technique for the swing volley approach, covered in chapter 5, is much simpler than it appears. Like any other tool in an advanced player's tool belt, this shot has to be developed and refined through repetition.

Steal a Volley

Current top players are beginning to make the old-school approach shot obsolete. Not only do they view the short ball as an opportunity to crush a winner, but they often skip the approach shot altogether. As educated players hurt opponents, they begin to look for defensive clues—for example, a grip change to a defensive Continental grip, lunging body language, or a shoelace-level strike zone—and actually bypass the approach shot entirely and simply bolt forward to steal the sitter volley. This transition drill incorporates stealing both traditional and swing volleys.

In sets of two, have a friend or coach randomly deliver

1. slice floating groundstrokes;

2. weak drives; and

3. defensive moonball feeds.

The net-rusher's job is to identify the high-percentage response and effortlessly merge the appropriate volley technique, movement, and stances into the play. Flexible skill training involves combining the proper techniques while under stress and on the move. This drill should be done with feeds coming from all three baseline positions (deuce-side alley, center, and ad-side alley). Once the player establishes proficiency, accelerate the drill to a live-ball exercise by adding an opponent and engaging in a point.

Slice Approach

The mechanics of a basic slice (described in chapter 4) remain the same for the approach shot version. The slice approach encompasses different variations, including the deep slice and the short-angle slice, as well as the drop-shot approach. All of these approach options have the same tactical function: to make the opponent bend low and elevate the ball so that the player receives a high, comfortable volley.

In today's game, a large emphasis is placed on lateral movement and topspin. From the Western grip forehands to the two-handed backhands, topspin dominates the spin wars. The goal for a creative net-rusher should therefore be to get the opponent to move forward inside the court, forcing him to produce a low, effective passing shot with his less practiced and less desired underspin grip systems. A short-angle slice approach shot will often reward a net rusher with an easy volley or an errant passing shot.

Movement

Movement varies greatly depending on the type of approach shot employed. Let's look at four common issues related to movement in the transition game.

Running Through the Ball Versus Stopping and Hitting

Coaches often bark, "Run through the ball," then minutes later howl, "No, no, no. Don't run through it! Stop and uncoil!" Sounds confusing, right?

The simple answer to this movement issue is to run through single-segment swings such as slices or traditional volleys. These backspin chip and punch shots occur when a player is seeking a positional court advantage and requires momentum for added power. When the player's feet stop on such shots, the abrupt deceleration of the lower body actually accelerates the upper body in a downward pull. This often drags the shot into the net.

On the flip side, if a player is looking to punish the ball, the best strategy is to stop and load because this requires the coiling and uncoiling of the full kinetic chain. This approach sequence is optimal when going for an outright winner.

Using an Open Stance Versus a Closed Stance

The open stance is terrific for uncoiling a short-ball kill. However, this stance is not recommended when a player is approaching the net. Here's why: The open-stance approach shot pulls the center of gravity around the opposite shoulder and back toward the center of the baseline.

When the player steps into the ball using the traditional closed-stance approach shot, this pulls the center of gravity inward toward the net. Studies show that players employing the closed stance get approximately 9 feet (2.7 m) closer to the net for their first volley.

Moving, Then Striking

A common miscue when capturing the net is spotting the short ball, then slamming on the brakes. Waiting for the weak ball to eventually arrive back on the baseline is an error in time management and positioning.

In advanced tennis, moving into no-man's land well before striking the approach shot pays off in two enormous ways. First, the attacker is taking away precious recovery and setup time from the opponent. Second, the attacker will be positioned well inside the service line, giving him the ability to dissect angles and receive higher volleys. A good general rule is to work hard on getting two or three steps into the court before hitting the transition approach shot.

Following the Ball

Teaching professionals around the world roll their eyes week after week as students at all levels repeatedly ignore this simple advice.

If the outbound approach shot is heading toward the opponent's deuce-side corner, the net player should take a position inside the ad service box (figure 8.3a). If the outbound approach shot is deep down the middle, the net player should move into a volley position straddling the center service line (figure 8.3b). If the approach shot is delivered deep into the opponent's ad corner, the player should simply progress into the deuce-side service box (figure 8.3c). This positioning allows the net player to successfully dissect the opponent's most attractive passing shot angles.

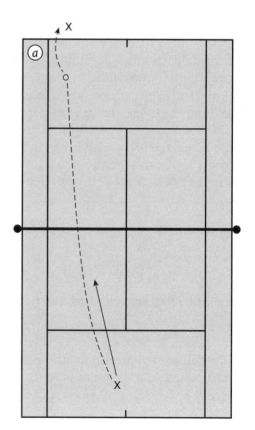

Figure 8.3 Following the ball: (a) to the opponent's deuce-side corner.

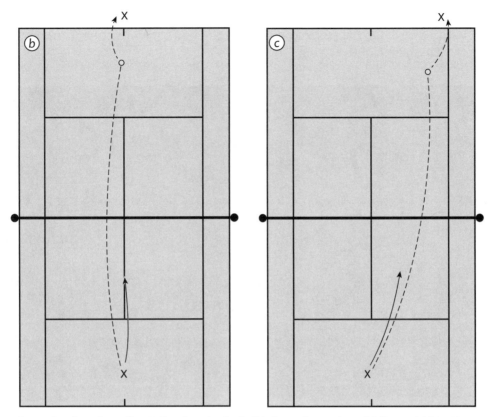

Figure 8.3 *(continued)* Following the ball: *(b)* deep down the middle, and *(c)* to the opponent's ad-side corner.

OVERHEAD

The overhead smash is a shot that puts fear in the hearts of most amateurs. It can result in occasional brilliance, but it often ends in predictable embarrassment. This section uncovers a handful of secrets that will transform an overhead avoider into an overhead hunter.

The primary cause of a misfired overhead is employing a service motion. Although the overhead shares some basic components with the serve—stance, grip, forearm pronation, and keeping the nondominant hand and head up until contact—the overhead is a little trickier. In a typical service motion, the racket head travels approximately 12 feet (3.6 m) of distance from the ready position through the "down together–up together" backswing, up into the loop, and through the contact phase of the stroke. It's one thing to do all of this off a controlled toss, but trying to time a two- or three-millisecond hit off an 80-foot lob dropping at the rate of gravity—often while the player is completely unbalanced—is quite a different proposition. Wherever I travel around the world for tennis workshops, I see amateurs attempting this nearly impossible task. They will invariably shank the ball and say, "You know, I just don't feel my overhead today."

Consistent overheads are a result of a two-part swing. The first part begins with the ready position (figure 8.4*a*). From there, the player executes a quick pivot, pointing the feet, knees, belly button, and shoulders toward the side fence. Simultaneously, the player moves the racket handle directly up to the dominant-side ear (figure 8.4*b*). (Imagine quickly picking up a phone and directly placing it up to your ear to talk.) The role of the nondominant arm is to aid in the coiling process by pointing to the ball with the elbow first (figure 8.4c), then extending the arm to point with the finger (figure 8.4d). This completes part 1 of the swing.

Figure 8.4 Overhead swing, part 1: (a) ready position, (b) pivoting with the racket handle by the ear, (c) pointing with the nondominant elbow, and (d) extending to point with the nondominant finger.

The second phase begins when the lob moves from ascending to the apex into the descent. This is the strike zone phase of the swing. The abbreviated backswing is restarted and moves into its remaining 3-foot (91 cm) swing. Approaching contact, the forearm should pronate (figure 8.5*a*) as the nondominant hand abruptly tucks into the belly to aid in blocking the shoulders and chest—also known as the third link of the kinetic chain—from rotating (figure 8.5*b*). After contact, a relaxed deceleration begins down through the follow-through phase (figure 8.5*c*).

By using this two-part overhead technique, a player can turn a defective liability into a picturesque thing of beauty.

Figure 8.5 Overhead swing, part 2: (*a*) forearm pronation, (*b*) nondominant hand tucking in, and (*c*) deceleration.

Four Boxes

Have a friend or teaching pro feed four lobs from the opposing baseline. The first lob is short into the hitter's deuce-side service box; the next lob is fed directly behind that spot into the deuce-side backcourt; the third is a short lob into the ad-side service box; and the last is a lob deeper into the ad-side backcourt (figure 8.6).

The hitter begins on the service T and moves into each of the four boxes, executing the two-part overhead smash. This pattern is repeated 10 times. The feeder then repeats the exercise from the advantage-side doubles alley and from the center of the court.

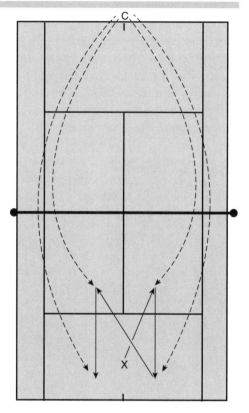

Figure 8.6   Four-boxes drill.

Cleaning Up Motion Blur

In the two-part overhead swing, proper movement includes a slight pause between part 1 and part 2. This critical freeze eliminates motion blur. What's motion blur? Improper core balance or excess head movement can cause motion traumas that produce millisecond drifts from the player's visual target (the ball). The resulting saccade is often the culprit for mishits. By freezing between the two-part swing, the player will have fewer ball-tracking errors.

In this drill, the player hits a basket of balls off a coach's or friend's feeds. The player executes overhead smashes while applying a two-count freeze in between part 1 and part 2 of the two-part swing. This results in fewer shanks and more smiles.

Strike Zone

A common flaw in the spacing component of the overhead smash lies in the actual name of the stroke. When struck properly, the overhead smash isn't really struck over the head. The natural uncoiling of a player's momentum propels the loose hitting arm off to the right (or dominant) side of the head. Trying to hit the overhead directly above the head—as the name suggests—destroys the smooth loop that the player seeks in a perfect serving motion. If anything, it's more accurate to call it an over-the-shoulder smash.

On the overhead, one of the key elements that separates intermediates from advanced players is movement and spacing to the ball. Typically, intermediates arrive at the net and expect the lob to come right to them. When that doesn't happen, which is most of the time, they struggle to strike a clean ball. Advanced players work hard to position themselves properly for the smash. They don't just kill overheads; they hunt them down first, and then kill them. Confidence around the net comes from a lack of fear of the opponent's lob.

Quarterback

Three methods are used to turn and track down a deep lob: the backpedal, the side shuffle, and the turn-and-run. The slowest of these methods is backpedaling. Which method is the most common at the club level? Backpedaling! The second slowest mode is the side shuffle. Which is the second most popular mode of transportation? Side shuffling! The fastest way to recover back for well-placed lobs is to turn and run, yet it's the least frequently used.

A good way to practice the turn-and-run technique is to simulate a quarterback's movement when he drops back to pass. To avoid defenders, the quarterback drops back five yards in five quick steps. This begins with the QB taking the snap from the center, which is similar to a tennis player's ready position (figure 8.7a). In the initial sequence, a left-handed QB begins with a large step back with his left foot (figure 8.7b), immediately followed by a right-foot crossover step (figure 8.7c). The crossover step initiates the quick, balanced run (figure 8.7d) back into the thrower's position (figure 8.7e). This four- or five-step drop-back is the turn-and-run sequence, or motor program, that advanced tennis players seek.

Figure 8.7
Quarterback drill.

Another similarity to the quarterback is that both athletes bring their dominant hand up to their dominant ear in the coiling phase of the turn (see figure 8.7e). This replicates the desired two-part swing mentioned earlier in this chapter. Keep in mind that repetition is needed in order to rewire an old flawed motor program and replace it with the correct one.

This holds true with this footwork drill as well. The player can begin with a simple throwing drill by performing the turn-and-run sequence while holding a tennis ball in the hitting hand. Once the player is comfortable with the proper movement skills, he can switch out the tennis ball for the racket; a coach or friend feeds lobs to the player, and the player smashes away.

Mind-Set

As with the approach shot and volley, the mind-set and intimidation factor are often the keys to a successful overhead. A positive, attacking attitude will often bully an opponent into donating unforced errors and shallow lobs. Taking an offensive court position and angling the overhead into the open court can apply more pressure than hitting the smash as hard as possible. This is known as playing with controlled aggression.

A common mental blunder is disrespecting the slow, easy lob. Often, players assume that the point is won, and they lazily keep their feet planted instead of closing in on the ball. This lapse in movement leads to the ball dropping below the desired contact height. From the mechanical side, the cement feet combined with the premature dropping of the nondominant hand, the eyes, and the racket face angle—the upper body essentially collapsing over—results in the ball smashing into the net. To avoid falling into this trap, players must get into the habit of moving aggressively and treating the easy overhead as though it has a high degree of difficulty.

LOBS

The lob is the most disrespected shot in the game. Macho competitors despise it, condemning its use as cowardly. In fact, the only players who actually admit to loving the lob are the ones with all the trophies. Cunning players use the lob as a means for managing both players' court positions through time management. They also expose flaws in an opponent's movement and stroke production. Lobbers even reveal underdeveloped mental and emotional skills (weeding out the weak) as they drive their uneducated victims crazy.

Lobs come in two general styles: offensive and defensive. With the offensive lob, the player is essentially attempting an outright winner. This type of lob is usually used when the opponent is caught too close to the net or is in a vulnerable, awkward position.

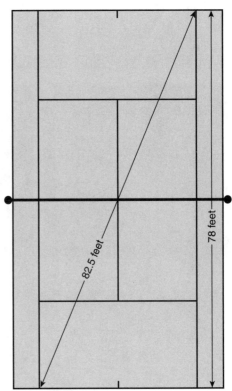

Figure 8.8 From corner to corner, the court distance equals 82.5 feet, whereas down the line, the court distance equals 78 feet.

A defensive lob is used to buy extra time, which enables a player who is in trouble to comfortably recover back into a safe home base position, essentially restarting the point. When possible, defensive lobs should be struck crosscourt. Measured from corner to corner, the length of the court is more than 82 feet (25 m). The distance measured down the line is 78 feet (23.8 m). This means that every lob that lands 4 feet (1.2 m) long on a down-the-line attempt would have landed inbounds if the crosscourt shot was attempted (figure 8.8).

Psychological warfare is at play here as well. Hard-hitting, athletic opponents most often enjoy pace and rhythm. Intelligent lobbers, understanding frustration and tolerance levels, intentionally take away both. This strategy baits an aggressive opponent into overhitting or attempting overly risky shots to finish the point. Once again, a winning strategy often involves hitting the shots that feel most uncomfortable to the opponent—as opposed to always hitting the shots that feel most comfortable to you.

Turn and Burn

Players sometimes receive high defensive lobs that are outside their overhead range. When this occurs, most players bow their head and concede the point. The secret to tracking down these seemingly impossible shots is actually quite simple. The mystery lies in the initial turn. To run back efficiently and receive an easy forehand, the player must ensure that her initial turn and crossover step are toward the backhand volley side. This turn and circle toward the backhand magically positions the player to strike an easier forehand lob or even an offensive stroke. An essential movement tip is that the player should run quickly past the landing zone of the incoming lob and proceed directly to the strike zone of the subsequent hit.

In this drill, the player starts at the net, and a ball is fed beyond the player's overhead smash range. The player must activate the proper turn-and-burn sequence: The player uses the half-circle approach (figure 8.9a), runs past the ball to the strike zone (figure 8.9b), and responds with an easy forehand relob (figure 8.9c). The player should repeat the drill enough times to sufficiently ingrain that initial turn toward the backhand side.

Figure 8.9 Turn-and-burn drill.

Topspin Lob

The topspin lob is used when an offensive opportunity is being presented. The opponent's court position as well as the incoming ball will play a big part in this choice. The topspin lob involves the same fundamental components as a topspin groundstroke (see chapter 4). The primary difference is the increased upward angle of the stroke's low-to-high flight path (figure 8.10). Effective lobbers often lean their center of gravity back as they increase the upward angle of the stroke. At the highest levels, players also commonly use the inverted follow-through. This is when the follow-through finishes on the same side as the contact point. The actual degree of racket face lift, the grip tension, and the racket head speed are dictated by the incoming ball speed, the landing zone, and the strike zone, as well as both players' court positions. A high, slower, and deep incoming ball offers the best opportunity to execute an effective topspin lob. This provides the court distance and time that are required to uncoil the full kinetic chain and unleash the steep-trajectory winner.

Note that a winning play with a topspin lob doesn't have to result in an outright winner. Simply causing an opponent to attempt an overhead from a deep, defensive position will usually achieve the same winning outcome.

Figure 8.10 Topspin lob.

Slice Lob

The slice lob involves the same fundamental components as a slice groundstroke (see chapter 4). The primary differences are the increased upward angle of the open racket face at impact as well as the stroke's low-to-high flight path (figure 8.11).

In beginner through intermediate competition, all relatively deep lobs are considered offensive plays. At the higher levels, this vital stroke is regarded as a defensive tool. Slice lobs are designed to neutralize an opponent's offensive situation. This emergency tactic is most dependable when a player is running forward, stretched wide, or protecting himself from body shots off well-struck overheads or volleys.

Figure 8.11 Slice lob.

Relob

The relob is a utility shot used to deliver a lob off an incoming overhead smash. The relob is essentially a traditional volley—same fundamental stroke production (see chapter 5)—used in an unconventional way. The primary difference is the increased upward angle of the open racket face at impact as well as the stroke's low-to-high flight pattern that is typical of a lob (figure 8.12).

Because of the time constraints and court positions, this is a purely defensive stroke used to neutralize a point. The key tactical play is to make the opponent hit two or three overheads in order to earn the point. Savvy defenders say to themselves as an opponent hits a smash, "Not bad, but I bet you can't do it again."

Figure 8.12 Relob.

Lob Strategy

The development of defensive skill sets is one of the key components that separates retrievers from other playing styles. The primary weapon of choice for defensive players is the use of various lobs and arced groundstrokes. It's a myth that the lob is only used against a net player. This is not so! All great lobbers share the ability to apply these seemingly hidden skills versus baseline players as well.

These five tips help identify when and why lobs should be applied. They also assist players in building shot tolerance while adopting both an offensive and defensive mind-set.

1. **Lob to change the pace.** Practice taking a well-struck groundstroke drive and returning it at half the pace with a higher arch. Hard hitters hate this tactic.

2. **Lob to expose an underdeveloped head-level strike zone.** Opponents who enjoy grooving for hours on end usually have solid primary strike zones. Simply moving the ball higher and out of their comfort zone disrupts their rhythm.

3. **Lob to buy time to manage the court.** When receiving a deep, penetrating ball, practice the art of arching it back deep, 8 to 10 feet (2.4 to 3.0 m) above the net. Keeping a ball deep neutralizes the hard hitter's advantage.

4. **Lob to tire out an opponent physically.** Pack drinks and a few snacks, and calmly elongate every point. While the opponent is saying, "If this guy pushes one more ball, I'm gonna kill something," you'll think, *Man, this is great. I could go to 50 strokes every rally!*

5. **Lob to wear out an opponent mentally and emotionally.** From the psychological side, when a player believes that an opponent will not miss, this causes a sense of despair and lost hope. A mentally and emotionally beaten opponent will often surrender and throw in the towel.

DROP SHOT

In nature, it's a fact that birds fly and fish swim. Occasionally, though, exceptions shadow the rules, and the opposite is true. The same applies to tennis. The swing volley is obviously a member of the volley family. It's defined as a volley because it is taken out of the air. However, the mechanics of the stroke are based on groundstroke fundamentals. Now, let's take the drop shot. By definition, a drop shot is a gently played shot that abruptly lands just after clearing the net. A great drop shot bounces twice before exiting the opponent's service box. This secondary stroke is found in the groundstroke family because the ball is struck after the bounce. However, the drop shot derives its fundamental stroke production from a volley technique.

The drop shot is essentially a volley struck after the bounce. Common components include the Continental grip, the abbreviated shoulder turn, and a compact, banana-shaped backswing. The racket head momentum of acceleration-deceleration at contact also plays an active role in the stroke's production. The primary difference between a drop shot and a traditional volley is the drop shot's elongated high-to-low flight pattern along with the soft, relaxed grip tension through impact (figure 8.13).

Figure 8.13 Drop shot.

Tap–Catch From the Baseline

To be successful at performing drop shots, a player must develop touch. To nurture correct form and feel, a player can use the tap–catch drill first discussed in chapter 5. In this variation, a player stands just inside the baseline in the ready position. A ball is fed to the forehand, and the player gently taps it using a high-to-low brushing motion to apply mild backspin. The ball should only travel about a foot (30 cm) up in the air. The player then catches the ball with the nondominant hand and repeats (refer back to figure 5.10). After a set amount of attempts, the player switches to the backhand side.

Once the player has established the proper feel, he should progress to applying the same technique while feathering the drop shot over the net.

Court Positioning

Court positioning plays a large role in the success or failure of a drop shot. Attempting a drop shot from behind the baseline or off a deep incoming ball is an extremely low-percentage shot. Percentages dramatically tip in a player's favor when the drop shot is played from the midcourt off an opponent's short ball. That's why, from a strategic basis, the drop shot is best implemented as a short-ball option. The opponent's court position also plays a role in the selection of this shot. Spotting an opponent 10 feet (3 m) behind the baseline makes the drop shot attractive, because it's now a high-percentage play.

When players need a physical, mental, or emotional out from a point, they may choose to hit a drop shot from a neutral or defensive position. In these circumstances, it's an all-or-nothing play that will either win or lose the point with one risky stroke.

Drop Shot a Drop Shot

The player begins by standing behind a cone on the center hash mark of the baseline (figure 8.14). A coach (or friend) is positioned on the other side of the net at the service line. The coach tosses a slow, underhand ball (a drop shot) over the net and shallow into the player's deuce-side service box. The player sprints in, hits a forehand drop shot off the coach's drop shot, and retreats back behind the cone. Without delay, the coach tosses another shallow ball into the player's advantage-side service box. The player sprints in and hits a backhand drop shot off the coach's drop shot, and the drill is repeated.

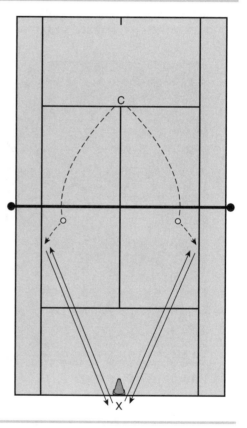

Figure 8.14 Drop shot a drop shot drill.

Drop-Shot Strategy

The drop shot is a delicate shot that requires a good deal of touch, but a well-disguised drop shot has many benefits. These three tips can help transform a drop shot into a weapon that will take backcourt retrievers off the baseline and out of their game.

1. **Drop shot to change the pace.** Great retrievers are at home 10 feet behind the baseline. Seek out short balls that allow you to apply the drop shot–lob sequence pattern. Retrievers aren't known for their dexterity or devastating overhead smashes. This draws them in before you lob over their head.

2. **Drop shot to expose underdeveloped volleys.** Opponents who enjoy a long patience contest are uncomfortable with rapid-fire volleys or quick decisions. Draw the opponent into the net with an abrupt drop shot, and then use passing shot sequences to finish the rally.

3. **Drop shot off the second serve.** Take an opponent's short second serves and use a drop shot to return the ball short and low. Pushers and counterpunchers often serve and then automatically retreat three or four steps behind the baseline to prepare for their defensive warfare. Stop it cold by immediately drawing them forward and forcing them to play in their least favorite part of the court.

The Mental Factor

chapter 9

Tactical and Strategic Execution

Mental toughness may appear to be an inborn talent reserved for the gifted few, but in fact it's a learned behavior. Just as no one is born with a topspin backhand, mental and emotional toughness are not automatic for any player. Mental toughness must be nurtured early in a player's development. Close matches generally boil down to tipping points: crucial games or situations that swing momentum and determine the outcome. These tipping points are usually decided by which player has the more fully developed mental game.

This chapter identifies the most common cognitive stumbling blocks and helps players turn them into stepping stones. Under stressful match conditions, players need to know how to control what's going on "upstairs." By doing so, a player can turn "I should have won" into "I won another tournament!" Earlier chapters focused on creating a tool belt full of primary and secondary strokes. Now it's time to dig deeper into applying those tools, providing insight into organizing game plans, understanding strategies and tactics, and constructing core points.

But what does having sound strategy and game plans have to do with mental toughness? A common misunderstanding is that mental toughness comes from competing hard, staying unflappable at crunch time, and controlling anger and emotions. True, these are characteristics of a mentally tough competitor. At their core, though, the mental components of the game are actually the Xs and Os. These include analytical match decisions such as the following:

- **Positioning:** Being in the right place at the right time to maximize success.
- **Shot selection:** Executing patterns and plays at the appropriate time.
- **Awareness and dissection of opponents:** Exposing the opponent's strengths and weaknesses.

At the higher levels of tennis, all players have dependable strokes. The head is often the most fragile and vulnerable part of a competitor's armor. It's also the main determinant between victory and defeat. Developing mental toughness is a twofold process.

First, the player must establish a series of protocols, and second, he must develop the ability to use those preset solutions for common problems. The speed of the game requires players to resolve emergencies in a millisecond—often in a decision-making frenzy. Therefore, mental toughness is a constant state of alert concentration sustained for hours at a time.

CONCENTRATION

At the center of mental toughness lies concentration; everything stems out from this one discipline. When players concentrate fully, they can better anticipate what comes next in a point. This recognition leads to appropriate reactions, which feed into proper execution of strokes and strategy. It's one connected chain that flows together. The ability to maintain a constant state of concentration often separates the seemingly great athletes from the actual champions. Like almost all things on the tennis court, concentration is a habit that can be learned and improved. Here are some keys to improving concentration:

- Practice in the manner in which you are expected to perform.
- Set task-specific goals and be accountable for them each training session.
- Train your mind to spot past, present, and future thoughts so you can perform "in the moment."
- In matches, focus on the task rather than your personal form.
- Apply rituals to avoid self-doubt and a wandering mind.
- Train your eyes to spot tendencies.
- When appropriate, listen carefully to digest a coach's information.
- Concentrate on work ethic and attitude.

Concentration is the cornerstone of high-level tennis. Hours before a match begins, a top competitor will commit his undivided attention to the upcoming match situation, organizing his tactical plans and the various functions of each component. To help my players visualize a working game plan, I teach them to apply three tiers of match strategy.

Concentrated Focus

The ability to screen out distractions is obviously important in match competition. Increasing the power of concentration requires time and commitment. Players should view concentration as an additional muscle that needs to be strengthened for success. To improve their ability to stay engaged in the task at hand, players should try these three simple exercises:

1. The player focuses on listening closely to every word of her daily conversations. She tries to spot when her attention strays from the topic, and she practices reeling it back in.

2. Once a day for a week, the player takes 10 minutes to sit quietly (with no distracting noises) and count backward from 100 to 1. She focuses on the singular task at hand.

3. The player completes brain games such as a newspaper's free crossword puzzle, Sudoku, or jigsaw puzzles.

THREE TIERS OF MATCH STRATEGY

Professional tennis players are keenly aware of their strengths and weaknesses. Tennis great Jack Kramer once said that if a player's A plan is better than the opponent's A plan, the player will win if he sticks to that plan. If the opponent's A plan is better than the player's A plan, the player will lose unless he adapts and applies a well-developed B or C plan. Following are what I call the three tiers of match strategy and how they should be used during match play.

Global Strategy   Players should begin every match by applying their global strategy, also known as plan A. For any player, the global strategy is to use his strengths early on to dictate the match. It is called the global strategy because it involves using the same winning patterns regardless of the circumstances. Whether in Miami or Moscow, on hard or clay courts, or in the first round or the finals, winners start each match doing what they do best.

Stylistic Strategy   Players should only slide to this secondary strategy, or plan B, when their global strategy is no longer working. Stylistic strategy begins with awareness of the opponent and her style of play. Each style of play has unique likes and dislikes associated with it (see the Assembling Game Plans section later in this chapter). The basis of stylistic strategy is to shift from hitting the shots that feel most comfortable to hitting the shots that pull the opponent out of her comfort zone.

Coach's Corner

It was late August 2004. The U.S. Open grounds provided a definite senses overload for my 15-year-old stepdaughter, Sarah. Sarah was the number 2 player in the junior national rankings. She had experienced a lot of success, winning 10 national singles titles, but this wildcard situation was a different story. In the first round of the Open, Sarah drew Barbara Rittner. The 30-year-old German had once held a career-high ranking of number 24 on the WTA tour.

The first set saw Barbara performing her aggressive baseline style. Her plan A didn't provide enough firepower as Sarah took the first set 6-4. At the start of the second set, Barbara came out with an all-out net-rushing style of play. Sarah comfortably defended the attack. Barbara soon realized that her predesigned plan B wasn't working either. Down 3-1 in the second set, Barbara looked to be on her way back to Germany. But then Barbara did what any experienced competitor would do; she shifted to her plan C. This was moonball city. In front of 2,000 fans, she elongated every point she could to 20- to 30-ball rallies. Barbara changed her trajectories and ball speed. She proceeded to hit only two speeds: slow . . . and slower. After Barbara won three games in that manner, Sarah screamed in disgust, "I hate pushers!" The wily veteran quickly turned to look at Sarah as if she couldn't believe her luck. *This punky kid's telling me how to beat her,* she thought. Barbara took the second set 6-3 and cruised to a comfortable third-set victory. Barbara earned a healthy paycheck that day because earlier in her career, she chose to develop more than one style of play.

Customized Strategy   This strategic plan goes one step deeper than stylistic strategy. Customized strategy, or plan C, takes into consideration the opponent's preferred style of play as well as his personal strengths and weaknesses (see the Assembling Game Plans section later in this chapter). This includes the opponent's movement likes and dislikes, stroke strengths and weaknesses, favorite short-ball option, and favorite patterns of play.

An important part of the mental game is deciding whether to make minor tweaks to a tactical plan or completely abort the global strategy and shift to a secondary style of play. The correct decision is based on how past points have been conducted. If a player is consistently controlling the court, the point construction, and the opponent—yet failing to execute the final blow in most points—the strategic plan is working. Minor adjustments in the player's physical strokes or emotional composure may be the cure. If a player isn't even in the match, however, a shift to plan B or C is probably the best option. Both changing and adjusting require depth of game. Employing secondary strokes and different patterns gives a player a critical edge over the competition. Challenging the opponent to provide answers to additional questions is an important tool in any champion's toolbox.

ASSEMBLING GAME PLANS

To develop the mental game, players begin by determining their preferred style of play. Players should develop strategy to accentuate their strengths while minimizing or avoiding their weaknesses. This is described earlier as a global plan of attack, or plan A; successful execution of this plan leads to winning matches.

The Four Main Playing Styles

Specializing in a certain style enables players to use their natural and nurtured strengths. However, circumstances sometimes dictate that secondary tactics be used. For instance, an opponent may have great success against a player's plan A, but that opponent may struggle mightily against another particular playing style. Therefore, as part of mental training, players need to identify their performance preferences and categorize them into a systematic plan A, B, C, and even D.

Organizing preferred styles of play from best to worse is a key to becoming a serious competitor. The four most common playing styles include the following (these styles were discussed in chapter 1):

1. Aggressive baseliner
2. Retriever
3. Net-rusher
4. Finesse player

Each individual player will determine which style is his bread and butter and will then adjust from there. For instance, hard hitters generally possess big serves as well. If they have respectable volleys, their plan B would be to rush the net. If they can't volley, they'll probably go into retrieval mode. A retriever without much pop or volley skill can turn to finesse. It all depends on a player's particular skill set.

Strategizing Versus the Four Main Playing Styles

In the previous section, we identified the four most common playing styles. A player can practice spotting these styles by visiting the courts and taking the time to observe every player there. While observing, the player should mentally categorize those players into their preferred approach to the game. When performing this exercise, I often ask students questions such as, "OK Kelly, what did you notice about Zoe over on court 6?" This training exercise helps players begin to learn the process of opponent classification.

Opponent match-ups are fascinating. How can Michael easily beat Steve, but Steve handles Mark, yet Mark whip Michael? Like the childhood game of rock-paper-scissors, a particular style of play in tennis often matches up more favorably against a specific opposing style (figure 9.1):

- Just as rock is beaten by paper, an aggressive baseliner's nemesis is the steady retriever.
- Just as paper is destroyed by scissors, a steady retriever is overwhelmed by a solid net-rusher.
- Just as scissors is defeated by rock, a net-rusher is often conquered by the aggressive baseliner.

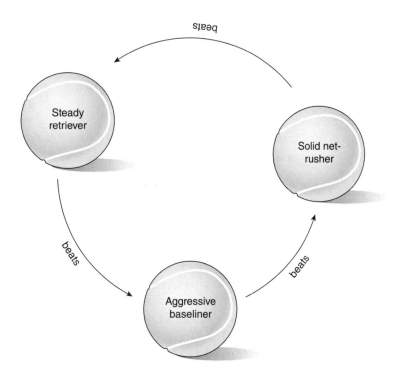

Figure 9.1 How style of play can affect a match-up.

Be aware that some crafty players are hybrids. These players can apply two or more approaches as their primary style of play. Other well-coached opponents will have developed more than one effective style and will also shift into plan B or C when necessary.

A player who wins the first set handily should be on the lookout for a probable shift in the opponent's style of play. If the opponent is well schooled, she will likely go to plan B.

The best players are comfortable with the strategies and tactics needed to dismantle any of the four common opponents. Establishing a basic protocol for each style in order to deprive opponents of their favorite weapons assists greatly in the physical, mental, and emotional battle.

How to Beat an Aggressive Baseliner

The modern game is full of intimidating hard hitters. Unless armed with the appropriate weaponry, engaging in aggressive baseline warfare isn't always in a player's best interest. The job of beating talented aggressive baseliners begins with understanding their frustration tolerance level. Are they comfortable with 2- to 3-, 5- to 6-, or 8- to 10-ball rallies? The second task is to identify the leading causes of their frustration. This is all about finding such flaws and pushing opponents over their limits. Here are a few terrific ways to draw errors from an aggressive baseliner:

1. Offer the opponent slower-speed balls. It's infinitely more difficult to hit a 90 mph forehand off a 35 mph ball compared to an 80 mph return.
2. Move the opponent. Hard hitters much prefer hitting hard over running hard.
3. Elongate the points to tax the opponent's emotional composure and ability to focus.
4. Alter the return of serve and general court position to allow more time to prepare the higher, deeper groundstrokes needed to force the opponent to contact the ball above his comfortable waist-level (primary) strike zone.

Once again, here's where the practical application of those secondary strokes comes into play. Notice that pulling an aggressive baseliner out of his comfort zone requires short-angle groundstrokes, higher-trajectory deep balls, low slices, and variations of serves. These tactics pay great dividends in destroying a hard hitter's desired rhythm. When not facing these variances in tactics, aggressive baseliners can make a match short and painful.

Here are a few patterns that a player can develop when playing against an aggressive baseliner:

Side-Door Angle   The side-door angle shot (see chapter 4) can be applied very successfully against aggressive baseliners. This shot is typically a short slice or dipping topspin crosscourt shot that lands close to where the service line meets the singles sideline. The shot pulls aggressive baseliners away from their comfortable home base and forces them to play some defense. Hard hitters enjoy making their opponents move, not the other way around. This tactic essentially takes the hard hitter away from her desired "boom ball" contest and into a speed contest. Aggressive baseliners often can't resist going for the low-percentage, down-the-line winner off the sharp-angle side-door shot. A player should offer them this risky opportunity and then smile as they crush ball after ball long and wide.

Mixing Spin, Speed, and Trajectories   Aggressive baseliners thrive on rhythm. They enjoy seeing the same clean groundstrokes arrive into their primary strike zone on a regular basis. A player should avoid offering these one-dimensional ball strikers a consistent ball by blending in secondary strokes such as low, slow slices and elevated topspin strokes. Changing ball speeds, spins, and trajectories forces opponents to alter their swing speed, timing, and strike zones. This disturbance of rhythm makes the opponent uncomfortable and results in indecision, which is a leading cause of errors.

Achieving a 70 Percent First-Serve Percentage   Aggressive baseliners usually return a first serve from behind the baseline in a neutral state of mind. However, they take full advantage of weak second serves by shifting their shot selection from neutral to offensive. Aggressive baseliners are known to step inside the court immediately after a missed first serve to crush an opponent's weak delivery. Therefore, intelligent competitors will replace their offensive—and low-percentage—first serve with a high-percentage spin first serve. Achieving a 70 percent first-serve performance helps keep the hard hitters from doing what they do best: crushing short balls.

Keeping Balls High and Deep   By now it should be fairly obvious that avoiding a hard hitter's primary strike zone is a crucial element in defusing his power game. Adjusting groundstrokes to a higher trajectory is another option; this forces the opposition to strike the ball at head level. Many players do not practice using the head-level strike zone enough, so it can be highly uncomfortable for them. Depth is also a critical factor in keeping a hostile enemy on defense. Pushing opponents deep behind the baseline gives them little angle to work with. When up against an aggressive baseliner, a player's battle cry should be "High and deep and watch 'em weep."

How to Beat a Retriever

When playing against a retriever, a player's first assignment is having respect. Competitors who fail to respect steady retrievers—often dismissively labeling them as "pushers"—will pay dearly. Beating these dogged competitors is a difficult assignment indeed. What do most of us do with life's tedious, annoying tasks? Avoid them! But remember, players must practice in the manner in which they are expected to perform. Retrievers are the gatekeepers to that shelf full of trophies. To beat them, a player must seek them out and play practice sets as often as possible. Why do players with solid primary strokes lose to pushers? They practice wrong. Grooving solid, waist-level groundstrokes back and forth, or worse, having a pro feed balls at waist level and directly to a player's primary strike zone will never help anyone beat those crafty retrievers. Instead, the practice routine should be modified so that the player develops the skills that are essential to the task—patience, concentration, composure, fitness, transition competence, and a variety of secondary strokes and shot-sequencing patterns. Being able to continually pull retrievers out of their comfort zone requires all of these components. If a player neglects to develop a complete game, this will exact a heavy toll when the player is facing a retriever.

Here are a few patterns that a player can develop when playing against a retriever:

Side-Door Pattern   The side-door pattern applies a one-two punch. The first stroke is the short-angle building shot (see chapter 4). As mentioned earlier, these are usually dipping topspin crosscourt shots or short slices that land near the spot where the singles sideline meets the service line. This shot pulls retrievers away from their comfort zone behind the baseline. The second shot delivers the offensive blow deep to the opposing corner or back behind the opponent. Applying the side-door pattern off a weak second serve can often be successful against high-level retrievers.

Moonball Approach Shot to Swing or Drop Volley   Retrievers are usually gifted counterpunchers. Rather than trying to attack them with a traditional approach shot, launching a moonball (see chapter 8) can cause them much more trouble. This terrific approach offers little pace and pushes the opponent well behind the baseline. Having banished the retriever from the playing field, the player now just needs to execute a simple swing or drop volley (see chapter 5) to win the point.

Drop Shot to Pass or Lob Once again, the drop shot (see chapter 8) followed by a pass or lob is another effective one-two combination. Retrievers often avoid the net—going to the net is a contrast of style from their slow, safe system of play. Pulling them out of their comfort zone and into the forecourt often proves successful. Keep in mind that a drop shot is a short-ball option. A player should use the drop shot off a weak second serve or a ball landing in her short-ball range. Players should not force a drop shot by attempting one off a high, deep incoming ball. Once retrievers are drawn to the net, they are essentially fish out of water. Passing shots or lobs are great complements to complete the shot sequence.

Remaining on the Baseline and Taking Balls on the Rise Instead of the development of a secondary stroke, this tactic requires the development of a secondary strike zone (see chapter 4). The moonball—a retriever's primary weapon—has an incoming trajectory that requires contact to be made most often at head level. Hitting the moonball on the rise at waist level is a more offensive yet risky option; doing so requires impeccable timing and hours of rehearsal. Otherwise, a player is forced to retreat to allow the ball to drop into the preferred primary strike zone. Having the ability to consistently handle the high ball prevents a player from being sucked into the retriever's deadly style of play.

How to Beat a Net-Rusher

Defeating a talented net-rusher requires a unique set of neutralizing tools and court positions. Players who are eager to take the net apply immediate pressure, giving opponents little time to feel comfortable stroking the ball. By shortening the court, net-rushers steal recovery time and allow no opportunity for proper decision making. To counter this suffocating style of play, variation is the key. The strategy once again lies in hitting shots that feel least comfortable to the opponent as opposed to simply hitting those warm and cozy primary shots that most players prefer to hit.

For example, net-rushers have a difficult time with opponents who employ the chip-and-dip tactical play. This variation of off-pace slice returns and slow topspin rollers causes havoc because the net-rushers are continually asked to supply their own pace and angle to shoestring volleys. Another good tactic is spinning serves wide to force return-and-charge opponents into transitioning to the net through the doubles alley, which opens up wide passing shot angles. Returning serves from varied positions—inside or behind the baseline, toward the doubles alley—is also very effective at putting a serve-and-volleyer in a constant state of adaptation and adjustment.

Here are a few other effective patterns for players to develop against the net-rusher:

Achieving a 70 Percent First-Serve Percentage Net-rushers are opportunistic on weak second serves, commonly using the second serve as their chance to approach. Just as with hard hitters, an effective strategic shift is to limit these openings by hitting fewer second serves. Instead of attempting offensive yet low-percentage first serves, the player should take pace off and apply more spin. The goal is to connect on 70 percent of first serves. This keeps the net-rushers from being offensive on their returns and establishing their desired attack.

Keeping Balls High and Deep Consistently keeping shots high and deep is never a bad strategy against anybody. Players who can do so generally win a lot of matches. But depth of shot is especially important versus net-rushers. The deeper in the court a net-rusher is forced to play shots, the more difficult it will be for her to transition forward. Elongating points while offering the net-rusher consistent head-level strike zones will cause her to become frustrated. This patience contest is a critical factor in keeping the attacker at bay. The player should repeat this phrase early and often: "Keep 'em back and watch 'em crack."

Using the Second-Shot Pass   A common pitfall when facing a net-rusher is attempting a crushing blow the moment the opponent transitions toward net. This often leads to errors without even forcing the opponent to produce a winning volley—a cardinal sin against a net-rusher. Instead of going for the knockout with one shot, a player should employ smart counterpunching tactics: He should place the first strike low at the feet of the onrushing player to force a defensive, weak volley in response. Now the opening is there for the player to attempt an aggressive passing shot or lob on the second shot.

Capturing the Net First   One of the best ways to counter net-rushers is to beat them at their own game. Obviously, this requires a player to have a certain level of comfort and skill with volleys and overheads, but it should be part of a plan B or C in a well-rounded player's arsenal. Keep in mind that net-rushers generally don't practice their defensive components because they'd rather be volleying. So by transitioning to the net first, a player not only forces net-rushers into a backcourt defensive position, but also forces them to use what could be their weakest cadre of shots.

How to Beat a Finesse Player

Drop-shot artists, junk ballers, spin doctors, hackers—these colorful labels describe a group of players who apply nonconventional offense. These mischievous opponents thrive on destroying rhythm. Their soft hands absorb pace and then redirect the ball, usually with irritating spin and location. In addition, they often possess hidden skills such as excellent anticipation and angle dissection, which helps them gain advantageous court positions.

However tempting it may be, trying to overpower players of this sort is ill-advised. Getting tangled up in their games of cat-and-mouse is also rarely a good idea. To beat the finesse player, players must rely on their own psychological warfare.

Players can apply the following patterns and plays to avoid being the next fly in a finesse player's web:

Drop Shot on a Drop Shot   The drop shot and pass or lob combination is a bankable play from the finesse player. A player can break this pattern early by essentially saying, "If I'm gonna run, so are you." By executing an effective redrop, players can take away the finesse player's intention of exhausting them physically and mentally (see the drop shot a drop shot drill in chapter 8). Anticipation is key: Players must spot the drop shots early by paying close attention to the depth of shot as well as the preparation phase of the spin doctor's backswing. If the opponent uses a high-to-low stroke pattern with slow racket speed, this is an indication that the drop shot is on the way.

Achieving a 70 Percent First-Serve Percentage   Finesse players don't overpower, but they will still take advantage of short-ball opportunities—such as a short second serve. Many will step in and carve a short, nasty angle or even feather a drop shot. Just as when facing other aggressive returners, it makes sense to avoid offering many second serves. The goal should be to put 70 percent of first serves in play to prevent the finesse player from starting the slow torture.

Keeping Balls High and Deep   Is there an echo in here? Yes, once again, depth of shot is a huge defense—maybe the cornerstone strategy—against drop-shot artists. For one thing, drop shots are a short-ball option. Keeping the opponent pinned behind the baseline dramatically increases the opponent's risk in hitting the drop shot. Plus, effective drop shots are often contacted around waist level. Elevating the strike zone to head level amps up the difficulty level and lowers the success rate. Unless they're willing to play low-percentage tennis the entire match, this tactic basically deprives finesse players of their favorite weapon.

Capturing the Net Finesse players may possess effective lobs, but they generally don't react well to being pressured by net-rushers. They prefer to use the forecourt area to manipulate opponents, and transitioning forward robs them of another favored play. Attacking the off-pace finesse player also provides players with the opportunity to transition forward on their own terms. Because finesse players aren't able to consistently manufacture their own power, the net-rushing pattern of the moonball approach shot followed by a swing or drop volley is a highly effective tactic against them.

Again, players must remember that their primary strategy should be applied first at the start of each match. But if the plan A is faltering, these preset patterns of play can save the day. Think of them as cheat sheets for match play. Each player should construct a priority list that ranks the styles of play—from one to four (most to least)—that cause him the most headaches. Players must set aside the appropriate amount of time to practice the tactical nuances needed to beat every style of play.

Customizing Play

Reactive players have little in the way of a game plan; they simply react to whatever the opponent delivers. Proactive players, however, come prepared. Their plan is based on not only controlling their own movements and actions, but controlling those of the opposing player as well. The patterns they envision are an optimal combination of their strengths playing into the opponent's weaknesses. This is especially true on mega points (critical points within a match). Running intelligent patterns on these game-turning points is a key factor in mental warfare.

Developing a customized list of proactive patterns begins with a script. By listing his favorite go-to patterns, the player begins to develop a systematic, higher-percentage approach to matches. An appropriate analogy is that of Hollywood actors: Once a script for a show is developed, dress rehearsals begin. Everybody practices exactly what they're supposed to do and say. This is followed by the actual shoot of the aired show. If it's a good script and everyone hits their lines, the show works.

Likewise, for a tennis player, proactive patterns should be developed and committed to paper. Then comes the dress rehearsal phase of repeatedly drilling these patterns along with using them in practice sets. Finally, after the appropriate amount of time, these proactive patterns are ready for the real show: a tennis tournament or league match.

Let's begin to expose the inner workings of proactive patterns. The following is a sample script of a junior player who is ranked in the top 10 nationally. She is a right-hander, visualizing playing against another right-hander. Her pre-tournament Proactive Patterns Worksheet looks like figure 9.2. (For a blank version of the form that players can fill out and customize before their next tournament, visit www.humankinetics.com/products/all-products/championship-tennis.)

Accelerated learning requires players to shift the focus of their practice from the fundamental strokes to pattern rehearsal. For example, for an entire hour session, players could shift the focus away from rallying back and forth to focusing 100 percent of their attention on a specific group of proactive patterns. A player should prioritize the pattern development sessions according to her strengths and weaknesses.

Figure 9.2   Proactive Patterns Worksheet

Serving Patterns and Percentage Frequency

Serving to the Deuce Side

1. Slice the serve out wide—hit to the opposite side or behind the returner. (30%)

2. Kick serve into the two-handed backhand—continue to attack the backhand. (50%)

3. Slice serve into the body—exploit the resulting opening. (20%)

Serving to the Advantage Side

1. Kick serve wide—hit to the open court. (60%)

2. Flat serve wide—hit behind the returner. (20%)

3. Slice serve down the center—hit into the backhand. (20%)

Return-of-Serve Patterns and Percentage Frequency

First Serve

1. Stand 5 feet back—arc the return high and deep down the middle. (50%)

2. Apply the big X pattern [see chapter 7]. (50%)

Second Serve

1. Start the point deep down the middle. (50%)

2. Punish it by running around backhand and crushing forehand. (25%)

3. Torture the opponent with a short-angle, side-door return. (10%)

4. Bring the opponent in with a drop shot followed by a pass or lob. (5%)

5. Turn up the heat with an approach shot–volley pattern. (10%)

Rally Patterns and Percentage Frequency

1. Isolate the opponent's backhand. (50%)

2. Hit deep and crosscourt until receiving a short ball. (10%)

3. Roll side-door patterns. (10%)

4. Mix the spin, speed, and trajectories to change the rhythm. (15%)

5. Get four balls in per point. (15%)

Net Rushing Patterns and Percentage Frequency

1. Serve and volley. (0%)

2. Drive and charge off weak second serves. (10%)

3. Approach off short balls and attack the backhand. (10%)

4. Moonball approach to swing volley pattern. (50%)

5. Spot the defensive slice and steal a volley. (30%)

REDUCING ERRORS

As everybody knows, tennis is a game of errors. Deciphering the actual cause of the error is the initial step in error reduction. A study that I conducted with nationally ranked juniors in Southern California found that in match play, there are four main causes of errors:

1. Poor shot selection (46 percent)

2. Below-par movement and spacing (32 percent)

3. Inadequate emotional control or rituals (12 percent)

4. Inferior stroke mechanics (10 percent)

What do most intermediate players focus on? You've got it: strokes! Up to the elite levels of the game, retrievers tend to have all the trophies, and it's not because of their elegant strokes. They win by developing their shot selection skills. Following are some practical tips for improving shot selection:

Offense

- Position inside the court to reduce the opponent's recovery time.
- Apply proper movement and spacing to contact the ball at the desired waist-level strike zone.
- Change the angle of the ball or attack the opponent's weakness relentlessly.

Neutral

- Simply match the ball speed.
- Apply secondary "building" shots to compromise the opponent's position.
- Use proper heights above the net to maintain proper depth.

Defense

- Position farther back behind the baseline.
- Elevate shots with heavy topspin to buy recovery time.
- Simply get the point back to neutral instead of going for an offensive shot.

How do players determine whether their next shot should be offensive, neutral, or defensive? One way is to make the decision based on their position on the court, or zonal tennis. As a general rule, the farther inside the baseline a player can play the ball, the more offensive options become available to him. Obviously, if a player is scrambling up to the service line to retrieve a tough drop shot, the return becomes more defensive. So in addition to positioning, a player's balance, the ball height, and preparation time will all affect the type of shot that can be produced.

Zonal Tennis

Zonal tennis has been applied successfully for decades. In the 1970s, zones were described as defensive, neutral, and offensive. In the 1980s, the popular terms were *defend, attack,* and *kill.* Recent catch phrases include "control, hurt, and finish." In the spirit of evolution, let's coin our own descriptions: the grind, torment, and obliterate zones. But before getting into the dynamics of these court zones, let's first cover air zones.

Air Zones

Air zones refer to the height at which the ball travels above the net. A player's court position dictates the height that the shot should travel above the net. Unforced errors and short balls multiply dramatically when players choose to ignore the laws of the air zones.

The rules are simple. When inside the court, a player should aim 2 to 3 feet (61 to 91 cm) above the net. On the baseline, a player should aim 3 to 5 feet (91 to 152 cm) above the net; and when 10 feet behind the baseline, the player should aim 8 to 10 feet (2.4 to 3.0 m) above the net (figure 9.3).

The higher a player hits the ball over the net, the deeper it will generally go into the opponent's court. The farther back a player is, the higher he needs to hit the ball to achieve the depth required to keep the opponent pinned to the baseline. Therefore, as the player moves up, less net clearance is needed.

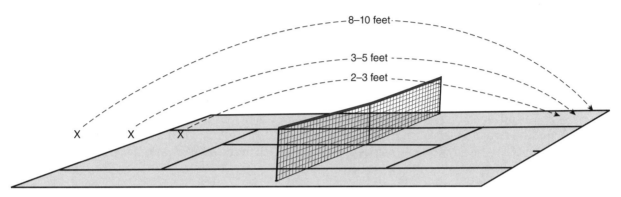

Figure 9.3 The three air zones in tennis.

Court Zones

Now that we have discussed air zones, let's move on to court zones. To determine the court zones, divide both halves of the court (39 feet [11.9 m] each) into three even zones (figure 9.4). The zone (location) in which the ball lands dictates the highest-percentage options for shot selection. Smart tacticians simply match their intentions with the landing zones.

Zone 1, or the grind zone, is located from the baseline inward about 13 feet (3.9 m). When a ball is about to land in the grind zone, the high-percentage shot would be a safe, deep return. Mature players avoid the temptation of going for an offensive shot from this zone.

Zone 2, or the torment zone, is the middle zone. It is located approximately 13 feet inside the court to approximately 13 feet from the net. When a ball lands inside this center zone, a player should apply building shots as well as attacking shots.

Zone 3 is the obliterate zone; it includes the 13 feet closest to the net. Groundstroke kills,

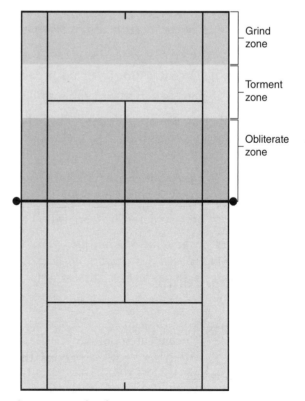

Figure 9.4 The three court zones in tennis.

approach-volley patterns, and deadly droppers should be applied in this zone. Finishing the point with an offensive play is the correct tactical move here.

Advanced players are keenly aware that the same zonal warfare applies on both sides. In other words, the location where a shot lands on the opponent's side dictates his options for a high-percentage shot. If a player dumps a short ball in the opponent's obliterate zone, it's time to defend. Playing zonal tennis greatly increases a player's anticipatory speed, court coverage, and shot variations. By shifting the focus to this mental strategy, players can dramatically improve their win–loss record.

Be aware that the zones are still "gray" areas depending on the incoming ball's spin, speed, and trajectory. Exceptions shadow every rule, so players must use their court sense and abilities in match play.

Offensive, Neutral, or Defensive Shot Selection

Beginners and intermediates are often taught to practice by calling their intended stroke as the incoming ball is passing over the net. This quick motor program drill is designed to eliminate hesitation so the player can calmly produce a smooth stroke.

The advanced version of this drill is to replace calling out the intended stroke with calling out the stroke's tactical intention: offense, neutral, or defense. This helps players shift their focus from the physical mechanics of hitting the ball to the mental task of identifying where and why they are executing a particular shot.

Charting Shot Selection

An effective live-ball exercise is to have two players play a tiebreaker while a third player charts their shot selections. The stat collector places a check mark in one of the three shot selection categories for each ball that a player strikes (table 15.3 can be used for this purpose). Statistical data may look like this:

- 70 percent offensive (going for a winner)
- 20 percent neutral (building, probing shots)
- 10 percent defensive (simply trying to get out of a compromising position)

Then those same players should chart the shot selection percentages of a WTA or ATP touring professional during a televised match. Here's what they usually calculate for the professional:

- 20 percent offensive (going for a winner)
- 60 percent neutral (building, probing shots)
- 20 percent defensive (simply trying to get out of a compromising position)

At advanced club levels and in high-performance junior tennis, improper shot selection is the leading cause of errors, and a clear cause-and-effect connection exists between improper shot selections and escalating emotional distress.

Consistency

In the tennis world, consistency is the granddaddy of strategy. The fewer errors committed, the greater the chance of winning. Consistency is developed through disciplined repetition of the physical, mental, and emotional components. But consistency is a lot like love: Confusion stems from the many meanings of the word. It would be shortsighted to limit its definition to "the ability to repeatedly put a ball in play." Consistency may mean that to a beginner, but it's something else to an ATP tour veteran. The difference lies in the customized application of the word. Successful consistency is dictated by a player's level of experience.

The seven phases of consistency are as follows:

1. Striking three balls consecutively "clean" on the strings
2. Placing five balls in a row inside the court boundaries
3. Continuously hitting on-court target areas
4. Consistently winning three points in a row
5. Performing at one's peak performance level three sets in a row
6. Performing at one's peak performance level four consecutive matches
7. Performing at one's peak performance level two events in a row

Novice players primarily seek consistency in the form of physical reliability. This includes achieving consistency in the fundamental strokes, movement, and stamina needed to compete. At the higher echelons of the game, competing requires mental and emotional endurance as well. These components may appear in the form of consistently making appropriate shot selections, continually choosing the correct pattern play, consistent concentration, consistent opponent awareness, and consistent between-point rituals, not to mention consistently winning matches.

MIND CONTROL

Players who haven't been educated in the importance of emotional control are often their own worst enemy in tournament competition. If competitors can't control their own wandering minds, how can they expect to control their physical skills, the ball, or the opponent?

Neurologists have suggested that an average person has roughly 58,000 thoughts in a 24-hour period. Inner dialogue is ever present. It aids us in how we process information and how we organize our lives. Self-talk used correctly can be a positive, calming, motivational force. Self-chatter that turns sour can also become the negative voices running the fun house. An age-old expression is, "Whatever we think about tends to multiply."

Over the course of a two-hour match, most players have approximately 5,000 thoughts streaming through their head. Yet in many prematch pep talks, the mantra is, "Remain performance oriented. Only think one point at a time and focus on three specific things." Great. But what about the other 4,997 thoughts?

Past, Present, and Future Thoughts

It's not easy to keep the mind quiet and focused. One of the more effective ways to do this is to remain performance oriented rather than fantasize about the outcome. A player's thoughts should be devoted to executing the next point pattern rather than focusing on the scoreboard. Outcome scenarios are irrelevant to the task at hand. Mental endurance is a factor that weighs heavily in tournament play. The ability to put everything out of one's mind except for the immediate relevant assignment is what often separates champions from almost champions. This goes for negative thoughts as well. During match play, three main categories of negative thoughts may cloud a player's mind: past, present, and future thoughts.

Here are some examples of past negative thoughts:

- *I'm playing Alexandra; she hooked me six times last match. She's going to cheat again.*
- *I'm playing the guy who won the Cleveland city title. He's going to kill me.*
- *Great . . . I always choke when I get these 5-2 leads.*
- *She's a pusher; I'm going to lose for sure. I've never beaten a pusher.*
- *I always wilt in the heat, and it's 100 degrees today.*

Here are some examples of present negative thoughts:

- *My volleys are terrible! I refuse to go back up to the net.*
- *Sarah's playing really well; I can't beat her when she's hitting like this.*
- *I'm so slow today. I can't get to any of his drop shots.*
- *I can't stand playing in the wind. My shots are going all over the place.*
- *Here he goes again, pushing. This could take all day! If this match goes three sets, I'm going to miss my dinner plans.*

Here are some examples of future negative thoughts:

- *OK, I'm up 4-1. It looks like Kate's up in the other semifinal match. What does their scorecard say? I'd rather play her in the finals.*
- *I'll never get that scholarship if I don't win today.*
- *What are my friends and parents going to say when I win this match?*
- *I'll surely get that wild card into the pro event now.*
- *What's my ranking going to jump to after this win?*
- *Where's that huge trophy going in my room?*
- *If I lose to this toad, I'll be the laughing stock of the club.*

Silencing doubts, fears, thoughts of accolades, and visions of postmatch scenarios involves a sort of self-hypnosis. It requires players to push aside their weaknesses and overemphasize their strengths. Players must believe in their superiority, without being overly confident to the point of not taking the match seriously. A player must make a continuous effort to treat stumbling blocks as stepping stones. The player needs to have the ability to mentally fix flaws without emotional attachment. This composure is one of the greatest tools of a gifted competitor.

Note that, when used correctly, past positive thoughts can act as a reminder of successful performances. These thoughts may include winning patterns and plays from previous matches. Repeating these plays is often part of the strategy found in the game plan of effective players. During a match, when a player focuses on the present task at hand, his odds of success will also dramatically improve. Devoting 100 percent of one's attention to the current assignment requires tuning out destructive thoughts and distractions. An effective way to do this is to focus on performance goals, which identify the specific tasks required for success in the match. Finally, although positive future thoughts distract a player from focusing on the task at hand during match play, these thoughts can be used after a match as a means of reflection.

Here are some examples of past positive thoughts:

- *I have beaten Angie before; I can do it again today!*
- *Wyatt's a net-rusher, and I love playing net-rushers.*
- *The finals are on stadium court. I always like to put on a good show on stadium court.*

Here are some examples of present positive thoughts (proactive performance goals):

- *Get 70 percent of my first serves in.*
- *Serve to the backhand; don't feed the forehand.*
- *Apply the short-ball options, including the side-door pattern and bringing the retriever in to the net.*
- *Slow down and employ between-point rituals.*
- *Use the moonball approach to swing volley tactic.*

Here are some examples of future positive thoughts:

- *If I keep training like this, when the opportunity comes, I'll be ready.*
- *The fastest way to become the best is by beating the best.*

Studies suggest that athletes with a focused agenda have a greater chance of elongating peak performance levels in competition. Therefore, proactive performance goals, or present positive thoughts, are the most important thoughts to employ throughout a match.

Focusing on Performance Goals Instead of Outcome Goals

Sport science research suggests that being performance oriented rather than outcome oriented increases positive motivation; improves focus; relaxes muscle tension; reduces anxiety, stress, and pressure; and increases confidence and concentration levels. Best of all, it increases a player's chances of achieving peak performance, which leads to the desired outcome.

Unfortunately, uneducated tennis parents and coaches are sometimes the leading cause of an athlete's poor match-day performance, and they don't even know it. While they drive their player physically to the match, their prematch banter also chauffeurs the athlete mentally and emotionally through the ringer. They inadvertently kill any chance of their player reaching peak performance. By placing extreme focus on the outcome instead of the performance, they unintentionally put their player in a mind-set that leads to losing the match.

Parental pregame motivational speeches often include statements such as the following:

- "We have the worst luck with these draws! You're playing the number 2 girl in the country."
- "We have to win this one! You may never get another shot like this."
- "Your mother and I just spent $2,000 to get here. Don't blow it."
- "If you don't win, don't expect your father and me to keep supporting your tennis."

Coaches' pregame speeches often include these types of statements:

- "We're going to nationals if you win today."
- "This is the most important match of the year! It's do-or-die; we have to win."
- "A win today will push us into the top 10! We've never been in the top 10."
- "If you don't win today, I'll have no choice but to drop you down on the team ladder."

In such situations, the player's pregame internal dialogue may include thoughts similar to the following:

- *Happiness depends on this win.*
- *If I fail, I'll disappoint my family, coaches, and teammates.*

- *If I lose, I won't get that college scholarship.*
- *If I don't win, I'll lose my spot on the ladies league squad and won't be invited to the luncheons any longer.*

The athlete is then so tense during competition that his muscles tighten and his heart races, leading to faulty execution, poor decision making, and subpar performance. Unfortunately, all the way home, the player gets all the blame for the loss.

However, players, parents, and coaches can all take positive steps to be performance oriented. Following are some ways that players can go into matches with the right mind-set.

Using Imagery   Players should mentally rehearse properly executed strokes, patterns, and protocols. This is best done at two specific instances on match day: during both the prematch and prepoint routines. Players should also apply these visualization techniques when falling asleep at night and waking up in the morning. Neurology studies have found that this is when the subconscious mind is easily accessible. Excellence doesn't have to be an occasional act; it can be a habit. Success on the court often depends on meaningful repetition off the court. The first step in performing great is to relive the process of performing great over and over in one's mind until it becomes natural.

Setting Reasonable Goals   A player must realize that even professionals lose almost every week. They go home unsatisfied yet comfortable because they've established reasonable goals. Nobody should feel the need to win every match in order to be happy. Winning 7 out of 10 matches is an excellent ratio. Players who win less than 40 percent of their matches may be wise to seek out lesser competition. All that losing can erode confidence. However, players who win 90 percent of their matches should look to move up a division to face better opponents.

Seeking Persistence   There is nothing more common than talented yet unsuccessful players. Innate ability can only be maximized through persistence and determination. Character and work ethic are the elements that push champions past the field. Having a house full of trophies requires the development of the physical, mental, and emotional components of the game. Proper planning prevents poor performances. If a player takes care of the small details and keeps looking to improve, the big picture will take care of itself.

Coach's Corner

For every match, the focus should be on the athlete's performance versus the athlete's potential, not the athlete's performance versus the opponent's performance. I regularly ask players, parents, and coaches to imagine that the athlete is a gymnast. This gymnast's highest score ever achieved in competition is an 8.0. Today, however, she performs above her peak performance level and receives a 9.5 from the judges. Ten minutes later, a very strong competitor scores a perfect 10 to win it all. Therefore, the gymnast does not win the competition, but she has nevertheless exceeded her previous level and performed brilliantly. While uneducated players, coaches, and parents will view the day as a failure, those who understand performance versus potential will view the performance as a shining success.

Improving Focus Management

A favorite saying of mine is, "You have to be comfortable being uncomfortable." For many athletes, focusing over the course of an entire match is uncomfortable. This is where discipline comes into play. Players can strengthen their focus by preestablishing and having confidence in their various game plans. Once focus goes adrift, the ability to restore it requires a plan to control internal and external distractions. A player must devise a predetermined code of behavior for handling stressors such as cheaters, pushers, and any unfavorable or uncontrollable elements.

Catch phrases can be used to assist in maintaining peak performance. Examples include "Tossing arm up" (on the serve), "Three balls in" (to elongate points), "High and deep" (for better depth), or "Move your feet" (to cover more court).

Manufacturing the pressure of match situations in practice is a superb way to rehearse handling stress. Following are some suggestions for on-court training:

- Use live-ball, pressure-packed simulation exercises with consequences.
- Practice patterns versus various styles of opponents.
- Lengthen training sessions to simulate a three-set or two-and-a-half-hour match.
- Train in inclement weather to simulate possible tournament conditions.
- Train at less desirable times of day to simulate matches with an 8:00 a.m. or 9:30 p.m. starting time.
- Practice between-point rituals and changeover rituals (when the mind wanders most in matches).

Controlling Mega Points and Mini-Mega Points

Playing "not to lose" and hoping that the opponent is going to simply hand over the trophy is rarely a good strategy. Sure, this occasionally works at the lower levels, but it isn't in a player's best interest over the long haul.

Controlling the mega points begins with being able to spot the actual game-winning points—six of the eight potential game-winning points are decided on the advantage side (40-0, 40-30, 0-40, 30-40, ad-in, and ad-out). Therefore, it makes sense for players to practice serving and returning strokes and patterns on the advantage side most often.

Players must also recognize the mini-mega points in a game. An example is when the score is 30-15. With this slight lead, players often ease their concentration level, giving the next point to the opponent and thus evening the score at 30-30. Recognizing this mini-mega situation requires absolute focus. A player must have conviction to run the smartest pattern and to "play to win." After all, a 40-15 lead offers a little more cushion.

A similar situation occurs when the game score is 4-2 in a set. Again, all too often with a break in hand, mentally soft competitors let their guard down and sloppily give a game back to their opponent. At 4-3, the opponent becomes engaged and dangerous. By staying focused on the importance of the mini-mega game, a player can build a 5-2 advantage.

Players can enhance their success on mega points by using video analysis to take a second look at their performance in these situations. Is the player spotting these situations? Is the player then executing the correct tactical plan? Is the player making the right decisions? Seizing the few precious match-altering points requires a heightened sense of awareness and the frame of mind to take the match. Players can control the mega points by turning up the concentration at the critical stages of a game, set, or match.

Brain Functions in Competition

Everything we do begins with a mental act. The tiniest move to wiggle an index finger begins with brain function. Lateralization of brain function refers to the specialization of functions between the left and right hemispheres of the brain. This "left brain versus right brain" theory has been used in sport science for decades. It includes the broad generalizations of labeling the left side as "logical" and the right side as "creative." Similar to the personality profiling covered in chapter 1, although there is a lateral dominance, both characteristics exist in both sides. For the purpose of this book, we'll look at each side's tendencies and trends as they relate to the art of winning tennis matches under stress.

A competitor who is analyzing every backswing and every follow-through is acting within the realm of left-brain dominance. A common misconception is believing that this hyper state of performance awareness is beneficial; it's not. Players who overanalyze and try to perform while in a constant state of criticism will never achieve mental peak performance.

The state of mind that leads to superior performance is achieved by using the right hemisphere of the brain. Tennis players who perform in this subconscious, creative mental state—often called "the zone"—report a flowing, trancelike lack of conscious effort. In this ideal mental state, they hit cleanly and accurately, and they make all the correct decisions. Today's players call this sensation "treeing"—as in the player was up in a tree, cracking winners all match and never coming down off the high. Players who are in the zone process information without criticizing and analyzing. They play without attaching negative emotions to their performance.

So, how do players perform at their peak levels without emotional judgment? The answer is simple: by keeping the left side of the brain busy with important tasks. If the analytical side is busy, it won't cloud the mind with critical and unnecessary thoughts.

Overanalyzing or criticizing performance is often carried out in between points and during changeovers. To help avoid these performance detractors, players should use proper rituals. Between-point rituals should include these three aspects in order to prevent the player from being pulled out of the "tree":

1. Getting over the previous point without an emotional attachment
2. Planning the next point's pattern of play
3. Performing a relaxation routine

If the player's mind is busy focusing on the proper process of the between-point ritual, there is no time nor room for negative or irrelevant thoughts to creep in.

The little devil in one's ear also rears his meddlesome head during changeovers. Most people have seen the external rituals of professionals, such as toweling off, drinking, and closing their eyes to focus. What isn't apparent is their internal routines. Smart players engage in internal dialogue throughout a changeover. This routine consists of a relaxed dissection of the previous two games along with planning for the two subsequent games. Again, the process has a unique purpose of keeping the left side of the brain busy and away from pulling the player into trouble.

Changeover dialogue should consist of a brief series of questions and answers: *Did I hold my last service game? Why? What's my plan in my upcoming service game?* After assessing the serve comes an analysis of the return game: *Did I break serve? Why? Why not? What should I be doing in the next return game?* Applying this type of internal ritual is the secret to quieting negative mental chatter.

Just as players can't expect to run a great pattern in matches unless they first do it over and over in practice, the same holds true for developing rituals. With this in mind, players should schedule practice sets in which the focus shifts from the actual points to the between-point and changeover routines necessary to quiet the overthinking, judgmental left side of the brain.

Tipping Point Tendencies

The dividing line between winning and losing tight matches is mental preparation. Each match has two or three defining moments that can tip the match in a player's favor. By incorporating preexisting strategies as go-to plans, a player can find quick answers and take the correct action to seize these critical points.

A player must learn why she loses before she can learn how to win. The player should think back to the last few times a winnable, tight match slipped away. Players often blame a loss on bad luck, a cheating opponent, a lack of "feel," or the lucky socks that were in the wash. In reality, those recurring defeats are most likely due to incomplete training.

Tennis is a terrific hobby, but players shouldn't expect to train like a hobbyist and get results like a champion. Accelerated learning takes place when a player shifts focus to specific tipping point tendencies. Here are 10 of the top tipping point tendencies that can help swing a close match in a player's favor:

1. Using emotional control techniques to calmly handle creative line callers
2. Applying patterns to beat a moonball player or pusher
3. Performing rituals to reach one's peak emotional state under stress
4. Closing out a lead by playing to win instead of playing not to lose
5. Hitting the shots that feel most uncomfortable to the opponent instead of hitting the shots that feel most comfortable to you
6. Learning to pay attention to match tendencies
7. Self-charting matches
8. Increasing fitness and stamina to compete at one's peak
9. Developing, rehearsing, and then executing proactive patterns under stress
10. Amplifying anticipatory skills such as going from narrow vision to broad vision

Tipping point tendencies are part of the art of winning under stress. Those seemingly little things are actually the extremely big things that make all the difference in tipping the odds in a player's favor. Players must understand the root causes of past losses and then establish a protocol for dealing with each match issue.

The key to winning is poise under pressure. To maintain internal balance while surrounded by chaos, a player must have confidence. Remaining calm, cool, and collected under stress comes from already having all the answers to the problems.

chapter 10

Environmental Intangibles

Most matches are decided by the performance, or lack thereof, of the participants. After all, for most of us, tennis is a game of self-destruction. How each player carries out a game plan and handles adversity goes a long way in determining the outcome. But within those parameters, various factors—such as court surface, atmospheric conditions, and ball properties—exist that can influence proper execution. A swirling wind can play havoc with a high service toss or defensive, floating slices. For players to adjust their game accordingly, they must understand the impact of these various elements.

Although every tennis court has the same dimensions, the environmental differences make each location unique. Tennis court surfaces have their individual characteristics, as do the slight variations of tennis balls. Mother Nature surely affects the playing conditions for outdoor tennis and, more often than not, affects the outcome of the match. Environmental intangibles bring a sense of uncertainty and unpredictability that shakes the very core of a competitor's game. On those unpleasant days, the battle cry begins with a singular goal: Today is not the day for classy tennis. As boring and unpleasing as it may be, today is about getting the job done in order to battle another day.

In this chapter, we uncover some of the most common environmental challenges and offer unique adjustments that will help players put more checks in the winning column.

COURT SURFACE

On the professional level, the four Grand Slam events are all played on entirely different surfaces. The Australian Open is played on Plexicushion, an acrylic surface that plays slower and softer than traditional concrete hard courts. The French Open is played on clay—white limestone, actually, with a sprinkling of red brick dust on top of the surface to give it the coloring. Wimbledon is played on 100 percent perennial ryegrass, which is considered the slowest playing type of grass. The U.S. Open is played on a hard surface (DecoTurf).

The International Tennis Federation (ITF) has a system in place—called a court pace rating—that rates the speed of a court. A rating of 1 is given to the slowest courts, while 5 is used for the fastest. Court speeds vary dramatically depending on installation factors, elements, and maintenance. For example, the speed of a hard court can be manipulated depending on the amount of sand added to the paint during installation; the greater the level of sand, the slower the court. An outdoor court has to withstand the elements, which eventually affects the court's performance. A clay court needs to be rolled, watered, and covered with calcium chloride to assist in "holding" the moisture. Because of these variables, a brand-new hard court can be rated extremely slow, and a clay court that has not been maintained can be incredibly fast. That's why a court's "personality" provides its own set of unique challenges.

Following are some specific surface characteristics and how a player can adjust to them.

Hard Courts and Indoor Courts

The typically quicker surface of a hard or indoor court often rewards offensive tactics. By taking offensive court positions and applying attacking tennis, a player can reduce an opponent's recovery time. For more success on a hard court or indoor surface, players should shorten their backswings, lower their swing speeds, and shorten their swing lengths. They need to adjust their timing because of the increased ball speed, lower ball trajectories, decreased spin, and increased speed of the court. They should also modify their footwork to accommodate the quick pace and the stickiness or slickness of the court.

Specific to indoors, players must adapt to the vision requirements of the site's lighting. Indoor courts may also require players to adjust to the proximity of between-court dividing nets and tight backdrops. Players must also get accustomed to the sounds of an indoor court, such as loud fans, heaters, and the echo of the ball at contact.

Clay Courts

On clay, neutral and defensive skills are usually accentuated and rewarded because of the surface's slower pace. A player can expect to see typical winners come back, but he can also expect to have enough time to return the favor against his opponent. Because of the higher bounce of the ball on clay, a player will see more shoulder-level groundstrokes. Players should construct points by establishing patterns; they should be ready to apply building shots before going for outright winners. A player must be emotionally armed with the patience needed for slow, lengthy points. In addition, the player should make sure he is in better condition than usual in order to endure extensive, grueling match play. Keep in mind that depth is more important than power. Players should apply narrow vision to spot erratic bounces off the uneven surface. On clay, line calls are under even greater scrutiny because of the ball mark left on the court.

Grass and Other Playing Surfaces

Although grass courts are still found at the professional level (there are currently six ATP and four WTA grass-court events on the calendar), amateurs will rarely play on this surface. Other rare court surfaces include indoor carpet, artificial turf (carpet covered by sand), and synthetic grass. Because these surfaces are so foreign to the everyday player, it makes sense to focus primarily on clay and hard courts.

That being said, players preparing for a grass-court event would be wise to psych themselves up for short, quick points. Players can lay the groundwork for grass-court competition by shortening backswings; flattening out groundstrokes; and prepping slice strokes, drop shots, and drop volleys. Because of the slippery surface, positioning on or inside the baseline is essential. Executing forward attacking movement, bending the knees, and using small adjustment steps are crucial in the assertive world of grass-court tennis.

BALL CHARACTERISTICS

A standard tennis ball is optic yellow. It is 6.7 centimeters (2.6 in.) in diameter and weighs 56.0 to 59.4 grams (2.0 to 2.1 oz). Various manufacturers produce a wide range of balls with varying characteristics. For example, Penn manufactures and sells over 10 types of tennis balls. But because the variance in ball weight is less than 4 grams and because so many similar materials are used in construction, it's extremely difficult to judge differences in ball performance. However, experienced players can recognize some subtle distinctions.

Balls described as "extra duty" have more felt so that they will last longer on a harder surface. Regular-duty balls are typically used on clay and don't absorb as much clay during play. Using an extra-duty ball on a clay court could result in the ball picking up more clay and feeling heavier than normal. Besides these basic delineations, playing with certain brands may reveal other tendencies to a player. One type of ball may feel lighter and livelier, while another feels heavier and more difficult to manipulate.

Generally, the elite players feel these differences and need to make minor changes to their games. Still, it's not unusual for even average players to enjoy playing with a certain type of ball because of perceived characteristics. The key is for a player to experience as many varieties as possible so that personal preferences and playing adjustments (if needed) can be established.

A completely different kind of tennis ball has been made specifically for 10-and-under tennis. England's LTA calls their 10-and-under program Mini Tennis, Tennis Australia calls their program Hot Shots, and the USTA calls their program QuickStart. Whatever the nomenclature, 10-and-under tennis programs attempt to introduce young players to tennis with the help of age-appropriate equipment: smaller rackets and larger, low-pressure balls that reduce the ball speed, bounce height, and distance. The balls generate less shock and are easier to track down. They also make it easier for players to time their strokes. The tennis balls for the 10-and-under age group are manufactured in various sizes and pressures, and they include red foam, red felt, orange felt, green felt, and green "dot" felt.

Although these programs are great for getting young players involved in tennis, an individual's rate of growth and development is unique, and age should be a secondary factor. Adults who have never played a sport in their lives would surely benefit from beginning their training with balls used for the 10-and-under groups. A player's coordination, maturity, and ability to focus should play the most significant role in determining his customized development. For that reason, any recreational player may want to consider low-pressure balls when starting out in the game.

However, just as some adults can benefit from starting out with the low-pressure balls, not all 10-year-olds should be lumped together. I teach a 7-year-old who competes in 10-and-under nationals. He wants to develop his ad-side kick serve and is pretty sure he can beat the club pros in straight sets. Having this player use low-pressure beginner balls would only hinder his progress. The quickest way to drive gifted youngsters away from the game is to stifle their growth.

Coach's Corner

Back in 1976, Vic Braden was doing a telecast in Las Vegas, Nevada. On the stadium court, a tiny tot was rallying consistently from the baseline with an old wooden racket. Vic quickly got the youngster on camera and asked his age. The young boy replied that he was six. Vic then asked, "What do you want to be when you grow up?" The little kid with bangs said, "Number 1." That six-year-old was Andre Agassi.

ATMOSPHERIC ELEMENTS

Common elements associated with outdoor tennis include wind, heat and humidity, and altitude. Educated tennis players are only mildly affected by these elements because they have established a protocol for how to perform in such conditions. These experienced players actually use the elements to assist them in obtaining the results that they want to achieve. This section contains information to assist players in mastering the elements.

Extreme Wind

The first thing to remember when playing in extreme wind—or any difficult weather condition for that matter—is that it makes no sense to complain. Both players have to deal with the situation, and there's no benefit in feeling persecuted by something that is out of a player's control. Instead, players should prepare beforehand by establishing protocols and practicing the tactical modifications needed to take advantage of the situation. My players love playing in the wind. This isn't because they actually love the wind—few players do—but rather because they are properly prepared for the elements and their opponents aren't.

To prepare for windy conditions, players should begin by understanding that tennis in the wind is essentially a game of error reduction. They must recognize that this is not the day for beautiful tennis; in these conditions, it's about winning ugly. Players should modify swing speeds and swing lengths to ensure clean contact with the goal being patient, disciplined, less risky tennis. Footwork becomes crucial, as small adjustment steps are required to reposition strokes within milliseconds. And finally, players must make the wind an ally. They should apply low slices or drop shots when hitting into the wind, apply extra topspin to groundstrokes when the wind is at their back, and use slow slice serves and short-angle groundstrokes when playing in a crosswind.

Extreme Heat and Humidity

When the sun is blazing and the air is thick, players must be sure not to waste energy. Efficiency under such conditions—in mind and body—can make all the difference. Players with well-constructed game plans and established protocols for extreme heat will enhance their performance and reduce heat-related problems come match day.

To prepare for high temperatures and humidity, players should begin by getting in great physical shape weeks before the scheduled event and by training in extreme heat to build tolerance for the conditions. If traveling to the event, a player should arrive three or four days early to get acclimated to the conditions.

Players should wear white clothes and hats to reflect the sun's rays. They should pack sunscreen, wristbands, and three extra shirts and pairs of socks per match. In addition, a player needs to bring two coolers and two towels. The first cooler is for drinking water; the second cooler is for ice water used to lower the player's body temperature in between changeovers. Towel 1 is a dry towel used to wipe sweat, while towel 2 is a wet towel kept inside the second cooler. The wet towel is used for applying ice water to the body, and it is placed over the head during changeovers. Lowering the body's core temperature is essential in managing extreme heat.

Before matches, players should stay inside in air conditioning as much as possible. Hydration must be managed in order to override the electrolytes lost through sweat. Players can begin this process the night before. They should plan on hydrating the morning of a match, before play, throughout the match or matches, directly after the match, and throughout the remainder of the day to replenish fluids.

Finally, players must familiarize themselves with the signs of heat-related problems such as heat exhaustion and heatstroke. Initial symptoms include the following:

- Headache
- Muscle cramping
- Weakness or clumsiness
- Shortness of breath
- Light-headedness or fainting
- Confusion or dizziness
- Nausea
- Blurred vision or inability to focus

If a player is exhibiting any of these symptoms, she must stop play immediately.

High Altitude

High-altitude tennis greatly affects two important elements: a player's body and the ball flight. Higher elevation means less oxygen in the air. Plus, the decreased barometric pressure makes it more laborious for the body to absorb that available oxygen. Less available oxygen along with the difficulty absorbing it results in less oxygen transported throughout the bloodstream. This lack of oxygen throughout the body can exact a toll and cause altitude sickness.

While the thin air can inhibit oxygen intake, it also increases ball speed and bounce height. So not only can players feel debilitated, but they also have to deal with faster, more challenging play. Naturally, players need to have some ground rules established to help them adjust to the conditions.

Players should begin this unique preparation by getting in great physical shape weeks before the scheduled event. If possible, they should train in high altitude to build tolerance for the conditions. Using high-altitude (lower-pressure) tennis balls for these prematch training sessions will familiarize the player with the low-pressure ball. A player may also consider stringing rackets at a higher tension to assist in controlling the ball in the thin air.

If traveling to a tournament, the player should arrive three or four days early to get acclimated; he can then gradually adjust to the elements. The player also needs to know the court surface for the event. Is it a hard- or clay-court event?

Offensive tennis pays off because of the consequences of the thin air. Players should abbreviate their backswings, lessen their swing speeds, and shorten their swing lengths to prepare for the quicker play. They should practice extra topspin, high-looping ground-strokes, and a wicked kick serve. These are age-old weapons in high altitude. Players need to modify their footwork to accommodate the quicker pace.

Hydration must be managed properly because of the dry, thin air (dehydration instigates altitude sickness). Once again, players can begin this process the night before. They should plan on hydrating the morning of a match, before play, throughout the match or matches, directly after the match, and throughout the remainder of the day to replenish fluids.

Finally, players must familiarize themselves with the symptoms of altitude sickness. Initial symptoms include the following:

- Headache
- Shortness of breath
- Weakness, light-headedness, or fainting

- Confusion or dizziness
- Nausea
- Blurred vision or inability to focus
- Improper judgment or decision making

Once again, if a player is exhibiting any of these symptoms, he must stop play immediately.

ADAPTABILITY

The common denominator in conquering environmental intangibles is adaptability. Adversity is an ever-present factor that comes in many forms in the course of competitive play. The successful athletes are the ones who have developed their preset protocols. These cunning competitors have a plan for handling the physical, mental, and emotional factors. They are conditioned to see adversity as an additional challenge rather than a threat.

Competitive tennis involves one obstacle after another. Players must embrace the challenge by scheduling time to organize and practice the unique protocols described in this chapter. Instead of complaining about the environmental difficulties, players should focus on the solutions that will enable them to overcome those hardships. Worrying about things beyond one's control is a counterproductive waste of time and energy. Players must control the controllables; no one can control the conditions, but players can control how they adapt their performance in those conditions. In many ways, winners adapt their game to the environment.

Emotional, Physical, and Mental Preparation

chapter 11

Emotional Factors

By now it should be clear that almost everything a player does on a tennis court is a learned behavior. Emotional toughness is no different. Emotions are at the very core of tennis. This is what makes the game so compelling. Humans innately enjoy drama. Drama stirs emotions, and tennis brings drama to our lives. The rush of adrenaline is alluring and contagious.

While tapping into emotions, a player must be able to manage and control them in order to perform at a high level. As discussed, close matches often boil down to tipping points, which are usually not decided by stroke mechanics. Top players have great strokes until their lack of emotional endurance triggers a breakdown under stress.

A common misunderstanding lies within the meaning of emotional toughness. To clarify, the emotional components of the game relate to the athlete's ability to handle competitive anxiety. Here are some examples of these hidden skills:

- Closing out a set or a match
- Concentrating for the duration of a set, match, or tournament
- Playing at a peak performance level against a perceived weaker opponent
- Overcoming choking or panicking
- Successfully handling hardship (injury, poor weather, or bad luck), gamesmanship, or an aggravating opposing playing style

At all levels, players often blame their lack of success on their inability to handle these emotional issues. We hardly ever hear a player walk off the court after a tough loss and say, "If I would have only followed through two inches higher on my backhand, I would have won." Instead, we often hear statements such as these:

- "I had 'em, but I choked."
- "I got cheated and went nuts."
- "I hate those pushers! They don't even play real tennis."

Emotional toughness is a player's hidden weaponry. In some cases, emotional toughness is the only missing piece of the puzzle in a seasoned tennis player's game. After all, handling emotions is at the very core of peak performance under stress. Emotional toughness is a player's ability to focus on the shot that the moment demands rather than on the perceived ramifications of the outcome. It's a constant state of remembering the positives and deleting the negatives.

Emotional toughness comes from the ability to be performance oriented rather than outcome oriented under stress. Failure under stress often begins when emotions control brain functions or actions. Successful players control their emotions even under stress. This brings us back to exploring the power of the mind. The mind should be considered a tennis player's greatest weapon. A player's preferred intelligence is the driving force behind accelerated learning and the player's ability to perform at her peak level under stress. Once a player's preferred intelligence is understood, a series of preset solutions to common problems can be designed in order to resolve setbacks.

UNDERSTANDING PREFERRED INTELLIGENCE

As mentioned throughout this book, there is no singular, absolute way to learn or teach tennis. Different players can take different routes to reach the same goal. These routes are shaped by players' learning preferences—another tenet of this book. Training within guidelines based on the characteristics of a player's preferred intelligence has been proven to accelerate the development of the physical, mental, and emotional components of the game. Players who use their preferred intelligence learn faster and see better results with greater joy and satisfaction.

Most people, however, are taught to accomplish tasks the same way that their parents or educators accomplished those same tasks. In this case, tennis coaches often expect each of their students to follow the same exact protocol; they require players to enter the coach's world. The more skilled and knowledgeable teachers, however, understand that students have their own individual learning styles. The one-style-fits-all approach is counterproductive. Getting inside the player's world is the surest way of consistently developing high-level, emotionally stable competitors.

Following are seven of the more common learning styles. Most often, players will have characteristics of more than one style. Each player needs to discover his preferred style and adjust the plan accordingly.

The Linguistic Linguistic-oriented players have a preference for verbal and written directions. These players use an expanded vocabulary and usually prefer detailed explanations for tasks at hand. Here are some good ways for language-oriented players to learn on the court:

- Reversing the coaching role and explaining the reasoning for each drill back to the coach.
- Verbally repeating strategies and tactics at the conclusion of a lesson.
- Writing down a lesson review in the last five minutes of every training session.
- Completing match logs after each match as well as daily focus journals.

The Logical Mathematic Logic-minded players prefer structure, order, and closure for each drill set. They want to successfully complete an exercise before moving on. These learners want to know not only how to hit a specific shot, but where and why to hit it. They enjoy working with numbers and facts. They are no-nonsense players who prefer training that stresses quality over quantity. Here are some effective ways for logical-minded players to learn tennis skills and strategies:

- Performing drills that employ negative scoring (losing points for committing mistakes); this keeps them accountable for unforced errors.
- At any match or tournament, classifying other competitors into their preferred playing styles and listing the patterns used to beat them.
- Learning how to chart opposing players and using the numbers to create a game plan.

The Elegant Kinesthetic The kinesthetic player gives meaning to the word *graceful*. These players possess excellent core balance and can easily master elegant-looking strokes. When kinesthetic players with gross motor skills receive balls in their strike zones, it's "lights out." Efficient ways for an elegant kinesthetic player to learn on the court include the following:

- Shadowing an instructor (or a professional on video) to learn new strokes or techniques.
- Using repetition of playing patterns in practice so the patterns can be re-created during match play.
- Training flexible skills; this is mandatory for kinesthetic players, because leaving their predictable comfort zones to simulate actual match conditions is key.

The Musical Rhythmic Musically in-tune players thrive on rhythm. They enjoy playing opponents who hit with the same ball speed, spins, and trajectory. These players find the zone when they sing their favorite song during play. Training with an iPod or with music on the court is like heaven to a player with this type of intelligence. Here are some good ways for a rhythmic player to learn on the court:

- Employing cadences and dance steps—for instance, a serve motion may have a five-count rhythm, while an approach shot and volley pattern may have a three-step split-step cadence.
- Performing the consistent rhythm of a clean rally; grooving strokes is what these players love to do best.
- Practicing how to handle players who have mastered the art of mixing the spin, speed, and trajectory of their shots; junk-ball artists frustrate rhythmic players to death.

The Spatial Brainiac Spatial brainiacs are great tacticians, but they are often not the most naturally gifted athletes. They have to work extra hard and are usually prepared to do so. They have an uncanny ability to dissect opponents accurately and create a detailed game plan. They enjoy spotting strengths and weaknesses. They easily master the use of broad vision to enhance their anticipatory skills. Here are some effective practice methods for this type of player:

- Purchasing a weekly planner and following the plan day by day; structuring all the mandatory components into a detailed, organized plan rationalizes the lesson or instruction for this type of learner.
- Trying to discover why a shot went awry rather than being told.
- Using video analysis of tournament and match play; developing the art of winning instead of working on simple stroke mechanics truly fits into the spatial brainiac's frame of mind.

The Interpersonal Personality profiling (Myers-Briggs) refers to this type of intelligence as "extrovert feelers." These people have emotional connections to almost everything and everyone. For this type of person, if there are 50 players in a group and 48 love him but 2 don't, his day is ruined. Interpersonal learners enjoy harmony and are highly sensitive to people and relationships. Here are some great ways for the interpersonal player to learn on the court:

- Including group clinics with plenty of peer interaction (note, however, that group workouts don't offer accelerated learning as much as social interaction).
- Closing out practice sets rather than rallying back and forth; because of their short attention span, these players often have an inability to focus over the long haul and frequently get bored with a commanding lead.
- Developing a protocol for handling opponents who apply gamesmanship; the interpersonal learner's sensitive nature necessitates this.

The Intrapersonal Personality profiling (Myers-Briggs) refers to this type of intelligence as "introvert thinkers." Players with this preferred intelligence are remarkable at controlling their own feelings, emotions, and attention span on the tennis court. Because tennis is an individual sport by nature, these players have a genetic advantage when it comes to distraction control. Effective ways for the intrapersonal players to learn on the court include the following:

- Using detailed explanations; these players prefer to reflect and think things through before making rash decisions, so "because I said so" doesn't cut it.
- Working alone in private lessons instead of in stressful group settings.
- Working on seeing the benefits of spotting and attacking a vulnerable opponent, because attacking the net isn't in the genetic design of these players.

OVERCOMING ADVERSITY

There are four sides to a complete player—stroke mechanics, physical fitness, strategy and tactics, and emotional control—and all are intertwined. If stroke mechanics are flawed, a player cannot compete because of the sheer number of unforced errors. This can trigger an emotional meltdown. If not physically fit, a competitor cannot keep up with others at the higher levels of play; this can cause emotional distress. Without a sound game plan, a player cannot control skilled opponents. This can also spur emotional collapse. And, once an emotional collapse occurs, any of the other three sides of a player that have not already broken down are then in jeopardy. So each part of the game feeds into the other; a weakness in one can easily cause frailty in another.

One thing that all athletes have experienced is the destructive effects that misplaced emotions have in competition. Anyone can steer the boat when the seas are calm—emotions are easy to control when things are going well—but it takes a tenacious competitor to regain composure when things are going awry. The key to doing this is establishing preset protocols. Just as motor programming is essential to reproducing consistent strokes, so too is programming solutions to common emotional pitfalls. Emotional development includes three phases:

1. Understanding how and why the component affects emotional performance.
2. Developing and practicing the solutions needed to remedy the flawed component.
3. Using live-ball simulation sets where players are required to repeatedly implement the solutions in competitive situations.

The depth of a player's resiliency stems from emotional development. This is the player's ability to endure hardship and persevere. Take a moment to look back at the evaluations in chapter 3. Which emotional issues did you grade as 3 or below? At the end of this chapter, solutions to various emotional issues are provided. These solutions will help you work through the three phases of emotional development in order to strengthen those underdeveloped skills.

But before identifying these, let's discuss the appropriate time for players to find these solutions during a match. When the ball is in play, tennis players have sheer milliseconds in between strokes. The human brain cannot solve two complex tasks—hitting the ball and controlling emotions—at once. This is called channel capacity, and it explains why people should not text on the phone while driving. For tennis players, attempting to focus their attention on the task at hand while at the same time analyzing past performance is a recipe for disaster.

Instead, analysis should be done during the short breaks in the action—namely, between points and during changeovers. (Prematch and postmatch routines and rituals are also essential for proper preparation and the discovery of opponent tendencies. They will be discussed further in chapter 14.)

Proper Between-Point and Changeover Rituals and Routines

As stated earlier, emotional toughness is a discipline that requires repetition and observation. When players are asked to describe their between-point rituals, the answers are often the same:

> "I look at my strings."
>
> "I walk to the back fence and go to my towel."
>
> "I bounce the ball four times before I serve."

Sounds constructive, doesn't it? Although these are fine examples of external rituals and preset routines, the players need to add a few internal rituals to assist in organizing the next point's pattern. The most skilled practitioners maintain a constant state of remembering the positives and deleting the negatives. Here's a true story that clearly illustrates the point:

Two high-performance players, Mark and Greg, were training with me in Southern California. (The names have been changed to protect the guilty!) Mark is an incredible athlete but tends to allow his emotions to control his problem-solving skills. This is the primary reason that Mark has yet to win a national title. Greg, on the other hand, is not quite the physical athlete but has spent a few years with me nurturing his mental and emotional components. Greg has won three national singles titles.

Serving in the first set, Mark hits a beautiful kick serve out wide to the ad side. Greg lunges for a defensive, high-slice backhand and barely floats it back across the net. Mark sees Greg's vulnerable reply and quickly darts in to steal a high forehand volley. Mark overhits the volley wide into Greg's deuce-side doubles alley. "SEE? THAT'S WHY I STINK!" he shouts. As I walk over to Mark's baseline, he puts his palm up. "I DON'T WANT TO HEAR IT. MY VOLLEYS ARE SO BAD." Mark walks away fast and angry to the deuce side, choosing to ignore his between-point rituals. Mark misses his flat-bomb first serve, then double-faults. On the ad point, he serves to the forehand and then sails a forehand six feet long to donate the game to Greg. During the changeover, Mark is still rambling on about his missed volley three points ago.

Fast-forward to the very next game: Greg serves the same penetrating kick serve wide into the ad box. This time it's Mark who floats a weak reply. Greg spots the floater and rushes in and nails the very same forehand volley wide into Mark's doubles alley. Greg simply turns, smiles, and walks toward the back fence. I walk over to him and ask, "Greg, what are you smiling about?" "Didn't you see it?" he replied. "Mark has no high backhand. Now I know what to do on big points." For the remaining three sets, whenever Greg had a critical point on his ad-side serve, he used the big kicker wide. Guess what shot Greg didn't even mention? You got it, his missed forehand volley.

Unfortunately, like Mark, most competitors spend the majority of their between-point time focusing on the past point, which is dead and gone. An effective technique is to keep one's mind occupied throughout the between-point phase. Try thinking of it this way: There are two glasses. The glass on the left is full of water. No unwanted liquids can enter that space. The glass on the right is empty. Like an empty brain in between points, anything can enter. By keeping the mind full (with thoughts of performance goals) between points, a player can prevent unwanted thoughts from casually creeping in.

Players can keep their glass full by walking through three "doors" in between each point:

1. Move past the last point by remembering the positives and deleting the negatives.

2. Plan the strategy and pattern of play for the next point.

3. Calmly revisit preset relaxation rituals before the next point begins.

Players should practice this by playing a few sets while focusing only on the ability to perform these between-point rituals. In these practice sets, the players disregard the score entirely. They let go of the actual outcome of the set and simply work on establishing a protocol for between-point focus control. Players should keep in mind that solutions are found when their mind is imbedded in performance goals rather than scattered in different directions.

Similar to the between-point rituals, changeover rituals consist of both external and internal routines. Examples of external routines include toweling off, taking a drink, and eating a few bites of a banana. Internal rituals should be added to improve emotional stability and enhance the ability to focus.

When adding internal rituals, a player should think only two games back and two games forward. After sitting down, she can begin the internal dialog by asking, *Did I break serve? Why or why not?* Then she proceeds to identify the successful patterns or make the appropriate adjustments. Second, she asks, *Did I hold serve? Why or why not?* Once again, she presets any adjustments needed. After a few drinks of water, a few calming deep breaths, and toweling off, the player quickly reviews her plan: *OK, how am I going to break serve? Got it. How am I going to hold serve? Got it.* Then she stands up and jogs back out to the court, prepared to do her best.

The Stress Balloon Theory

Imagine a small balloon floating just above a player's head throughout the course of each match. Each time the player makes a mistake, frustrations begin to accumulate inside the balloon. If a player fails to let the hot air out of the balloon, it will quickly reach its breaking point and burst. The key to controlling emotions is to religiously take the time to let the hot air out.

This imaginary release is carried out with the application of between-point rituals. Players struggling with emotional demons should take the time to actually walk through the three doors of between-point rituals, systematically de-stressing the balloon. This practical application is used to great success in controlling garden-variety emotional meltdowns. Table 11.1 describes some of these common emotional issues.

Fear of Failure or Success

Losing is never enjoyable, but it can't always be avoided. Champions have lost hundreds of matches. Does this make multimillionaire tennis pros—with hordes of titles—failures? Of course not. At the higher levels of the game, titles are taken, not easily given away. A player should project an image of indestructibility while secretly understanding that every professional tennis player loses almost every week. Bravery helps a good player

Table 11.1   Controlling Common Emotional Issues

Emotional issue	Release during rituals
Mistakes	Identify, control, fix, or simply avoid mistakes.
Adversity and stress	Regulate or endure misfortune.
Lack of a game plan	Preset strategy and tactics, then actually perform those tasks.
Frustration	Identify the number of shots per rally that disrupt an opponent's comfort zone.
Bad temperament	Control one's emotional climate, heart rate, and pace of play.
External distractions	Avoid external stimuli often found around tournament sites (avoid having wandering eyes).
Internal distractions	Eliminate internal distractions that can cloud one's mind.
Ego or arrogance	Limit presumptuous or overconfident attitude and behavior.
Nervousness	Use prepared emotional solutions and protocols to conquer the feelings of inadequacy that cause nervousness.
Self-condemnation	Before matches, review video playback of an actual performance and chart the instances of negative facial expressions, negative body language, and negative self-talk. Then focus on cutting that number in half during the next match.
Bad anger	Remember that not all anger is bad. Anger occasionally leads to increased adrenaline and an upward spiral of effort and fight. Negative anger, however, can zap energy, and it needs to be released.
Unforced errors	Take the time to identify the cause of each error you make. Two is the magic number. It's nearly impossible to compete while committing more than two unforced errors per game.
Choking	Choking is a state of overarousal brought about by overthinking. It most often appears when thoughts about the future outcome of the match precede one's actual performance goals. Don't think about the finish line. Devise a plan for and focus on each individual point. Continue to duplicate the attitude and execution that has resulted in the lead.
Panicking	Panicking is caused by a lack of adequate problem solving. This mental turmoil is often outwardly displayed by fast walking and the lack of between-point rituals. Slow down and perform them!
Lack of patience	Ignore impulses and calmly wait for the right moment to attack.
Negative body language	Negative postures and gestures demonstrate vulnerability. Act as you want to be perceived instead of acting the way you feel.

sleep at night. Players should view losses as stepping stones, not stumbling blocks—as a way of learning to discard unproductive behaviors and to approach the game more intelligently. The key to avoiding failures in the future lies in one's ability to avoid repeating mistakes. Error containment involves fixing and avoiding past mistakes instead of hoping that the opponent will crack and give the match away.

Fear of failure is often acknowledged, but fear of success is much more common than one might think. Success brings about change. Winning matches and tournaments can result in new competition, opportunities, expectations, and pressures. To some people, this type of change is scary, uncomfortable, and something to be avoided. The bar has forever been set higher. This means that the old habits and the old work ethic won't do. Winning means more on-court practice, more hours in the gym, more travel, and less time for pursuing other interests. High-performance players realize that reaching the top is easier than staying at the top. The unknown can be intimidating, but players must welcome and embrace the challenge.

How to Handle Creative Line Calling and Gamesmanship

When someone yells, "Are you blind?" after a close line call, the player making the call should just smile. After all, calling lines is primarily a guessing game. Studies we did back in the 1980s at the Vic Braden Tennis College showed that the human eye cannot register a two- or three-millisecond event. This means that no human can actually see the ball hit a racket or hit the court. The eye is greatly affected by two variables: perspective angles and motion blur.

Perspective Angles   During a seminar at the 2012 Australian Open's International Coaching Conference, I conducted an interesting line-call study with 233 high-performance coaches on court at Hisense Arena. Even with all the coaches' experience and knowledge, the results were typical: 95 percent misread the line call on the opposite side of the net.

Perform this line-call test yourself: Stand at the back fence on one side of a court. Turn and face the fence so that you can't see the court. Ask a friend to place four balls on and just beyond the service line on the other side of the net. Ask this person to repeat it with four different balls on the opposing baseline. When all the balls are in place, walk slowly to your baseline and try to make eight correct line calls. Which balls are in and which are out? Next, walk toward the other side. As you take a sideline view, the perspective changes. Now stand behind the other baseline. Things will again have a new perspective. And don't forget that in match play, the ball is only contacting the court for about two or three milliseconds (two one-thousandths of a second)!

This test proves that, when competitors think they are being wrongfully hooked on a call, most often they have misread the situation. The next time this happens, they may need to ask themselves if they are sure before accusing the opponent of making an incorrect line call.

In match play, players do occasionally get bad calls by the opponent, but they also cheat themselves. Often, incoming balls landing slightly long appear to be right on the line from the perspective angle of a player standing behind his own baseline. In live-ball drills, I've found that players actually fall into the common trap of cheating themselves more often than cheating an opponent.

Coach's Corner

I begin my usual on-court tennis lessons by asking a dozen or so questions to gain an understanding of the player's personality, frustrations, and knowledge of the game. While teaching 15-year-old Petra, I was quick to notice that her father interrupted every question with his version of the answer. He then proceeded to tell me, "Her problem is that on the court, she's not a problem solver. She can't manage her mistakes or her emotions. In school, she gets straight *A*s, but on the tennis court she acts like she's stupid!" My response was this: "Do you realize you didn't allow your daughter to answer one of my questions? At school, she has developed the skill sets of an independent thinker. In her tennis world, she may be so used to you supplying all the answers that she's become a dependent thinker. Tennis champions are independent problem solvers; it's the nature of the sport."

Petra loved the idea of having the opportunity to be an independent thinker. But for the initial two to three weeks, she really struggled. She had to find her own practice partners, take her rackets to be restrung, book her own court time, and even come up with her own game plans. Petra was so accustomed to her father doing everything for her that she was overwhelmed. After she developed the organizational skills needed to be self-sufficient, however, her self-trust and confidence grew, she began problem solving on the court, and there was no stopping her. Now she's competing on the pro challenger circuit.

Motion Blur Motion blur occurs when an athlete is moving. In this state, the eyes actually move in their sockets as well (that's why it's so difficult to read when going for a vigorous run). In this condition, a player could be considered "legally blind" and in no position to accurately call lines.

So calling lines is largely an imperfect endeavor. Still, handling the creative line caller is a very common emotional trigger. At the amateur level, tennis is a sport essentially without referees, umpires, and official scorekeepers. Imagine the consequences for football or basketball games if the participants ruled the fun house. In the heat of battle, pressure occasionally causes generally nice people to go to the dark side and cheat as a way to cope with the game of a talented opponent.

Here are some other common antics used in the business of gamesmanship:

- Stalling
- Changing the score
- Belittling the opponent
- Taking several extended bathroom or trainer breaks
- Having temper tantrums (including breaking rackets)
- Fighting with playing partners, coaches, or parents during the match
- Accusing opponents of cheating or changing the score

Why Do Cheaters Often Win?

The reasons why cheaters do their evil deeds may never be fully understood. But the important thing is discovering how these dishonorable players win and how to overcome their antics and the ensuing drama.

Cheaters win because they force their victims into channel capacity. Remember, depending on the complexity of the demands, the human brain cannot handle two complicated tasks at once. Focusing on the motor programs required to execute the skills that the moment demands (based on the appropriate performance goals) forces a player to primarily use a certain side of the brain. Channel capacity is evident when the victim attempts to handle the additional demands of confronting the opponent, dealing with the emotional trauma, and inventing a protocol to handle the situation. This disruption in focus is often more detrimental than the three or four stolen points that a cheater may gain with questionable line calls. The outcome of the match is generally determined by the victim's inability to handle the stress and by the three or four additional points donated by the victim as a result of being pulled into channel capacity.

Solutions for Handling Suspect Line Calls

An inability to cope with cheaters has been known to drive many talented players to the sidelines. The sheer frustration overshadows the joys of match play. But savvy competitors know how to shield themselves from dishonest opponents. Following are a variety of solutions for dealing with line-call controversy on the court.

Avoid Prematch Speculation Occasionally, a player's prematch preparation is based on speculation that the upcoming opponent has a bad reputation and will surely cheat. The stress caused by this belief can be so overwhelming that it results in the loss of sleep the night before the match. Players should not let expectations of possible drama pull the focus of their preparation away from their performance goals.

Center Your Attention on What Can Be Controlled Players should establish this protocol: Expect a few bad line calls per match. A few years back, I was curious to see if cheating is a more modern problem, so I asked Jack Kramer. He said, "It was about the same back then. I'd plan on expecting six bad calls a match." Because it's impossible to control the moral compass of the opponent, players should plan on devoting attention to things within their power—for instance, limiting the number of unforced errors per set. If players keep that number to 10 or below, the opponent can have a few hooks without hurting them.

Focus on Not Cheating Yourself   In my travels coaching nationally ranked or ITF (International Tennis Federation) juniors, I ask tournament referees at every site what is more prevalent, players receiving bad calls from opponents or players missing line calls and playing out balls. The answer is always the same: players missing line calls and playing out balls. Most players unknowingly hook themselves more than any opponent does. They simply play out balls and then proceed to lose the point. If players tighten up on the calls on their side of the court, the other side of the court will be less of an issue.

Remember That Cheaters Know That Their Skills Are No Match for Yours
Why do cheaters cheat? Most often they resort to cheating because they fear that their physical skills are no match for the opponent's. In this state of desperation, they probe for an underdeveloped or weak mental link to attack. Sadly, once they spot a victim who does not have a preset protocol for handling emotional trauma, the hookfest is on.

Inquire About the Umpire's Availability (When Playing in Tournaments)   At check-in for a tournament, players should ask about the availability of an umpire. As the tournament desk official hands both players the balls and relays the court number and scoring procedures, a player can gently ask (in front of the opponent), "Is there an umpire on-site who is available if needed?" This sends a powerful message to the opponent: "Antics will not be tolerated."

Try the Standard Procedure for Handling Cheaters   First, the player should question the initial bad call. If this does not work, he should get an official. When the umpire or line judge leaves after a game or two, the player has two options: One, he may repeat the procedure and be an enabler, letting the cheater steal the match; or two, he may take matters into his own hands and fight fire with fire. The manner in which a competitor handles confrontation will depend on his personality and his preset protocols.

After a Confrontation, Do Not Begin Play Right Away   If an argument over a line call occurs, a player should take a few moments to regain composure and get her thoughts back to the task at hand. An effective way to do so is by taking a legal bathroom break. Once there, the player can take the time to reshift focus back to the performance goals and away from the drama. Champions can compartmentalize, simply deleting the negatives and getting their thoughts back to executing the shots that the moment demands.

Rehearse Sets Versus a Cheater   Players should plan some practice sets with this unique twist: Every time a ball is hit on the line, the ball may be called out. This establishes two important protocols: First, the players become comfortable with the emotional turmoil of being hooked and how to deal with it. Second, the players learn to win without painting the lines. By aiming 2 feet (61 cm) inside the lines, players not only remove the cheating scenario, but they also give themselves more room for error.

Tournament Personnel

For competitive players—even those in the 10-and-under or 2.5 NTRP divisions—understanding the roles of tennis tournament personnel can be the difference between winning and losing a war against creative line callers and opponents who employ gamesmanship. When confronted with a cheater, players can approach any of these individuals for assistance, depending on which ones are available at that particular event.

Tournament Director   Tournament directors wear many hats. They are responsible for the general operations of the event. Their job description includes hiring and overseeing the paid and volunteer staff (including officials), creating and updating the draws, monitoring financials, promoting and marketing the tournament, handing out trophies and awards, tracking and updating ranking stats, and securing event sponsorships.

Officials   *Official* is a loose term used to identify anyone working the tournament. This includes line judges, chair umpires, roving umpires, and the assortment of referees. Referees may include site referees, deputy referees, desk referees, and often the tournament director and her staff.

Umpires   These people are responsible for monitoring the warm-up time, performing the coin toss, overseeing play, calling time violations and foot faults, and resolving on-court player disputes during match play. If the resolution is not satisfactory, a player may ask the umpire to speak with the referee. The referee has the final word on all conflict resolutions.

Referees   Referees are usually found at or around the tournament desk. They are responsible for creating the court and match schedules, appointing officials or umpires to court stations, postponing or canceling match play because of inclement weather, and generally overseeing all tournament play.

Video Analysis of Matches

For decades, players have been using video analysis as a valuable tool for spotting mechanical flaws in their strokes, but video can also provide feedback in the emotions department. Granted, many people hate to see themselves on camera. But if players want to achieve accelerated growth, they should break out the video camera. The most common learning style is visual, and seeing is believing. By sitting down and reviewing match performances monthly via video, players can gain valuable insight.

Here are some specifics for players to look for when they are reviewing match video to identify their emotional strengths and weaknesses:

- Emotional control
- Causes of over- and underarousal (discussed later in this chapter)
- Focus control, such as lapses in concentration
- Between-point and changeover rituals

Error detection is the first step in achieving growth. Essentially, a player must spot the cause of errors before those flaws can be fixed. For tennis players to develop at the quickest rate, they should analyze video playback of one match every tournament with the well-trained eye of a professional. At the higher levels of the game, players commonly ask a teaching professional to conduct nonhitting lessons to evaluate their actual performances.

Universal Tennis Stressors

Becoming a champion requires more than building strokes. An important emotional component is the ability to identify common stressors. These are often the leading causes of players quitting the game. Stressors are divided into two distinct categories:

1. Organizational and developmental stressors
2. Competitive and match-day stressors

Organizational and Developmental Stressors Organizational and developmental stressors are those that are part of everyday living in relation to tennis play. Organizational stressors may relate to time management and scheduling or logistical planning (e.g., travel). Attempting to balance tennis around work, school, or educational requirements—as well as personal or family time—can cause stress for a player. Financial concerns may also come into play. Developmental stressors can come from component development or coaching conflicts, or they may result from the amount of work and perseverance required of a tennis player.

Competitive and Match-Day Stressors Perfectionism is a common stressor on game day. Other stressors include losing to pushers or cheaters, failing to close out matches, choking, or panicking. External sources, such as a parent's or an opponent's behavior, are also triggers for stress. Preparations for match play—including video analysis and charting (chapter 15) as well as pre- and postmatch routines—are also examples of competitive and match-day stressors.

Note that beginner and intermediate players may not struggle with these issues until they reach the competitive stages of the game.

Adrenaline and Peak Performance

Adrenaline is a naturally occurring hormone that is produced when a person is experiencing intense emotions. High-performance players understand that pumping up the adrenaline at the end of games, sets, and matches is a crucial element of winning. These "self-induced" adrenaline bursts assist in increasing a player's heart rate, focus intensity, muscle strength, and speed.

Champions know that they can't simply wait for the adrenaline to find them; they have to bring it on at the crucial stages of a match. Emotionally screaming, "Come on!" and pumping a fist in the air are signs that a player is calling on an adrenaline burst to pump him up for the next few points. Using this highly advantageous protocol to improve performance is a key emotional ingredient in successful tennis.

Recognizing Tennis Burnout

Tennis burnout is caused by a prolonged period of exhaustion. This emotional state of diminishing interest and cynicism originates from a reduced sense of fulfillment and accomplishment. One of the leading causes of burnout is an athlete's perfectionism. (Remember, a common emotional stressor is the need to be flawless.) Burnout is seen in two polar opposite displays: overarousal and underarousal.

Signs of overarousal include the following:

- Reduced concentration
- Fear of failure
- Lack of emotional control
- Lack of strategy and judgment
- Poor opponent awareness
- Inability to think clearly
- Negative verbal outbursts
- Racket banging and throwing
- Pessimism
- Stressful and forced play

Signs of underarousal include the following:

- Lack of motivation
- Poor equipment preparation
- Lack of energy
- Poor racket preparation during play
- Lack of anticipation and timing
- Negative facial expressions
- Negative body language
- Short attention span
- Eyes wandering outside the court
- Lack of concern about performance goals
- Low patience
- Lack of enthusiasm
- A sense of hopelessness

The good news is that there are some solutions for burned-out players. One is to refocus on improvement goals rather than on winning. Target goals, such as winning 65 percent of the points in matches or winning 70 percent of matches monthly, are also helpful. Burned-out players can also benefit from understanding and rehearsing solutions to choking, panicking, and tanking.

Changing up the player's schedule is another solution. This can be done in a variety of ways depending on the player's specific needs; for example, players may redesign their weekly schedule to improve periodization training, modify their tournament schedule, or even add rest and recovery time to their training schedule—providing physical, mental, and emotional time away from the sport.

Perfectionism: A False Belief System

Perfectionism afflicts some of the most gifted players. Its consequences have stopped cold many a promising player who neglected to perform mental and emotional training. Helping perfectionists get the most out of their talent isn't necessarily about fixing strokes; it's about designing a new belief system. Here are some of the most common consequences of perfectionism and how to rectify the problem:

Believing Only Perfect Execution Will Lead to Victory Successful tennis players are satisfied with winning about 65 percent of the points in each match. Doing so allows for imperfection. It also allows the opponent to have a little glory in defeat. This provides a less anxious environment where playing at peak performance is possible.

Fearing Adversity Good athletes should actually be seeking adversity by means of a worthy opponent. After all, a player has to beat the best in order to become the best. Adversity should be thought of as a challenge to seek out. It's not a threat. Perfectionists should focus on recognizing the solutions and executing what's needed instead of focusing on the possible outcome of the match.

Playing Not to Lose Playing to win is a proactive approach to closing out stressful situations. It's not a frantic behavior; it's a methodical attack. Unfortunately, for most perfectionists, the fear of losing is so great that they fall into the trap of "playing not to lose." Pushing is caused by the fear of missing, which actually makes a player play worse.

Having Unrealistic Expectations   Nationally ranked juniors enter, on average, 30 tough tournaments a year. If they win 3 or 4 of those events, it's a great year. That means they go home losers 26 weeks a year. Winning over 50 percent of matches is terrific; winning 70 percent of matches is way ahead of the curve.

Becoming Angry   Anger quickly comes into play when people are facing adversity. When players become angry, they become extremely vulnerable. They overthink or shut down mentally, they can't focus, and they can even lose muscle control. A more effective strategy is to view adversity as something to learn from. Players who struggle should know that it's because they still need to develop their skills. A player can avoid anger issues by confronting adversity slowly with calmness, courage, and positive action.

Exhibiting Self-Critical Behavior   A player must realize that it's okay to have a Gatorade stain on her untucked shirt. Her hair should be messy. There's nothing wrong with shanking a few winners or rolling a few off the net tape for winners. A player can play slow and decrease ball speed. The player should give opponents what they hate rather than what looks like "good" tennis. A player should allow herself to miss some. It doesn't always have to be pretty. Often, perfectionists would rather lose than win ugly.

Coach's Corner

Here are a few ways to spot a perfectionist:

1. Perfectionists believe that there is only one way to do it right. After hitting a great shot, a perfectionist may say, "Sure, I hit a winner, but didn't you see it? My follow-through was 6.5 inches too low! Why can't I do it correctly?"

2. Perfectionists obsess over basics. They often say things like this: "I can run a Fortune 500 company and manage 2,000 employees, but I can't control this ball toss!"

3. Perfectionists love to share their disease. They not only spot their own errors but also enjoy spotting—and sharing—their opponent's flaws.

4. Perfectionists demand perfection in others. They may say to their children, "Honey, I know you're only seven years old, but you should be able to get more kick on that second serve! Dinner will wait—do another basket."

5. Perfectionists' tennis outfits are organized to a fault. No true perfectionist would consider wearing a Nike top with Adidas shorts. Their shorts are often pressed, along with their matching shirt that is perfectly tucked in. In addition, their matching socks, wristbands, and headbands are spotless. If you see players like this, ask to see their tennis bag. Without a doubt it will be organized to—you guessed it—perfection!

6. Perfectionists find things to worry about. They might say, "I checked the forecast every 15 minutes last night; what if it rains? What if we end up playing Martha? She's the world's biggest pusher. Or we could play Harold. Everyone knows he cheats."

7. Perfectionists constantly second-guess themselves. In a match, they are often thinking, Oh, here comes a short ball—I should go in. No, maybe not; it's possibly a trick. I'd better wait and analyze the situation . . . too late!

8. Perfectionists are so detail-oriented that they may take this list and rewrite it!

Demonstrating Negative Body Language   Players should think about how they want to be perceived. Do they want to be perceived as vulnerable and weak or as focused and relentless? Negative body language leads to poor performance. A player who appears helpless will play helplessly. Players should act the way they want to be seen, not the way they feel. The wall that players build around themselves is truly felt by their competition.

Failing to Focus on Rituals   One study that I've been conducting for the past 20 years at every level shows that about 75 to 80 percent of the time that players spend on court is actually between points. When do most meltdowns occur? They occur in between points. Instead of focusing on results, players need to focus on the process of proper internal changeover and between-point rituals.

Forgetting to Self-Trust   Confidence comes from self-trust, and self-trust has to be earned. Self-trust comes from building the four components of top-level tennis—stroke mechanics, physical fitness, strategy and tactics, and emotional control. Developing these four parts of the game—and therefore self-trust—is a learned behavior. Players shouldn't expect to own these facets in stressful matches without cultivating them.

Displaying a Negative Attitude   Players must understand that attitude is a choice. This means that a player has the freedom to change it. Just because stress has caused negativity in the past doesn't mean this has to be repeated in future adverse situations. A positive attitude not only makes a huge difference in players' performances, but it also has a constructive effect on those who play with or coach those players.

Overcoming Performance Anxiety

Do any of these situations sound familiar?

- "I have no issues closing out matches on the practice court, but in league or tournament play, I tighten up as if I'm trying not to lose."
- "I get so nervous on match day that I can't perform."
- "I want to win so bad that I can hardly swing my racket."

Fear and extreme nervousness often show their strain dramatically when a player is positioned to close out a lead. Picture a race car driver in the lead who sees the finish line. Instead of sticking with the game plan that got him the lead (keeping the right foot firmly on the gas), he eases off the gas pedal to avoid overheating the engine or spinning out of control and protect his lead. The trailing race car maintains its speed and blows by to steal the victory.

Most of the anxiety felt by athletes is caused by perceptions, not facts. The way that players interpret the ramifications of the situation is most often the culprit. Players feel anxiety before or during a match because they are fixating on the outcome and the social ramifications. Remember, wanting to win or not wanting to lose is a terrific motivational force. But focusing on having to win or hoping not to lose instead of focusing on performing the task at hand is a recipe for disaster.

Overcoming performance anxiety is tricky business. Confronting these questions can help:

- What is the underlying cause of my lack of performance in matches?
- What is causing my prematch nervousness?
- What is causing my tension and fear in matches?

- Where is the pressure to win coming from?
- Are my match-time mistakes stemming from technical stroke mechanics, lack of strategy, movement and fitness issues, or emotional issues?
- Why am I scared to play my game in the heat of battle?
- How is my monthlong pre-tournament preparation?
- How is my match-day preparation?
- What are my A, B, and C game plans?
- Am I dissecting the opponents efficiently?
  - Do I recognize their style of play and go-to patterns?
  - Do I spot the strengths and weaknesses of their strokes and strike zones?
  - Do I notice any flaws in their movement skills (backcourt versus net)?
  - Are they inconsistent with their emotional or focus control?
- What do I need to do in order to enjoy the battle?

Gathering the answers to these questions helps players stay in the process rather than worry about their performance. Their attention is directed toward something constructive, and they are proactively seeking solutions. This can positively affect a player's outlook on an upcoming match or tournament.

Following is a checklist of solutions to review:

- Keep in mind that even world-class athletes fight the same nerves, fears, and anxieties that plague all of us. The solution lies in the ability to fight off fear and play to win anyway.
- Be aware that opponents are most dangerous when they are about to lose. In the winning position, players often let their guard down and play with decreased intensity because the outcome is almost decided. At that very same time, most opponents relinquish the outcome and play loose, relaxed, and fearless. The combination of exchanging an attacking system for a slower, safer style along with the opponent's newfound courageous style of play is trouble waiting to happen.
- To understand the feeling of letting go of the outcome, recall those times when an opponent hit a serve long. While bellowing "out," players relax because the outcome has already been decided, and they often proceed to hit a scorching return. They become detached from the outcome and just let their body react without allowing the mind to get in the way. Players usually follow with the lament, "Why can't I do that when the serve is in?" The reason is that in those situations, the outcome enters the picture. That's why—although not easy to do—an effective technique is to play "in" balls as if they were "out."
- To prevail over choking, simply stick to the plan that earned you the lead. Play the system that has been working and accept that a few points will be lost by attacking on the way to victory. Be aware that it's not just "you" who has a lead; it's "you playing a certain style of tennis" who has the lead. That singular style of play can possibly win 50 out of 60 sets versus this opponent. The "other you" playing a different style of game may actually lose to the very same opponent 50 out of 60 sets. Stick to the style that has proven to be successful.
- Remember that increased confidence comes from preparing more effectively in all facets of the game, including the physical, mental, emotional, and stroke production sides. Preparing properly also means practicing the art of closing out sets.

- Decrease anxiety by smiling and laughing during competition. Laughing is no joking matter; it actually releases endorphins from the brain in a process known as the stress release response. This soothes tension and relaxes muscles.

- Decrease anxiety by staying in a frame of mind that is focused on performance goals rather than outcome goals. Apply proper between-point rituals and consistently plan the next point's pattern.

- Even if playing an important match or tournament, pretend that the stakes are low—nothing more than a little hit with old friends.

- Review match performance at peak level via imagery or actual video footage. Focus on mastered skills, not the strokes that need work.

- Replace the old habit of "undercooking" under stress with "overcooking." Essentially win or lose by avoiding the preset pattern of playing scared at crunch time.

SELF-DESTRUCTION RECOVERY TECHNIQUES

Problem solving is a function of high-performance tennis. Often, the problem isn't the opponent at all; it is simply a matter of self-destruction. Continually applying the same invalid, crippled solutions or no solutions at all while hoping for a different result is unsound strategic play. Following are the most common problems that cause players to self-destruct on the tennis court, along with their solutions.

PROBLEM: Making poor decisions regarding shot selection. Video analysis of club players and juniors often shows shot selections averaging 80 percent offense, 15 percent neutral, and 5 percent defense. Even at the higher levels, improper shot selection is repeatedly the leading cause of unforced errors.

SOLUTION: Apply the proper use of offensive, neutral, and defensive shot selections. Studies of the pro tours show that professionals often hit on average 60 percent neutral, 20 percent offense, and 20 percent defense.

PROBLEM: Donating points with first- or second-strike errors.

SOLUTION: Simply focus on hitting three clean balls straight down the center of the court. Switch from handing opponents matches to making them earn seven-ball rallies.

PROBLEM: Allowing a mistake to ignite an anger tantrum. Anger leads to increasing ball speed, and increasing ball speed often leads to more errors.

SOLUTION: To steady up, simply match the opponent's ball speed until your game is back to a controllable level. Yes, champions simply match the ball speed.

PROBLEM: While sneaking a peek at where that beautiful stroke is going to land, pulling out of the strike zone and shanking balls off the frame.

SOLUTION: A new twist on an age-old tip is to simply say "one" when the incoming ball lands on a player's side of the court and "two" as the player begins to uncoil the kinetic chain into the ball. This tricks players into thinking that they can see the ball hit the strings. Guess what? No more shanks!

PROBLEM: Assuming that "hooking" is occurring and allowing that speculation to cloud physical, mental, and emotional performance. The human brain cannot complete two complicated tasks at once. Remember channel capacity?

SOLUTION: Revisit the eight-ball line-call test described earlier in this chapter. The human eye cannot pick up a three-millisecond event clearly, especially while moving.

Redirect the focus to executing the correct shot rather than dwelling on the drama of the possible stolen point.

PROBLEM: Spending 99 percent of practice time on stroke mechanics, even though the most common cause of errors in tournament play is usually shot selection.

SOLUTION: Use the Cause of Error chart (chapter 15) to identify the source of errors. Identifying the cause of the error is the first step in error correction.

PROBLEM: Self-destructing, as demonstrated with quick walking or serving and frustrated play. This mindless play is known as panicking.

SOLUTION: Recommit to applying the three pillars of between-point rituals: Get over the previous point (and stop for a few seconds), plan the next point's pattern, and then apply your rehearsed relaxation rituals.

PROBLEM: Ignoring changeover rituals. Many players use their external routines but ignore their internal rituals.

SOLUTION: A proper internal changeover routine is designed to stop a wandering mind. Simplify the thoughts to focus on just the past two games. Mentally fix flaws and design proactive plans, then organize how these modifications will be applied during the next two games. This changeover routine is designed to redirect the focus to the task at hand.

PROBLEM: Failing to close out a lead. This overthinking situation is commonly known as choking. Thoughts about things such as where that cool trophy is going to sit in your room, the award presentation, a possible new ranking, or what friends are going to say after you beat the "seed" are a surefire path to Loserville.

SOLUTION: Focus on executing the next point's pattern instead of on the sociological ramifications of winning or losing. Remember, fear inhibits muscle movement. Under stress, muscles contract, breathing becomes shallow, and problem solving stops. Start by employing positive corrective steps such as taking a few shadow swings in between points to break down that excess muscle tension, listening to your feet, and focusing attention on simply winning three points in a row.

PROBLEM: Going into a match without match notes.

SOLUTION: When champions self-destruct, they don't passively succumb to the adversity. Smart players have notes prepared before a match, and they pull them out and read them if needed. Important notes may include patterns to use against various styles and two or three solutions that may stop the player from self-destructing.

Tournament finalists often don't possess the fastest serves or biggest forehands. They may not even have the cleanest strokes, but they generally share one undeniable trait: an unwillingness to concede. This competitive spirit is part of the emotional component of a champion. This "never surrender" attitude is nurtured on and off the court through relentless effort. This readiness to go the extra mile is evidenced in the choices the athlete makes every day. The simple truth is, a player can't be a champion without making sacrifices.

chapter 12

Movement and Fitness Factors

One of the more interesting facets of the game is how the development of individual components harmonizes together into a mutually beneficial, upward spiral. A more effective serve leads to increased short-ball opportunities. Sharpened approach shots result in easier volleys and overhead winners. Well-defined game plans produce a confident attitude that makes a player less prone to mental implosion. One skill grows and feeds into the other. Being agile and physically fit, especially in the modern game, is undoubtedly a synergizing factor that raises each component to a higher level. The key ingredient to this chapter is preparation. Consistent winning is preceded by consistent off-court physical training. Preparing the physical components of tennis requires commitment, planning, and action.

MOVEMENT

The most notable evolutionary factor in the modern game is ball speed. Simply put, chasing down faster balls requires quicker anticipatory speed and accelerated foot speed. Footwork is just that: work. This section digs deeper into the movement components of the game, beginning with some universal blunders.

Universal Movement Blunders

Improvising shots "on the fly" is surely an occasional necessity of the game, but proper movement and spacing are essential for winning tennis. Developing elegant, clean strokes requires the ability to position oneself properly. Efficient court coverage is the mandatory beginning step in a domino effect that results in winning tennis: Cleaner movement leads to cleaner strokes; cleaner strokes lead to consistency; and greater consistency leads to more victories. Movement blunders, however, have a way of disrupting the sequence before it ever gets started. Following are some of the most common movement mistakes and how to avoid them:

Not Moving Forward Before Returning a Short Ball   Short balls are opportunities to hit a punishing shot. Rather than remain on the baseline, players should advance forward because this improves their hitting angles and decreases the opponent's recovery time. Players should apply broad vision to spot the anticipatory clues needed to get a better jump on the ball.

Failing to Back Up to Hit a Defensive Shot off an Offensive Deep Ball   Moving back allows players to strike the ball in their preferred hip-to-chest strike zone instead of attempting a half-volley groundstroke from the baseline. Applying defensive positioning when forced into defense is intelligence in action.

Taking an Initial Step Backward When Running Down a Drop Shot   Stepping back adds two extra steps to the process. The first step is the flaw; the second step simply returns the player back to the starting position. Keep in mind that a drop shot is a short-ball option; avoiding opponents' drop shots requires consistent groundstroke height and depth. Spotting drop shots requires the ability to read the opponent's racket manipulation—specifically, the opponent's stroke length, stroke speed, and stroke path.

Circling In to Short Balls   This occurs when a player processes the width of the stroke first, then the depth. Dissecting the angle shaves off two or three steps, which allows players to arrive in plenty of time to strike the ball closer to their comfort zone rather than at their shoelaces. The common blunder is to begin tracking down the ball with three small, hesitating steps followed by a mad rush through the contact phase. The solution is to use the opposite footwork. As the player spots the short ball, he should take three large sprinting steps first, followed by smaller adjustment steps just before contact. This fast-to-slow method produces smooth, controllable strokes and consistent kills within the short-ball range.

Shuffling to the Ball   This is a flaw that is consistently seen in players at the beginner to intermediate levels of the game. Shuffling around the tennis court is a method that was often encouraged in old-school lessons. However, crossover steps are a much faster mode of transportation.

Running With the Racket Back   This is another unfortunate old-school method that is still seen today. Anatomically speaking, it is severely inefficient to run with the dominant hand and racket trailing behind. Players should pump both arms for a cleaner, more natural stride into the proper coiling position. (Training for explosive speed will be covered later in this chapter.)

Not Decelerating on an Incoming Ball   This causes players to overrun wide balls. Learning how to properly judge an incoming ball and slowing down the lateral movement can be a huge energy saver. Let's say a player takes 3 extra steps to stop momentum after hitting the ball. If the typical point averages four shots, that equals 12 unwanted steps per point. Multiply that by a 200-point close match, and that player is taking 2,400 more steps than an efficient opponent. Now, multiply that by the five matches required to win a 64-player event, and the player has taken 12,000 more steps than an economical mover would. Who's going to be tired, sore, and possibly injured?

Discovering One's Body Type

Tennis is a demanding sport that requires players to learn and advance what is not uniquely inherited. Discovering "who you are" is an essential step in accelerating the learning curve. To increase the odds of winning at the higher levels, a player should begin by gaining an understanding of his body's natural strengths and inherent limitations. How a body functions on the court is directly related to its innate structure.

Think back to the discussion of the two unique body types in chapter 1; it will prove useful when organizing an off-court regimen. Players with a genetic predisposition for dominance of fine motor skills are wired from the elbows to the fingertips. They possess fast hands but often find their wristy play to be both their greatest blessing and greatest curse. These players would do well to increase the development of the larger muscle groups used for gross motor skills. This includes the legs, trunk, and shoulders. The opposite approach should be taken by players with dominant gross motor skills. These graceful players possess calmness through the strike zone, but they often lack the firepower to put opponents away. Developing explosive speed is usually in their best interest.

An educational tool that I recommend for any player, gross or fine motor skilled, is the Vibrex Whistling Dampener (by Unique Sports Products). When placed at the top of the racket head, this device acts as an auditory clue that provides feedback on racket head speed. The slower the swing speed, the quieter the whistle; the faster the swing speed, the louder the whistle. Players with dominant gross motor skills can apply the tool to assist in increasing hand speed, while players with dominant fine motor skills can use the device to quiet the hands and swing more effectively with the body.

Cognitive Processing Speed

One of the most common complaints from players is that they're too slow. Yet when these same players are asked to perform a simple preset sprint—such as going from the baseline to the net—they run like the wind. There's nothing inherently wrong with their quickness. It's not a problem of conditioning or muscular underdevelopment. The lack of velocity is found in the processing speed rather than the actual foot speed; they're slow off the mark because of sluggish reaction time.

Cognitive processing is an interesting element in the speed process. Think of the brain as a muscle that can be enhanced. To increase "brain" speed on the tennis court, players must use flexible skills training methods (as opposed to consistent skills training). Players who are educated in flexible skills training perform their cognitive skills in three distinct parts:

1. Information flows into the brain.
2. Relevant information is processed.
3. Essential motor programs are sent.

Slow cognitive speed appears when an athlete does not apply selective processing. Selective processing means only assimilating information that is relevant to the task at hand. Thoughts about the player laughing on the next court or a debated close line call from a previous point should not be part of the reaction equation. Players who haven't been training with flexible skills may be using six distinct parts of their cognitive skill sets:

1. The competitor's brain is already cluttered with irrelevant thoughts.
2. Information flows into the brain.
3. The preexisting internal dialogue is still in deep conversation.
4. Relevant data cannot be processed quickly enough because of channel capacity.
5. Essential motor programs are not sent in time.
6. This appears in the form of hesitation, indecisiveness, and slow footwork.

Increasing brain speed is not about adding more; it's about trimming the fat. One defining characteristic is eliminating inner chatter (discussed in detail in chapter 11). These thoughts muddy the brain, which hinders movement. The second characteristic is learning to apply flexible skills. This is the hidden secret to quicker court coverage.

Flexible Skills Training

Static skills training, also called consistent skills training, is an elementary training method that is essential in the early development of motor programs. This is most commonly referred to as stroke development through repetition. A player is continually fed balls in his preferred strike zone in order to build proper stroke mechanics.

A sample half-hour lesson using consistent skills training may go something like this: "OK Arthur, let's hit 50 forehands. . . . Nice job! Now 50 backhands. . . . OK, now come over and hit 50 serves. . . . Terrific! See you next week!"

However, after these skills are ingrained, in order for players to enhance their movement, they must practice in the manner in which they are expected to perform. Players who want to improve their anticipation, foot speed, and general court coverage should trade in their static skills training for flexible skills training.

A sample half-hour lesson using flexible skills training may sound like this: "OK Arthur, today we're going to run service patterns for about 50 points. Hit your second serve into the backhand corner of the deuce box, and then I'll quickly feed in two random groundstrokes; hit those to the opposing corner. Then we'll shift to the advantage side."

In both sample lessons, Arthur hit 50 forehands, 50 backhands, and 50 serves. Which session improves cognitive processing speed as well as foot speed? Which lesson also incorporates the additional benefit of presetting second-serve patterns? Advancing beyond static drills is a prime example of smarter training, which accelerates the learning curve.

Four-Star Flexible Skills

The four-star drill combines cognitive processing speed with foot speed, agility, and stamina. It's designed to accelerate the learning curve by simulating the actual conditions of match play. Instead of the static practice of simply playing catch (hitting back and forth), this exercise involves playing keep-away with a coach, parent, or friend.

Court speed is twofold: It is composed of brain speed and foot speed. This training regimen accelerates both. The player starts on the baseline, in the center "home base" position (figure 12.1). The feeder stands in the center of the opposing baseline and hits balls to each of the four corners of the player's court:

Star 1—high and deep to the forehand corner

Star 2—short into the forehand-side service box

Star 3—high and deep to the backhand corner

Star 4—short into the backhand-side service box

The workout begins with the player establishing the consistent pattern of tracking down and controlling all four balls in order. After each hit, the player is required to recover back to home base. After the pattern is established, the coach takes the drill to a new level by feeding the four balls randomly to all four corners. Now cognitive processing speed is really tested and developed.

Advanced versions of the four-star drill include having the feeder hit from behind the doubles alleys to change the incoming–outgoing angles or asking the player to hit to court targets or zones.

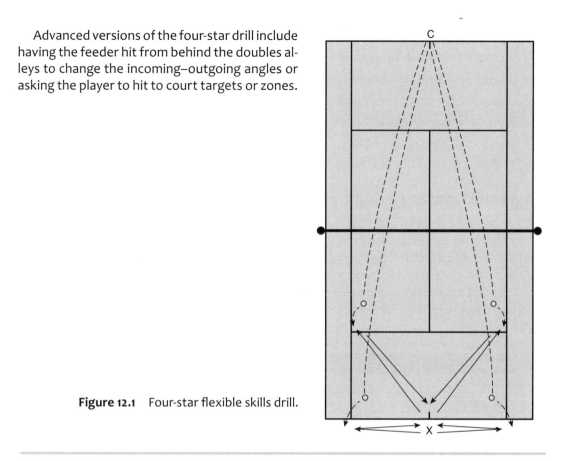

Figure 12.1   Four-star flexible skills drill.

FITNESS

Tennis players who are weekend warriors can socialize, have a ton of fun, and get some fresh air without the need for serious off-court training. However, serious competitors must recognize and embrace the pivotal role that fitness plays in high-level tennis. Just as stroke production and mental training have evolved, so too has the increasing physical demands of the game. Having a brilliant forehand is only effective if a player has the strength and stamina to be in position to hit it for the duration of a gruelling match. Athletes who are interested in entering tournament play should review this chapter's physical endurance reality check. Whatever a player's goal, one common denominator in every level of the game is always true: When conditioning is ignored or compromised, so is the standard of play.

Being physically fit has these benefits for a player on the tennis court:

- Elevates physical energy
- Enhances endurance
- Raises cardiovascular performance
- Improves agility, acceleration, and deceleration speeds
- Improves positioning for cleaner technical strokes
- Increases power
- Shortens recovery time
- Enhances balance, coordination, and flexibility

- Prevents injuries
- Reduces fatigue and soreness
- Strengthens muscles, tendons, ligaments, and bones
- Contributes to emotional stability
- Elevates concentration, proper shot selection, and problem-solving skills
- Swells confidence
- Adds to the intimidation factor

Physical Endurance Reality Check

This is directed primarily at those players who participate—or plan to participate—in competitive tournaments. But even for other players, this information is still worth noting for future consideration. How many sets does a singles and doubles champion have to play in order to win a 64-player event?

Table 12.1 provides an example of the physical requirements that may be involved in winning a five-day, 64-player event:

Table 12.1 Potential Number of Sets in a 64-Player Tournament

Round	Singles	Doubles
First round	6-2, 6-3	6-4, 6-4
Second round	6-4, 6-2	4-6, 7-6, 6-3
Quarter-finals	1-6, 6-4, 6-1	6-2, 7-6
Semifinals	6-4, 6-3	6-7, 6-4, 6-1
Finals	4-6, 6-4, 6-4	7-6, 7-6
Total sets	**12**	**12**

In this example, the total number of sets played in a week is 24. Now ask yourself, "When was the last time I played 24 grueling sets over five days?" Mindful competitors focus on controlling the controllable. Being defeated by a superior opponent may be out of one's control, but losing a match because of a lack of fitness is unacceptable.

Fitness Training

Tennis requires a combination of aerobic and anaerobic fitness. Aerobic fitness (long-term stamina) is required because the game is essentially long in duration but moderate in intensity. Anaerobic fitness (short-term, explosive movements followed by short periods of rest) is required because of the constant demands of solving emergencies. These are the random points that are relatively short in duration but high in intensity. A player needs to be both a long-distance runner and a sprinter. Off-court training that builds strength, speed, and stamina plays an integral part in helping a player assume both roles.

Table 12.2 is a sample one-hour workout routine that simulates the physical requirements of real match-play conditions. Completing this workout—or better yet, customizing a version (a blank form is available for download at www.humankinetics.com/products/all-products/championship-tennis) based on the various types of training covered in this chapter—will be a big boost to a player's conditioning and confidence. Regardless of time, once the player completes all reps for a given exercise, he should move on to the next exercise listed. If a player cannot complete the number of reps provided for a particular exercise in the amount of time stipulated, he should give that exercise extra attention until he can.

Table 12.2 One-Hour Workout Routine

Activity	Time
Light jog or jogging in place (warm-up)	3 minutes
Dynamic upper- and lower-body stretches	3 minutes
Jump rope	2 minutes
Push-ups (50)	4 minutes to complete
Jump rope	2 minutes
Sit-ups (100)	5 minutes to complete
Jump rope	2 minute
Break	5 minutes
Jump rope	2 minutes
Medicine ball toss against wall (50 forehand, 50 backhand)	5 minutes to complete
Jump rope	2 minutes
Medicine ball overhead slams against wall (50)	5 minutes to complete
Jump rope	2 minutes
Lunges (50 per leg)	10 minutes to complete
Jump rope	2 minutes
Static upper- and lower-body stretches	3 minutes
Light jog or jogging in place (cool-down)	3 minutes

Off-court training is not only valuable for strengthening the body to prevent injuries and building the necessary endurance to compete in lengthy matches and tournaments, but it also plays a critical role in player improvement. For instance, building a stronger core fosters increased trunk rotation, leading to greater racket head speed and more destructive groundstrokes. So by performing resistance and explosive exercises, players can amplify their playing attributes, which in turn boosts confidence. The best exercises focus on improving a player's power and speed.

Coach's Corner

Although it's difficult to believe, tennis players over the ripe old age of 35 are officially categorized as "seniors." Some seniors remain incredibly competitive, but for most, tennis is simply a wonderful hobby. Athletes with a touch of gray who are ready to reap the benefits of fitness would be wise to start with small steps and consult a physician before beginning an off-court training regimen. Cardio tennis—offered at many clubs around the country—is a great starting point.

Training for Increased Power

Although equipment and improved technique can help increase the power of strokes, the greatest gains are brought about by physical improvements. In the sample one-hour circuit provided earlier, notice that most of the resistance training, or strength training, is done with a player's own body weight. What makes this so effective for the sport of tennis is that it forces players to control their body through space, just as an athlete would during competition.

This is not to say that free weights such as dumbbells, barbells, and kettlebells have no value. Far from it. They are great for building strong muscles and developing power. Some players worry that using free weights will make them bulky and rob them of speed. This is a misconception. The fact is, very few people—without the help of pharmaceuticals—are predisposed for developing large, brawny muscles. Plus, it takes a significant increase in caloric intake to help those muscles grow. For most people, the result of resistance training is actually a leaner physique. However, simply lifting more on the bench press isn't necessarily the way to achieve a faster serve or a more explosive forehand. Tennis players need their fitness to mirror what they need on the court (once again, practicing in the manner in which they are expected to perform). There will never come a time when a player will stop in the middle of a point, lie on a bench, and push weight up and down.

For this reason, the most practical and valuable tool for developing massive power for tennis-specific movements is the weighted medicine ball. Medicine ball exercises work the five regions necessary for massive power: the core, legs, chest, arms, and shoulders. What's also great about the medicine ball is that it can easily transition between the three primary planes of sport movement (figure 12.2): forward and back (sagittal plane), side to side or lateral (frontal plane), and rotational (transverse plane). A single tennis point can demand a player's body to travel several times through each of these planes, and using a medicine ball can replicate the movements with the power-building benefit of added resistance.

The following medicine ball exercises can be conducted with a partner or solo. In addition to being part of a complete off-court regimen, these exercises can also be performed as part of a brief prematch routine. Using a rubberized medicine ball is recommended because the ball will often be thrown against a wall. Medicine balls generally run anywhere from 4 to 25 pounds in weight; the size used should depend on the player's fitness level. A typical routine consists of 3 sets of 10 repetitions, but modifications should be instituted to suit the individual.

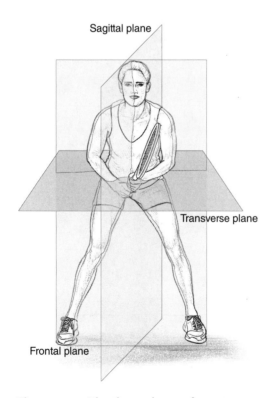

Figure 12.2 The three planes of sport movement: sagittal, frontal, and transverse.

Stationary Closed-Stance Groundstroke Simulation Throw

In a ready position, hold the medicine ball with both hands about chest high (figure 12.3a). Keep the medicine ball high as the body coils to the right (to simulate a right-handed forehand or a left-handed backhand). Transfer the body's weight from the right foot to the left as the traditional closed-stance platform (stepping into the ball) is applied (figure 12.3b). Drop the medicine ball low in the backswing to simulate a groundstroke's low-to-high flight pattern (figure 12.3c). Release the medicine ball at the contact zone and finish by following through over the left ear (as if throwing a bucket of water; figure 12.3d). Repeat on the left side (to simulate a right-hander's backhand or a left-hander's forehand).

Figure 12.3 Stationary closed-stance groundstroke simulation throw.

Stationary Open-Stance
Groundstroke Simulation Throw

As in the previous drill, assume a ready position, and hold the medicine ball with both hands about chest high (figure 12.4a). Keep the medicine ball high as the body coils to the right (to simulate a right-handed forehand or a left-handed backhand). This time, transfer the body's weight by stepping out to the right with the right (back) foot, using an open-stance platform (figure 12.4b). Drop the medicine ball low in the backswing to simulate a groundstroke's low-to-high flight pattern (figure 12.4c). Release the medicine ball at the contact zone and finish by following through over the left ear (figure 12.4d). Repeat on the left side (to simulate a right-hander's backhand or a left-hander's forehand).

Figure 12.4 Stationary open-stance groundstroke simulation throw.

Moving Closed-Stance Groundstroke Simulation Throw

Begin with a coach or friend tossing a medicine ball a few steps to your right and then to your left to simulate proper spacing and movement on both the forehand and backhand. As the coach prepares to toss the ball to your right, begin with a crossover step (figure 12.5a). Lightly jog into position to catch the medicine ball (figure 12.5b). After catching the ball, toss the ball back to the coach using the procedure described in the stationary closed-stance groundstroke simulation throw (figure 12.5, c-d). Be sure to apply small spacing steps while positioning the body for the catch and release.

Figure 12.5 Moving closed-stance groundstroke simulation throw.

Moving Open-Stance
Groundstroke Simulation Throw

As in the previous drill, begin with a coach or friend tossing a medicine ball a few steps to your right and then to your left to simulate proper spacing and movement on both the forehand and backhand. As the coach prepares to toss the ball to your right, begin with a crossover step (figure 12.6a). Lightly jog into position to catch the medicine ball (figure 12.6b). After catching the ball, toss the ball back to the coach using the procedure described in the stationary open-stance groundstroke simulation throw (figure 12.6, c-d). Once again, be sure to apply small spacing steps while positioning the body for the catch and release.

Figure 12.6 Moving open-stance groundstroke simulation throw.

Stationary Chest Press

Stand with the feet about shoulder-width apart. Place the hands on the sides of the medicine ball and press it close against the chest (figure 12.7a). Bend the knees, sit the hips back into a squat position (figure 12.7b), and, with an upward thrust, throw the ball skyward by extending and pronating the palms away from the body (figure 12.7, c-d).

Figure 12.7   Stationary chest press.

Stationary Overhead Slam

Stand with the feet about shoulder-width apart. Place the hands on the sides of the medicine ball and place it high above the head (figure 12.8a). From this position, accelerate the medicine ball down into the ground (figure 12.8b), causing a high bounce.

Figure 12.8 Stationary overhead slam.

Moving Chest Press

Begin with a coach or friend tossing a medicine ball a few steps to your right and left to simulate proper spacing and movement in an open stance. As the coach prepares to toss the ball to your right, begin with a crossover step (figure 12.9*a*). Lightly jog into position to catch the medicine ball (figure 12.9*b*). After catching the ball, toss the ball back to the coach using the procedure described in the stationary chest press (figure 12.9, *c-d*). Be sure to apply small spacing steps while positioning for the catch and release.

Figure 12.9 Moving chest press.

Moving Overhead Slam

As in the previous drill, begin with a coach or friend tossing a medicine ball a few steps to your right and left to simulate proper spacing and movement in an open stance. As the coach prepares to toss the ball to your right, begin with a crossover step (figure 12.10a). Lightly jog into position to catch the medicine ball (figure 12.10b). After catching the ball, bounce the ball back to the coach using the procedure described in the stationary overhead slam (figure 12.10, c-d). Once again, remember to apply small spacing steps while positioning for the catch and release.

Figure 12.10   Moving overhead slam.

Stationary Overhead Slam to Push-Up

This exercise requires a coach or friend and an aerobic mat. Begin on the knees with the back straight, holding the medicine ball high above the head (figure 12.11a). Throw the medicine ball down into the ground (figure 12.11b) and quickly move into a push-up position (figure 12.11c), with knees still on the floor. Stronger or more advanced trainees may want to perform a standard push-up. The coach or friend catches the medicine ball on the bounce and will toss it back to you (figure 12.11d). Complete the push-up before rising up to catch the medicine ball, then begin another rep.

Figure 12.11 Stationary overhead slam to push-up.

Training for Explosive Speed

Three forms of explosive speed are required in the competitive levels of the game: core rotational speed, hand speed, and foot speed. Following are descriptions of each form and some exercises designed specifically for improving them.

Core Rotational Speed   The initial movement for almost any action on the court originates in the core (which essentially encompasses everything outside of the arms and legs). The turn of the core instigates and ignites the hands and feet. It's not glamorous, but to maximize this rotational speed, players need to work this hugely important part of the body.

Numerous movements can be used to strengthen this region, and the following are two that are particularly good for tennis. The number of sets and repetitions should be customized to suit the player's ability level; a typical routine consists of 3 sets of 10 reps.

Stationary Mat Twist

Kneeling on a mat while holding a weight or medicine ball (figure 12.12*a*), rotate to the right (figure 12.12*b*). Return to the center, then rotate left, performing the same movement to complete the repetition.

Figure 12.12   Stationary mat twist.

Dumbbell Torso Rotation

Holding a dumbbell in the right hand, coil and touch the weight to the ground in front of the left foot (figure 12.13*a*). Then explode from low to high, finishing with the dumbbell above the head on the right side (figure 12.13*b*). After performing the appropriate number of repetitions, repeat the exercise for the left side of the body.

Figure 12.13 Dumbbell torso rotation.

Hand Speed   Greater hand speed creates faster racket head speed, which results in enhanced ball speed. Various methods can be used to increase hand speed, including cross-training with boxing. Hitting padded targets, hitting a heavy bag, or even shadow boxing can help develop explosive shoulder, forearm, and hand speed. Players can perform the following for a specified number of repetitions (3 sets of 10) or a specified amount of time (punch for 30 seconds straight).

Boxing While Stationary

This drill requires padded targets or a heavy bag, held in place by a coach or friend. While standing still, begin by loading the back foot with your body weight (figure 12.14a), then uncoil. Remember to drive forward when you punch (figure 12.14b). This will increase the power and accuracy of the punch.

For every action, there is an equal and opposite reaction. As one hand extends toward the target, the opposing hand travels inward toward the body, essentially blocking the third link of the kinetic chain, which aids in accelerating the punch.

Figure 12.14   Boxing while stationary.

Boxing on the Move

Dancing in either direction, uncoil and hit randomly moving padded targets or a heavy bag held by a coach or friend. While on the move, begin by loading the back foot with your body weight (figure 12.15a), then uncoil. Remember to drive forward when you punch (figure 12.15b). This will increase the power and accuracy of the punch.

Again, for every action, there is an equal and opposite reaction. As one hand extends toward the target, the opposing hand travels inward toward the body, essentially blocking the third link of the kinetic chain, which aids in accelerating the punch.

Figure 12.15   Boxing on the move.

Foot Speed   In tennis, explosive foot speed involves a variety of distinct muscle requirements. A player needs to be able to accelerate, decelerate, stabilize the body, and rotate in various directions—usually several times in a typical point. Note that sprinting in a straight line does not simulate the actual start-and-stop, multidirectional conditions of high-performance tennis. Explosive tennis speed requires an athlete to continually change directions, essentially turning on a dime.

Following are some drills to help maximize foot speed. They can be done for reps or time, beginning at the low end of the spectrum and then building toward a goal. Customization is key.

Arm Drive

Arm drives are used to assist in synchronizing the body in order to run more efficiently, thus encouraging more explosive running. Begin with the arms out in front of the body and parallel, just below chest level (imagine that you are holding the racket in the ready position). Raise the right hand up to ear-level while simultaneously lowering the left hand down to the left-side pant pocket (figure 12.16*a*). Then pump the arms in a reverse fashion to complete the rep (figure 12.16*b*). Here are a few variations on the arm drive:

- *Seated arm drive.* This time, perform the same movement while seated in a chair. The seated position isolates the upper-body rotation and intensifies the arm drive.

- *Jogging-in-place arm drive.* Perform the arm drive while jogging in place.

- *Uphill arm drive.* Perform the arm drive while jogging uphill.

Figure 12.16   Arm drive.

Colored Cones Circle

Place randomly colored (or numbered) cones in a circle that is 20 feet (6.1 m) wide. Stand in the center and apply flexible skills training by having a trainer or friend randomly call out a colored cone. Sprint to the appropriate cone, then perform a crossover step and recover back to home base (figure 12.17).

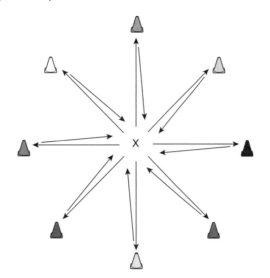

Figure 12.17 Colored cones circle.

Uphill Acceleration Sprints

Perform a set number of sprints on an uphill incline for a specific distance. Customize the sprints (for example, 4 × 15-yard sprints with a 30-second break) according to your fitness level.

Training for Rapid Agility

Agile players always look in control. To shift the body's directional course effectively, players must have a nimbleness found in the combination of coordination and reflexes. These quick adjustments are in direct response to the situation or stimuli at hand. Incorporating an agility ladder into training can maximize this type of quickness. Ask a coach or friend to randomly interchange ladder drill sequences. This advanced technique builds cognitive processing speed and the flexible skills required in the higher levels of the game. Players should perform 3 sets of 10 reps (down and back) of the following footwork drills. These drills can also be performed as part of a brief prematch routine.

Forward Inside-Out Agility Ladder

Begin in a sprinter's ready position in front of an agility ladder. Step inside the first square of the ladder with the left foot, then step alongside the next square with the right foot (figure 12.18). Continue through the length of the ladder and back. Next, reverse the drill, beginning with the right foot.

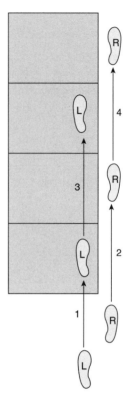

Figure 12.18
Forward inside-out agility ladder.

Forward Reverse Agility Ladder

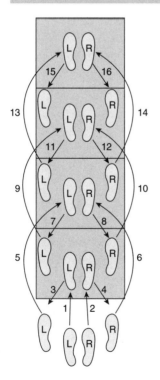

Begin in a sprinter's ready position in front of an agility ladder. Alternate stepping forward into the first square with the left foot followed by the right foot, then stepping backward outside the square with the left foot followed by the right foot (figure 12.19). Proceed to step (first with the left foot and then with the right foot) two squares ahead and repeat the drill to the end of the ladder and back. Next, reverse the drill, beginning with the right foot.

Figure 12.19 Forward reverse agility ladder.

Carioca Agility Ladder

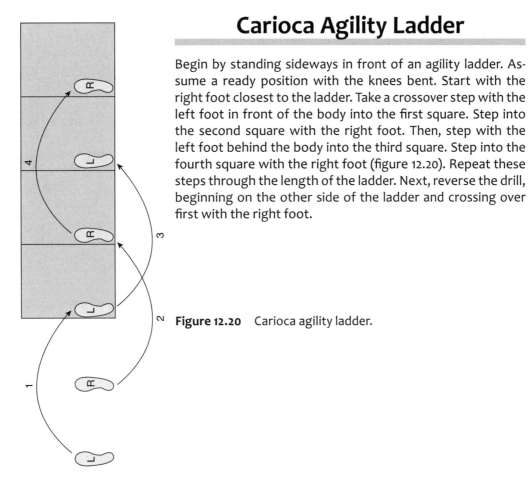

Begin by standing sideways in front of an agility ladder. Assume a ready position with the knees bent. Start with the right foot closest to the ladder. Take a crossover step with the left foot in front of the body into the first square. Step into the second square with the right foot. Then, step with the left foot behind the body into the third square. Step into the fourth square with the right foot (figure 12.20). Repeat these steps through the length of the ladder. Next, reverse the drill, beginning on the other side of the ladder and crossing over first with the right foot.

Figure 12.20 Carioca agility ladder.

Lateral Agility Ladder

Begin by standing sideways in front of an agility ladder. Assume a ready position with the knees bent. Start with the right foot closest to the ladder. Place the right foot followed by the left foot inside the first square. From this position, step into the second square first with the right foot followed by the left, and so on (figure 12.21). Proceed down each square to the end of the ladder and back. Next, reverse the drill, beginning on the other side of the ladder and starting with the left foot.

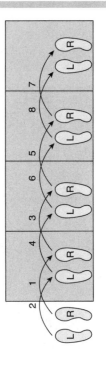

Figure 12.21 Lateral agility ladder.

Training for Long-Suffering Endurance

There's an old joke used for beginners and intermediates: Once the server steps up to the baseline to serve, the point is almost over. It's different for professionals, but in club-level tennis, most points last around 3 to 5 seconds on faster surfaces and up to 10 seconds on slower surfaces. This means that players need to train aerobically and anaerobically by using interval training to systematically tax their energy reserves. A training technique that many players like to use for this is plyometrics (also known as plyos). This is a type of jump training that improves the long-term performance of muscle responses. Players should perform 3 sets of 10 reps of the following exercises; in addition to being part of a training regimen, these exercises can also be performed as part of a brief prematch routine. Note that for the exercises involving a stable box or platform, players who don't have a platform to jump on may consider sprinting up a 30-yard hill, then lightly jogging down to begin the sequence again.

Stroke Rotation

Stand with the feet shoulder-width apart, facing a 6-inch (15 cm) plyo platform (figure 12.22a). Squat, load, and jump, transferring your energy quietly up onto the platform (figure 12.22b). Once you are stable in a power position, uncoil the kinetic chain and perform a forehand shadow-swing groundstroke (figure 12.22, c-d). Repeat the next jump while applying a backhand shadow-swing groundstroke, and so on.

Figure 12.22 Stroke rotation.

Sky Jump

Facing a 6-inch to 1 foot (30 to 61 cm) plyo platform, begin in a ready position with the arms straight out in front (figure 12.23a). Jump up and bring the knees toward the chest (figure 12.23b), landing on the plyo platform (figure 12.23c). From the platform, jump backward, landing in a balanced position on the ground, and repeat.

Figure 12.23 Sky jump.

Single-Leg Box Jump

Facing a 6-inch to 1-foot plyo platform, stand with the feet shoulder-width apart (figure 12.24a). Squat, load, and jump, transferring the energy to the right leg only (figure 12.24b). Land in a balanced position on the platform on the right leg only (figure 12.24c). Once stable, jump back down, once again landing on the right leg only. Next, repeat the sequence with the left leg.

Figure 12.24 Single-leg box jump.

Lateral Box Jump

With the feet shoulder-width apart, stand along the right side of a 6-inch plyo platform (figure 12.25a). Squat and load, jumping up to the left (figure 12.25b) onto the platform in a power position (figure 12.25c). Once stable, jump back down alongside the right side of the platform. Next, repeat on the left side of the plyo platform, jumping to the right.

Figure 12.25　Lateral box jump.

Single-Leg Lateral Box Jump

With the feet shoulder-width apart, stand along the right side of a six-inch plyo platform (figure 12.26a). Squat and load the body weight and jump up to the left (figure 12.26b), landing only on the left foot on the plyo platform (figure 12.26c). Jump back down alongside the right side of the platform, again landing only on the left foot. Next, repeat on the left side of the plyo platform, jumping to the right onto the right leg only.

Figure 12.26 Single-leg lateral box jump.

Rapid-Fire Tuck Jumps

Starting in a squat position with the arms straight out in front (figure 12.27*a*), jump as high as you can and tuck the knees into the chest (figure 12.27*b*). As soon as your feet hit the ground on the landing, repeat.

Figure 12.27 Rapid-fire tuck jumps.

Pre- and Postmatch Off-Court Routine

Anyone who spends some time on the professional tours will quickly see that no two players are exactly alike. This especially holds true for their pre- and postmatch routines. Tour stops typically have elite gyms that adjoin the player lounge. Players can often be seen riding stationary bikes, tossing a light medicine ball, or performing a full variety of stretches. Common tools found in pro players' bags include elastic bands and jump ropes. One thing, however, is certain for all: They have their pre- and postmatch rituals and routines, and they never deviate from them.

A good place to start a prematch routine is with a light jog. After the heart rate is lifted, the player should shift to dynamic movements, including upper- and lower-body exercises. Advanced players may also include a more intense routine. After each match, a player should perform a brief and light static stretching routine.

Dynamic Movements

Before match play, dynamic movements are preferred over static stretching. These movements reduce muscle tightness and therefore help reduce strains, tears, and other injuries. The best strategy is to perform dynamic stretching just before competition. A common blunder that many tennis players fall into is completing their dynamic movement routine too early before play. Then they sit, allowing the muscles to actually get stiffer than if they hadn't stretched at all. Following are some examples of popular dynamic exercises that will improve match-day results.

Lower-Body Warm-Ups   To warm up the lower body before engaging in competition, players need to get the blood flowing through jogging-related exercises. The following exercises in particular are great for warming up the glutes, quads, hamstrings, and calves.

Butt Kicks

This exercise is similar to lightly jogging in place. While jogging, keep the knees low. Increase the height of the heel of each foot as you individually kick them up behind you—until the heel touches the butt (figure 12.28, a-b).

Figure 12.28   Butt kicks.

High Knees

Again, this exercise is similar to lightly jogging in place. Place both hands out in front of the body, waist high, as you begin to jog. Increase the height of the alternating left and right knees until each almost touches the corresponding hand (figure 12.29, a-b).

Figure 12.29 High knees.

Monster Walk

Begin with the feet shoulder-width apart. Keeping both legs straight and minimizing any excess hip rotation, walk forward and back (figure 12.30). Ankle bands are often used for greater resistance. The movement of the legs is exaggerated, as they should be at least parallel, if not higher, to the court.

Figure 12.30 Monster walk.

Upper-Body Warm-Ups   Stretch bands and resistance cables are popular tools for helping to warm up the chest, arms, and shoulders. The player can anchor the band to a fence, pole, around the back, or under the feet. Players should customize a series of dynamic resistance band stretches to systematically warm up the upper body before doing battle on the court. Following are a few favorites.

Standing Fly

Wrap a resistance band around a fixed object (e.g., a fence or pole), making sure that the band is at shoulder height. Facing away from the cable, place one end of the band in each hand. With the band at shoulder height and the arms out (figure 12.31a), bring the hands together in front of you (figure 12.31b).

Figure 12.31   Standing fly.

One-Arm Shoulder Press

This exercise requires a resistance band. Stabilize the band by standing on the middle of it, holding the ends at shoulder height (figure 12.32*a*). Arms should be out with elbows facing down. Begin the exercise by raising the left arm straight up overhead, band in hand (figure 12.32*b*). After bringing the left arm back to its starting position, perform the exercise with the right arm, then repeat.

Figure 12.32   One-arm shoulder press.

One-Arm Overhead Triceps Extension

This exercise requires a resistance band. Stabilize the band by standing on the middle of it, holding the ends at shoulder height, with both hands facing the ears and elbows pointing up (figure 12.33*a*). Begin the exercise by raising and pronating the right arm straight up overhead, band in hand (figure 12.33*b*). After bringing the right arm back to its starting position, perform the exercise with the left arm, then repeat.

Figure 12.33 One-arm overhead triceps extension.

Lateral Raise

This exercise requires one resistance band. Stabilize the center of the band under the arches of both feet, holding one end of the band in each hand. While standing on the band, bend the knees into a slightly tucked position (figure 12.34a). Raise both hands up and out to the sides, keeping the palms down, until the arms reach shoulder height (figure 12.34b). Repeat.

Figure 12.34 Lateral raise.

Static Stretching

Static stretches are simply that—stretches that a person performs while remaining still. Old-school static stretching requires the athlete to hold a stretch for at least 30 seconds and up to 2 minutes. The benefits of this are to lengthen and elongate the targeted muscles. However, results from more recent studies indicate that static stretching performed before competition is detrimental to performance. These studies clearly show that static stretching weakens muscles, lessens explosive speed, and increases joint instability. Therefore, experts now recommend that athletes perform static stretching after competition as part of a cool-down routine to maintain flexibility.

Ankle Stretching Routine

The ankle stretching routine is composed of three exercises, including flexing, extending, and rotating. Sitting in a chair, straighten out both legs in front of you. From this position, flex the feet, pointing the toes upward toward the head (figure 12.35*a*). Hold for 30 seconds. Next, extend the feet, pointing the toes downward toward the ground (figure 12.35*b*). Once again, hold for 30 seconds. For the final exercise, with the legs still straight out in front of you, slowly rotate the left foot in a circular motion (figure 12.35*c*), followed by the right foot (figure 12.35*d*). Start the rotation in a clockwise direction; then, after 30 seconds for each foot, switch the direction to counterclockwise.

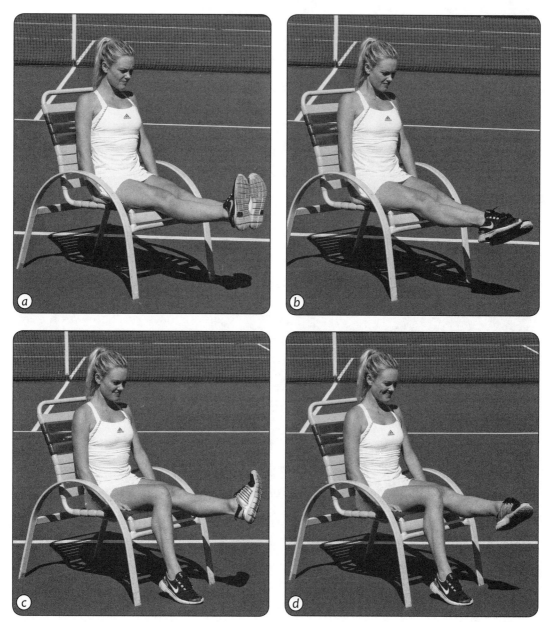

Figure 12.35   Ankle stretching routine.

Knee Stretch

Standing tall, pull the right knee up and into the chest (figure 12.36). Hold for 30 seconds, and then repeat the stretch with the left knee. Not only does this stretch lengthen the muscles around the knee, but it also strengthens core muscles and improves core balance.

Figure 12.36   Knee stretch.

Hip Flexor Stretch

Begin in a lunge position with the left foot forward and the right knee on the ground. Grab the back (right) ankle with the right hand and slowly lift it as you lean forward (figure 12.37). After holding the stretch for 30 seconds, switch legs and repeat.

Figure 12.37   Hip flexor stretch.

Core Stretching Routine

The core stretching routine includes three basic static stretch exercises. To begin the first exercise, stand straight up with feet together. Bend to touch the toes, elongating the lower back (figure 12.38a). Hold the stretch for 30 seconds. Moving into the second exercise, cross the left leg over the right (figure 12.38b). Again, hold the stretch for 30 seconds, switch legs (crossing the right leg over the left), and repeat. For the third exercise, return to a standing position, with the right hand on the right hip and with the left hand above the head. Stretch the left hand toward the right side of the head (figure 12.38c). Hold for 30 seconds, and then repeat the stretch with the left hand on the hip and the right hand above the head.

Figure 12.38 Core stretching routine.

Arm Stretching Routine

The arm stretching routine includes two static stretch exercises, one for the biceps and one for the triceps. In a standing position, begin the triceps stretch by raising the right arm above the head. Pull it down slowly behind the head, reaching for the opposite shoulder. With the left hand, reach to the right elbow and pull it over, deepening the stretch (figure 12.39*a*). Hold the stretch for 30 seconds, and then repeat the routine with the left arm. After completing the triceps stretch, begin the biceps stretch by straightening the right arm out in front of the body with the palm turned up toward the sky. With the left hand, slowly pull the fingers of the right hand downward (figure 12.39*b*). Again, hold the stretch for 30 seconds, and then repeat with the opposite arm.

Figure 12.39   Arm stretching routine.

Rotator Cuff Stretching Routine

The rotator cuff stretching routine is composed of two exercises. In a standing position with arms straight out in front of you, perform the first exercise by gently pronating (palms facing downward; figure 12.40*a*) and supinating (palms facing upward; figure 12.40*b*) the forearms for 30 seconds. After finishing the first exercise with the arms in a pronated position (figure 12.40*c*), raise the arms up until both hands point toward the sky (figure 12.40*d*). From this position, lower the arms back to the palm-down horizontal plane (figure 12.40*e*), then continue to drop them downward to your sides so the palms face behind you (figure 12.40*f*).

Figure 12.40 Rotator cuff stretching routine.

Neck Stretching Routine

The neck stretching routine contains three static stretches. Standing tall, place the left hand down along the left thigh. Gently tilt the head down toward the right to stretch the back of the neck (figure 12.41a). Next, lightly tilt the right ear to the shoulder to stretch the mid scalene muscles (figure 12.41b). Finally, look up toward the right to slowly stretch the front of the neck (figure 12.41c). Hold each stretch for 30 seconds, and then repeat the series on the opposite side.

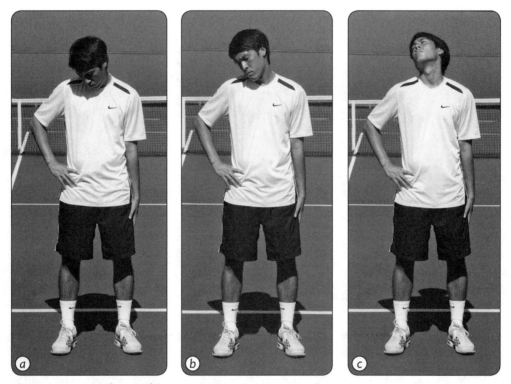

Figure 12.41   Neck stretching routine.

At the club level, prematch routines should involve similar concepts for all players but should be slightly customized to each player's needs. Some players are so naturally hyper that they need to go for a run before a match in order to calm down enough to perform at their peak level. Others may just need to perform a customized routine of dynamic movements like those described earlier to prepare for play. For those who are routinely slow starters in competition, the best plan is to experiment with overcooking the warm-up routine rather than undercooking it.

Remember, one size does not fit all. The exercises included in this chapter are meant to provide a starting point from which a player can customize his routines. If a reader is interested in exploring off-court training further, I recommend looking into training-specific tennis books such as *Tennis Anatomy* and *Complete Conditioning for Tennis* (both published by Human Kinetics). Self-discovery is the best way to customize a routine that will provide the best chance of starting a match in that crucial peak-performance state.

Practice and Planning

chapter 13

Organization and Scheduling

The first thing that any athlete must determine is how far he wants to go in the sport. Tennis attracts players with varying degrees of ambition. Some just want a good workout and time with friends; others want to lift trophies. Goals of junior players may range from "I want to make my high school squad!" to "I want to go pro!" Adult rec players' goals could be anything from "I just want to beat Harold on the club ladder" to "I want to be good enough to make the ladies' 4.0 league team."

Identifying one's motivational factors and ambitions provides the initial step in creating a structured blueprint for success. No matter what the goal, all players looking to improve can benefit from having an organized plan. The world is full of talented athletes with big dreams but with little design on how to achieve them. This chapter provides information that will assist players in turning their vision into a reality.

When putting together a customized navigational plan, players should focus on two distinct courses of action. One is developing the player's tool belt. This involves building primary and secondary strokes, as well as off-court skills such as movement, fitness, and agility. The other is the art of winning matches. This involves the development of the mental and emotional competencies. It also includes developing the ability to consistently implement those tools under competitive, stressful situations. A typical misstep is to simply focus year after year solely on the betterment of the strokes without addressing the critical mental aspects. Players need to address both aspects if they want to reach their goals in tennis (whatever those goals might be).

TIME MANAGEMENT

I have worked with thousands of players—from nationally ranked juniors to weekend warriors—and a common myth that I routinely destroy is, "I don't have enough time." Competitive players at every level all share one undeniable truth: They all get the same 168 hours per week. The difference for those who show greater improvement stems from the acceptance of a customized, organizational blueprint. Whatever time they can devote to the tennis court, they make the most of it.

The 168-hour question is this: How much time does a player truly have available to dedicate to tennis? Figure 13.1 is what I call the 168-hour time-management schedule; I give this to my students to help them assess their time in a week. (A blank version of this form is available for download at www.humankinetics.com/products/all-products/championship-tennis.)

Figure 13.1   168-Hour Time-Management Schedule

__56__ hours for sleep

__30__ hours for school + 10 hours for homework OR 40 hours for work

__12__ hours for meals

__7__ hours for driving and incidentals

__53__ **hours remaining:**   __20__ hours for high-performance training

__33__ hours for socialization, relaxation, and recovery

While filling out the 168-hour time-management schedule, athletes should keep in mind that customization of their weekly blueprint is required. Life throws us curves, and weekly adjustments and modifications are recommended.

The first step in customizing a schedule is determining how much time the player can truly devote to the developmental plan. For instance, players with the goal of hitting the pro tours must keep in mind the 10,000-hour rule, which states that success in any endeavor lies in practicing that endeavor for a total of 10,000 hours. Although there has been research showing this to be an arbitrary number as well as examples refuting its legitimacy, I believe that the actual number is not the point. The fact is that in order to reach a world-class level, a player must have dedication—a love for the game and a devotion like that to a lifetime ambition rather than a hobby. Designing a developmental plan of approximately 20 hours a week for 10 years is a barometer for high-level success. Guess what Wayne Gretzky, Bobby Fischer, Yo-Yo Ma, Bill Gates, The Beatles, Mozart, Michelangelo, Michael Jackson, and Tiger Woods all have in common with Roger Federer. You guessed it, the dedication and desire to reach and exceed the 10,000-hour rule.

This much dedication may seem unrealistic for many beginner and intermediate-level players. Managing a schedule is a juggling act—with family, work, school, other sports, and so on. And when a person already has so many balls in the air, adding another seems daunting. Still, the players who show intense commitment to their development enjoy great rewards.

ORGANIZING A WEEKLY PLAN

The analogy I like to use is this: Would you train your dog to compete in the National Obstacle Course Championships by simply having Fido run five miles a day in a straight line? Not if the goal is winning. Fido would be far better served by training in an obstacle course environment and working on developing all the tools needed to master each unique barrier and hurdle. The same philosophy holds true when developing tennis players.

If you haven't done so already, go back to the book's initial evaluation sections (chapters 2 and 3) and rate your general performance level for each integral component and its list of subcomponents. Once that's done, purchase a weekly planner and schedule time to bolster any areas of weakness. This would be any area that was graded a 3 or below.

Using this chapter's match logs, in addition to analysis of match video, can be extremely useful for discovering weapons as well as identifying unwanted behavioral patterns that creep up in match play conditions. (Video analysis will be discussed in chapter 15.) A player should use the data collected to customize the percentage of training time devoted to building strengths and repairing flaws.

Figure 13.2 provides sample lesson plans and weekly developmental plans for beginner, intermediate, and advanced players.

Figure 13.2   Sample Lesson and Developmental Plans

A beginner's lesson plan may consist of the following:
- 40 percent primary stroke proficiency
- 20 percent on-court movement and agility
- 10 percent comprehension of scorekeeping, rules, and court diagram
- 10 percent basic strategic development
- 20 percent live-ball play

A beginner's weekly developmental plan may consist of the following:
- One-hour private lesson
- Two-hour group clinic
- Two hours of shadow swinging (at home)
- One hour of repetition with ball machine

An intermediate's lesson plan may consist of the following:
- 30 percent primary stroke proficiency
- 20 percent secondary stroke proficiency
- 20 percent mental maturity
- 20 percent emotional improvement
- 10 percent off-court training

An intermediate's weekly developmental plan may consist of the following:
- Two hours of private lessons
- One-hour group clinic
- Two hours of match play
- One-hour cardio tennis class
- One hour of repetition with ball machine
- One hour of tennis-specific off-court training

An advanced player's lesson plan may consist of the following:
- 20 percent secondary stroke proficiency
- 20 percent pattern repetition
- 20 percent mental growth and maturity
- 20 percent emotional improvement
- 20 percent off-court training

An advanced player's weekly developmental plan may consist of the following:
- Four hours of private lessons
- Four hours of group clinic
- Six hours of match play
- One hour of repetition with ball machine
- One hour of serving repetition
- Four hours of tennis-specific off-court training

So how does a player construct a blueprint for success? Players can begin by completing the weekly planner (see the example in table 13.1). (A blank version of this form is available for download at www.humankinetics.com/products/all-products/championship-tennis.) A player should enter information for his old regimen on the left side of the form and then revise a new and improved weekly plan on the right. The player should then apply the school methodology training described in the following section.

Table 13.1 Customized Weekly Planner

Date _____ May 7–13 _____

Essential components of world-class training	Old	New
Off-court gym (core and upper body)	0 hours	3 hours
Off-court cardio (speed and stamina)	0 hours	3 hours
Primary stroke production	6 hours	2 hours
Secondary stroke development	0 hours	2 hours
Pattern development	0 hours	2 hours
Complete practice matches	1 hour	2 hours
Video analysis	0 hours	1 hour
Hitting with friends	3 hours	0 hours
Ball machine	0 hours	0 hours
Serving basket	0 hours	1 hour
Clinics or academies	4 hours	0 hours
Total	14 hours	16 hours

SCHOOL METHODOLOGY TRAINING

When it comes to organizing long-term training, players should think of their tennis regimen as going back to school. School exists to educate and produce well-rounded individuals. Various subjects of study—math, English, science, and foreign language—are introduced and expanded on to broaden the student's knowledge and intellect.

Maximizing player potential at the quickest rate employs the same methodology. Begin by replacing the school disciplines with tennis components. These components include tennis-specific off-court training, primary and secondary stroke development and repetition, pattern development and repetition, the mental sides of strategy and tactical awareness, and the emotional control elements found in routines and rituals.

People generally enjoy doing what they are good at. Just as students favor certain subjects in school, tennis players on the practice court are often too content with continually grooving their primary strokes. This feels and looks good, so they stick to it. Coaches can unknowingly contribute to the problem by orchestrating the same handful of lesson plans on a weekly basis. This safe, nonthreatening environment is comfortable, reassuring, and even fun; but it seldom produces results.

Champions, however, are always eager to learn. They focus their practices on the development of the tools that they have yet to master. As mentioned previously, accelerating the learning curve requires that players leave the comfort zone and enter the learning zone.

PERIODIZATION TRAINING

Players need to balance their preparations for short-term goals—such as an upcoming tournament—with their long-term improvement schedule. Managing these training phases is called periodization. When preparing for an upcoming match, a player's plan for training to reach a peak level at the event should be customized to the player's current comfort and ability level. Trying to perform skills that have not yet been securely ingrained is a recipe for disaster. Following are examples of both poor and intelligent prematch preparations through periodization.

Poor prematch preparation:
- Changing fundamental grips or strokes, which leads to not having the old stroke any longer and not having the new stroke ready for match play.
- Cramming for the event by overloading the practice schedule, which leads to drained, low batteries on match day.
- Overdoing the off-court training, which leads to soreness, fatigue, and injuries come match day.
- Adding unfamiliar things to routines, which leads to physical and mental confusion.
- Playing only superior competition in practice matches, which leads to low self-esteem and zero confidence.
- Warming up past the point of diminishing returns, which leads to less confidence.

Intelligent prematch preparation:
- Including repetition of primary and secondary strokes, which grooves the timing and increases confidence.
- Including repetition of proactive patterns, which leads to fast cognitive processing speed and faith in the patterns.
- Performing light off-court training, which leads to strength and stamina.
- Presetting mental protocols, which leads to dependability in the problem-solving skills.
- Presetting emotional protocols, which leads to self-assurance and trust under stress.

Players who are unfamiliar with periodization often unknowingly sabotage their performance. They think they're preparing properly by practicing hard and challenging their game, but this actually hurts their chances of playing at their best.

ORGANIZING PRACTICE SETS

Being totally prepared for tournament play doesn't happen by accident; there's a science to it. To win an event, a player will usually have to defeat several types of opponents. These adversaries will apply a variety of playing styles along with their own unique strategies, tactics, ball speeds, and playing tempos. Therefore, players should schedule their practice matches in a way that best prepares them for these assorted players and situations. Before a big tournament, a player can try this formula: Schedule "up" matches approximately 50 percent of the time, and schedule "down" matches the other 50 percent of the time.

For "up" matches, the player should seek out higher-level players of different styles of play. Practicing against superior competition reaps these benefits:

1. Exposure to higher levels of focus and intensity
2. Experience facing players who move quicker and have faster decision-making abilities
3. Experience against superior strategists and tacticians
4. Exposure to faster ball speeds and incoming spins

Note that if a player happens to win a set under this scenario, she should fight the urge to celebrate or read too much into the victory. It's quite possible that the opponent is using the "down" practice set to work on weaknesses or a secondary game plan rather than trying to win.

Scheduling "down" matches and battling lower-level players of varying styles can have the following beneficial effects:

1. Repetition of secondary strokes under stress
2. Rehearsal of underdeveloped proactive patterns of play
3. Practice of B and C game plans in pressure situations
4. Experience in overcoming the inability to play at peak level and actually win two out of three sets for five days straight

If players occasionally lose a few sets to a lower-ranked player, they need to keep the bigger picture in mind. In these sets, the players are working on and improving secondary strokes and game plans that would normally be avoided under the strains of real competition; therefore, these losses are actually gains in the steps toward winning at higher levels. Losing a few practice battles is often necessary in order to win the real wars.

Players must avoid the age-old advice of only seeking superior opponents for practice matches. When a player only plays "up" and suffers loss after loss, this actually kills the player's competitive confidence. Being constantly stuck in reaction mode—always scrambling and feeling pushed around—is counterproductive and can lead to considerable frustration. By facing less skilled opponents, players have the opportunity to practice developing proactive patterns, which leads to growth as a competitor. Plus, it feels good to close out a set. Players must have the memory of winning. Confidence stems from succeeding, and winning breeds winning.

Another great way for players to begin scheduling practice sets is to choose opponents who play the most challenging style for them to compete against. (Refer back to the match cheat sheets in chapter 9 to review the patterns needed to beat the various styles of opponents.) For example, if a player struggles against a retriever, the player's first choice for practice matches should be a dogged retriever. If players have trouble finding a player who plays a certain style, they can ask a stronger player to assume the role. If that proves unsuccessful, paying top juniors a couple of bucks an hour to do their best retriever impression (or whatever style one struggles most against) is always a good option.

Coach's Corner

Justin is 16 years old. He's a sectionally ranked junior in Southern California. He loves the camaraderie of the academy environment, so he chooses to hit at a particular academy six hours a day, five days a week. Unfortunately for Justin and his parents, he loses in the first or second round tournament after tournament.

Justin's father, Steve, e-mails me every few weeks venting about his son's lack of results and current training regimen. "Justin has emotional issues closing out sets and matches," Steve states. "He always gets a lead each set only to let the opponent back in to steal the match at crunch time." I e-mail back my advice, which is to devise a new developmental plan that shifts the focus to Jason's weaknesses rather than let him simply rally back and forth for hours on end. Steve says, "Justin's on a scholarship saving me 15 percent! Also, his coach will get really mad if he finds out he's training somewhere else." So they ignore my advice of developing a new organizational training plan and simply return to the academy.

One of this book's recurring themes is that players must practice in the manner in which they are expected to perform. Justin can't close out sets, yet he keeps returning to his group classes and their daily routine of rallying back and forth. In this situation, Justin has no plan, no organizational blueprint to actually solve the issue that is holding him back. What's going to happen to Justin? Most likely, absolutely nothing. He'll simply run out of time, age out, and attend a mid-level college with no hope of receiving a tennis scholarship.

USING MATCH LOGS

Judging a match based solely on the outcome is a mistake. Although the score line usually reveals which player had the better day, it is not always indicative of performance. Match logs are essential to serious players who are interested in analyzing their games. Performing this 5- to 10-minute postmatch exercise helps document a player's accomplishments and pitfalls. This self-analysis is a constructive habit that can have significant positive effects on future performances.

Figures 13.3 and 13.4 are customizable match log forms (blank versions are available for download at www.humankinetics.com/products/all-products/championship-tennis). These forms enable players to complete a postmatch analysis by documenting their personal opinions regarding their competitive performance. Players can benefit greatly by sharing these conclusions with coaches, hitting partners, and parents—anyone who has knowledge of their games. Players should be on the lookout for "recurring nightmares": stumbling blocks that continually trip them up match after match, tournament after tournament. These hurdles come in numerous forms; some of the most common include inefficient prematch routines, lack of performance goals or plans, overabundance of unforced errors off a particular stroke, inability to close out leads, issues competing against retrievers, inability to handle gamesmanship, and roller-coaster (up-and-down) performances.

Figure 13.3   Beginner or Intermediate Tournament Match Log

Tournament: _The Houston Challenge Tennis Classic_

Date: _August 14-19_

Opponent: _Kelly Crawford_

Ranking: _None_

Set 1

Results: _6-3_

Improvement: _I need to serve to the backhand more and get more arch on deep balls._

Opponent's style: _She was a hard-hitting baseliner._

Set 2

Results: _4-6_

Improvement: _I need to hold serve more often and maintain consistency in my groundstrokes._

Opponent's style: _She started to simply retrieve and steady up her game._

Set 3

Results: _6-2_

Improvement: _I still served to her backhand, but I got more stingy and didn't self-destruct._

Opponent's style: _She continued to retrieve, but she got tired and sloppy._

Notes: _I have to work on a more reliable second serve and develop spin. My defensive backhands can use work, too. I hit too short._

From *The Tennis Parent's Bible* (www.thetennisparentsbible.com). © Frank Giampaolo.

Figure 13.4   Advanced Tournament Match Log

Event: _Orange Bowl_   Date: _December 4_

Opponent: _Marcio Granger (Netherlands)_   Ranking: _28 ITF_

Conditions: _Warm, wet clay_   Match time: _11:00 a.m._

Prematch Preparation

Grade your degree of accomplishment for each of the following details of prematch preparation. For instance, assessments could be "didn't bother," "gave little effort," or "gave 100% effort."

30-minute warm-up _100% effort_

Proper nutrition and hydration _Little effort (I get too nervous to eat before a match.)_

Stretching _Little effort_

20-minute visualization _Didn't bother_

Equipment preparation _100% effort_

Scouting (live or Internet) _Didn't bother_

Short run before check-in _Didn't bother_

Prematch Performance Goals

1. Get 65 percent of first serves in.

2. Keep deep balls deep and remain steady.

3. Attack balls inside my short-ball range with my offensive forehand kill.

Match Results

Score _2-6, 6-7_

Parent and Coach Assistance

Did they video the match for video analysis? _Yes_

Did they chart the match? _Yes (on their phone app)_

Which type of chart was used? _Unforced errors to winners_

Did they reduce stress or add stress to the day? _Added stress_

(continued)

Figure 13.4 *(continued)*

Postmatch Analysis

Personally grade your level of satisfaction with your performance in the following 20 areas (1 = lowest, 10 = highest):

6 Attitude

7 Effort or fight

4 Calmness

9 Stroke mechanics

6 Shot selection

7 Focus control

0 Reading notes (when losing)

7 Use of patterns

7 Properly applying offensive, neutral, and defensive play

4 Limiting unforced errors

4 Spotting mega points

6 Attaining performance goals

6 Enjoying the battle

7 Spotting tendencies (own and the opponent's)

8 Self-charting

9 Between-point rituals

5 Mistake management

3 Anger management

5 Focusing on the here and now

6 Relaxing under stress

Dissect the opponent (list the opponent's strengths, weaknesses, and tendencies):

Strokes *Consistency was his strength, and his transition game was his weakness. His hitting tendency was to only hit the appropriate shot that the moment demanded.*

Patterns *Kicked serves to my backhand, arched deep to get short balls, and then crushed them.*

Style of play *Counterpuncher*

Movement and fitness *Excellent*

Emotions *Excellent*

USING DAILY SUCCESS JOURNALS

Daily success journals are used by world-class leaders in every walk of life. Not to be confused with a personal diary, these journals are an integral part of any developmental plan. Contributing nightly to a success journal takes roughly five minutes, but it plays a critical part in turning a player's negative self-talk into positive, reinforcing statements. When documenting the day's accomplishments, the player should end each entry with an optimistic, inspiring note. Like match logs, listing these encouraging events will have an accumulative effect and help improve future performances.

Whether a player's day has consisted of a simple practice or an important match, the player should use the success journal to describe her accomplishments on the court. Figure 13.5 provides an example of a nationally ranked junior's daily success journal. (A blank version of this form is available for download at www.humankinetics.com/products/all-products/championship-tennis.)

Figure 13.5 Daily Success Journal

Day: _Saturday_   Date: _August 25_

List your successes for the day. Include the reason for completing each entry, along with information on further progress you'd like to make or the next action you'd like to take.

1. I got my rackets restrung; the strings on two were broken.

2. I worked on my kick second serve alone for 1.5 hours; I need a more reliable second serve under stress. I should do it again twice next week.

3. I went to the gym and did 1 hour of medicine ball training and took a yoga class to improve my core strength and core balance.

4. I did a 3-hour training session, focusing on my swinging volleys and my proactive patterns versus pushers. I need to play practice sets versus pushers twice before next week's tournament.

5. I went for a 2-mile run, varying my speeds. I need to improve my aerobic capacity. I will run again Saturday night after tennis.

DEVELOPING A QUARTERLY SYSTEM

Trying to plan for the entire year can be tricky. Certain unexpected events—such as an injury, a coaching change, a new tournament that the player now qualifies for, or job or family commitments—may occur that cause a player to reevaluate priorities or change goals. Breaking up the year into quarterly blocks is a more realistic strategic plan. A quarterly organizational plan provides structure, comfort, and confidence. A player's quarterly plan should be formally committed to paper but should remain flexible. Each player's customized plan should include the following:

- Short-term objectives and their attainable due dates (e.g., the development of a competent slice backhand by February 15 or qualifying and entering the sectional championship by February 18)
- Long-term objectives (e.g., reaching a certain ranking in the section, attaining a full tennis scholarship for college, or winning a team championship) and their attainable due dates, as well as the progress needed to attain those goals
- A training schedule (see the weekly planner earlier in this chapter) with each division and any subdivisions organized in detail
- A tentative tournament list or team tennis schedule of matches
- Rest and relaxation periods built into the schedule
- The player's entourage and each member's job description
- School or work schedule and family obligations
- Quarterly expenses (see figures 13.6 and 13.7)

Figure 13.6 Sample Quarterly Expense Report of a Top 20 Nationally Ranked Junior in the United States

Transportation: $720

Meals on the road: $1,200

Tennis academies: $1,440

Off-court training: $1,200

Tennis lessons: $2,400

Strings and grips: $600

Clothes (three outfits, one pair of tennis shoes): $350

Tournament registration: $450

Two nights in a hotel: $300

Total: $34,640 annually, $8,660 quarterly, $95 per day

Figure 13.7 Sample Quarterly Expense Report
of a Local Recreational Player in the United States

Transportation: $100

Meals on the road or at the club: $200

Tennis clinics (group): $80

Gym membership or off-court training: $150

Off-court trainer: $150

Tennis lessons: $240

Strings and grips: $75

Clothes (one outfit and one pair of tennis shoes): $220

Tournament registration: $100

One night in a hotel: $150

Total: $5,860 annually, $1,465 quarterly, $16 per day

As the old saying goes, failing to plan is planning to fail. Can a player without a plan enjoy his time on the tennis court and even show marginal improvement? Sure. However, this book's goal is to accelerate the learning curve at the quickest possible rate, and a player interested in significantly developing his game has to have a preset blueprint for success. A player must have the foresight to set up reachable goals and effectively break up the calendar in order to attain them. The player must also have the dedication to stick to the organizational plan in order to achieve the desired results. Being conscientious enough to organize a detailed developmental plan isn't for every player—it's only for the ones seeking to accelerate their level in the shortest amount of time.

chapter 14

Match Preparation

There is often a very thin line between competitive success and failure. A poor start, an initial lack of focus, or a bout of wavering confidence can cause a seemingly winnable match to quickly slip away. The will to properly prepare for competition usually makes the difference. For players to achieve consistently positive match results, their preparation must include ritualistic, inflexible routines. A player who is ready for battle creates an impenetrable wall that keeps all the human elements of fear away. Remember, for a tennis player, *FEAR* stands for "false expectations appearing real." Players who disregard prematch rituals often unknowingly start a downward spiral that inevitably results in a loss. Their lack of self-discipline leads to self-doubt, a condition that fuels nervousness and then causes a lack of confidence and low self-esteem. These negative forces have a way of fostering a lack of self-control on match day. Although not preparing properly for competition may provide short-term fun, it comes with long-term consequences.

Getting geared up for a match involves a type of self-hypnosis. Players use a series of internal processes to spur a metamorphosis—to put on their game faces. The physical, mental, and emotional components are all ready for competition. Confidence is high, and all energy is devoted to the task at hand. This chapter contains information to help players of all levels find this state of readiness that enables them to transform from a normal person into a tennis warrior.

PREPARATION CHECKLIST

Readiness breeds confidence. When players know that they are fully prepared for an upcoming event, their belief in their chances of winning skyrockets. Nothing has been left to chance—equipment is ready, game plans have been rehearsed, prematch routines have been followed—and all their focus can go to the task at hand.

Equipment Preparation

A serious competitor's tennis bag should consist of two or three rackets (freshly strung and regripped if the player is starting a tournament); extra sets of string and grips; a first aid kit composed of Band-Aids, athletic tape, elastic bandage, aspirin, and plastic bags for ice; extra shoelaces, socks, and shirts; a towel; water, sports drinks, fruit, and energy bars/gels or nuts to be used as a bridge between meals; match notes and cheat sheets; match logs for post-performance analysis; and, if in a tournament, past opponent notes (to possibly assist with matches in future rounds).

Opponent Profiling

Observing an upcoming opponent can provide a player with a valuable strategic advantage. Areas to scout include the opponent's primary style of play; preferred serve and return patterns (especially on mega points); dominant short-ball option; stroke strengths and weaknesses (advanced players should consider strike zones); movement, agility, and stamina; and frustration tolerance, focus, and emotional stability. Opponent profiling should continue from the prematch phase, all the way through the actual match, and into the postmatch.

Nutrition and Hydration

Proper eating and hydration are an essential component for optimum performance. Although a sound diet is a critical everyday endeavor for the high-performance athlete, match-day nutrition is especially important.

Hydration begins the day before the match, especially if a player will be performing in excessive heat. The player should hydrate before bed the night before the match, after rising on match day, and before the match. This will help ensure adequate hydration.

Meal planning is dependent on match time. If a player has an early-morning match, she should begin the day with a light breakfast of lean protein or a good fat, along with complex carbohydrate. If the match is later in the day, the player should avoid eating a heavy meal within one hour of the scheduled start. It's best to plan the meal for two to three hours before match time.

The goal is to provide carbohydrate for quick energy and a small portion of lean protein and good fat to maintain level blood sugars. Foods high in simple sugars—sodas, packaged fruit, and cereals—lead to a spike in blood sugars, followed by a crash. Eating a high-fat or high-protein meal can delay digestion, making a player feel sluggish, which may impede performance. That's why a good source of clean carbohydrate is the most essential match-day fuel. Carbohydrate is the most efficient source of energy and the best fuel for the brain. Recommended carbohydrate foods include whole grains, oatmeal, low-sugar cereals, rice, pasta, fruits, and vegetables.

Experiment with carbohydrate loading the night before a match, which may help the body store glucose for quick energy during play. Bananas, sports drinks, and glucose supplements are excellent snacks for a player to consume during the match to maintain energy. And a postmatch meal of lean protein and carbohydrate is essential for proper muscle repair and recovery.

Improper nutrition and hydration can lead to the following:

- Lethargic play and decreased strength and reaction time
- Low physical, mental, and emotional endurance
- Impaired concentration, court awareness, and problem-solving skills
- Emotional breakdowns

- Delayed muscle repair and recovery
- Serious risk of dehydration and possible heatstroke (with as little as 1 to 2 percent dehydration)

Match-Day Stretching

For all-around better performance as well as a decrease in potential injury, players should incorporate a three-part stretching routine. Part 1 is an active warm-up to elevate core body temperature. A light jog with slow windmill arm rotations, jogging in place, or light jump roping will work wonders to loosen up the body. Part 2 is a progression into a series of dynamic stretches: tennis-specific movements that incorporate fluid mobility. Suggestions include shoulder circles, trunk rotations, and squats and lunges for the lower body. Part 3 is postmatch static stretching during the cool-down phase. While the body is at rest, the player elongates muscles and holds the position for 30 seconds to 2 minutes. This allows the muscles to be stretched farther in order to increase range of motion. For the upper body, the player should stretch the shoulders, chest, and triceps. For the lower body, the player should stretch the glutes, hamstrings, quads, and hips.

Prematch Warm-Up Rituals

Sam Sumyk, coach of Victoria Azarenka, says, "Vika's prematch routine consistently includes a 45-minute stretching ritual followed by a 45-minute hitting routine." While the pros have more of an opportunity to indulge their prematch routines, players who routinely warm up both their primary and secondary strokes have a major advantage in tightly contested matches. Grooving forehands and backhands before a match is important, but a first-set tiebreak can often come down to a player executing a winning swing volley or topspin lob. Confidently performing such shots at crunch time without hesitation stems from properly warming them up before the match. Players who neglect their secondary strokes have a very different mind-set when faced with the same exact situation. Instead of instinctively moving forward to hit the swing volley, they hesitate and are caught thinking, *I don't remember the last time I hit one of these.*

Prematch Visualization and Imagery

What we think about often dictates what we create. This is commonly referred to as the universal law of attraction. Players need to build up their "wall of defenses" in preparation for the continuous onslaught of challenges that competitive tennis delivers. Responding correctly to those challenges does not happen automatically; it's a learned behavior that results from constant, positive imagery and visualization training. Consistent, daily repetition is required in order to make a change in a player's mental image. Automatic pattern play grows the same way that muscles do, building with repetition and withering with inactivity.

For prematch visualization, a player should put aside 20 minutes before the match to mentally rehearse the performance goals for the upcoming competition. The player starts this self-hypnosis by seeking out a quiet area away from other competitors and distractions. With closed eyes, the player takes several deep, relaxing breaths. He then creates a vivid mental image of numerous tasks being performed successfully. This enhances the player's mental awareness and builds his confidence. The player should mentally rerun the "movie" several times to reinforce the thoughts. This visual experience actually trains a player to perform the skills imagined. Prematch visualization topics are unlimited, but some favorites include the following:

- Perfectly executed primary and secondary strokes
- Groups of perfectly executed proactive patterns
- The three pillars of between-point rituals
- Successful patterns of play against the four main styles of opponents
- Preset protocols for common emotional issues

Performing nightly visualization also maximizes efficiency come match day. As a player goes to sleep, the conscious, analytical, judgmental side of the brain shuts down while the creative, dream-state side of the brain awakens. This near subconscious state is when the positive images are deeply ingrained.

Visualization works best when players are very peaceful, such as when they are falling asleep, waking up, or simply relaxing in their rooms. Positive visualization produces an optimistic outlook that can change negative attitudes, boost moods, and decrease toxic levels of competitive stress.

Short, Calming Prematch Run

As match time draws near, players often experience a wave of apprehension and nervousness. This fear triggers an overflow of adrenaline; it's time for fight or flight. When players feel this sensation, they can burn off their performance anxiety by going for a short run. Players should do this the night before the match, in the morning before they hit a ball in warm-up, and again just before the match begins. If a player is not the overly nervous type, she may only need to take a short run before the match.

The prematch run or runs should be customized based on the player's fitness level and emotional stability, as well as the amount of time available. Raising the body's core temperature warms up the muscle groups and relaxes the tension as it burns off the excess adrenaline, calming the mind and helping the player begin the match in a peak-performance state.

THE COMPETITIVE EVENT OR TOURNAMENT PATHWAY

All this preparation won't mean anything if there are no tournaments or events to get ready for. Seeking out competitions that suit a player's skills and objectives is an important element for planning a schedule. In the early stages of a player's tennis career, the competitive events are most often loosely structured and extremely social. In these fun, friendly community events, eligibility, registration, scoring systems, and rules may vary. These nonsanctioned events are run through park and recreational departments, organizations, and clubs. Players competing at this novice level have the opportunity to gain hands-on experience with the rules of the game, basic strategies and tactics, the scoring system, and the code of ethics associated with good sportsmanship. In this early stage of competition, adult and junior tennis events can share social formats. They include local leagues, ladders, round-robins, club exchanges, flex leagues, tennis on campus, tournament play, and weekend match-ups.

For those adults and juniors seeking elevated competition, the U.S. Tennis Association, or USTA, offers singles and doubles players a chance to chase rankings points virtually every weekend. Players compete in age- and ability-appropriate events, ranging from local events to sectional tournaments to national-level competitions. The USTA's NTRP (National Tennis Rating Program) system is designed to ensure that athletes compete with players of their own level. Established in 1979, this system rates players on a scale of 1.0 (absolute beginner) through 7.0 (touring professional); see table 14.1 for the various NTRP levels and their descriptions. Specialized divisions are even available for wheelchair participants. For the truly ambitious who want another shot at the dream, the USTA conducts a national playoff that gives players an opportunity to earn a coveted spot in the U.S. Open.

Table 14.1   USTA NTRP System

Rating	Description
1.0	Player is just starting to play tennis.
1.5	Player has limited experience and is still working primarily on getting the ball into play.
2.0	Player needs on-court experience. Player has obvious stroke weaknesses but is familiar with basic positions for singles and doubles play.
2.5	Player is learning to judge where the ball is going although court coverage is weak. Player can sustain a short rally of slow pace with other players of the same ability.
3.0	Player is fairly consistent when hitting medium-paced shots but is not comfortable with all strokes and lacks execution when trying for directional control, depth, or power. Most common doubles formation is one up and one back.
3.5	Player has achieved stroke dependability with directional control on moderate shots but still lacks depth and variety. Player is starting to exhibit more aggressive net play, has improved court coverage, and is developing teamwork in doubles.
4.0	Player has dependable strokes, including directional control and depth on both forehand and backhand sides on moderate shots, plus the ability to use lobs, overheads, approach shots, and volleys with some success. Player occasionally forces errors when serving, and teamwork in doubles is evident. Rallies may be lost because of impatience.
4.5	Player is starting to master the use of power and spins and is beginning to handle pace; player has sound footwork, can control depth of shots, and is beginning to vary game plans according to opponents. Player can hit first serves with power and accuracy and can place the second serve. Player tends to overhit on difficult shots. Aggressive net play is common in doubles.
5.0	Player has good shot anticipation and frequently has an outstanding shot or exceptional consistency around which a game may be structured. Player can regularly hit winners or force errors off short balls and can put away volleys. Player can successfully execute lobs, drop shots, half volleys, and overhead smashes and has good depth and spin on most second serves.
5.5	Player has developed power or consistency as a major weapon. Player can vary strategies and styles of play in a competitive situation and can hit dependable shots in a stressful situation.
6.0	Player generally does not need NTRP rating. Rankings or past rankings will speak for themselves. Player has obtained a sectional or national ranking.
6.5	Player has extensive satellite tournament experience.
7.0	Player makes living from tournament prize money.

ENTOURAGE SUPPORT

I spend much of my professional life working with national and international juniors. It is fun, fulfilling, and a constant challenge. This section of the book is dedicated to those players and their parents and coaches (for further information on the subject, refer to my book *The Tennis Parent's Bible*). For a junior to have fun and thrive in tournaments, this threesome must function as a cohesive team. A coach must realize that educating doesn't stop with the player. The coach needs to be the catalyst for developing unity within the player's entire entourage. This holds true all the way through a player's junior tennis journey and well into the high school, college, or even professional career.

Coach's Corner

Mark and Martha have a talented 15-year-old daughter named Kelly. Mark wants mental and emotional training for Kelly. He claims that she is the most gifted player in her division but can't seem to win a real match. As part of the mental and emotional training, the family videotapes one tournament weekend from prematch preparation to postmatch analysis. Interestingly, here's what they see:

DAY 1

Kelly's mom, Martha, is scheduled to take Kelly to the tournament site. Here's some of the things included in Martha's prematch routine:

- Martha wakes up tightly wound.
- She shakes her head in disgust at Kelly's choice of outfit.
- She becomes upset about Kelly's chewing at breakfast.
- Once in the car, Martha screams at the traffic.
- She is peeved about the poor directions.
- She is annoyed about catching every red light.
- She yells at a guy trying to get into his lane.

Martha is at the end of her rope, and Kelly's match is still three hours away. After Kelly's first-round main-draw loss, guess who gets all the blame. Yup, Kelly!

DAY 2

This time, Kelly's dad, Mark, is scheduled to take Kelly to the event. Here are snippets of his prematch pep talk:

- "OK, Kelly, she's ranked 98 spots ahead of us."
- "She's top 3 in the nation and just won the Florida Nationals. This will be a huge win for us."
- "If you win. your ranking will skyrocket into the top 20 . . . if you don't blow it."
- "Remember, she cheats and is going to push. So focus."
- "This is by far the most important match of the year for us—by far. You have to win."
- "Remember, I spent $2,000 on lessons, so don't expect me to keep on forking over my hard-earned money if you lose."

After Kelly's back-draw loss, guess who once again gets all the blame. Poor Kelly.

Seasoned coaches know that an uneducated tennis parent can easily derail the countless hours spent preparing a student to reach peak performance on match day. Ill-chosen words from a parent can hinder a player's self-esteem while increasing her nervousness and self-doubt. And poor communication occurs not just through words, but actions as well. A child can detect a stressed-out parent, which compounds the tension of an already anxious situation. An unrealistic, unhealthy parental philosophy often pulls the athlete into an outcome-oriented frame of mind rather than the desired mind-set of being focused on performance goals. This negative performance philosophy holds true for adult recreational players as well, whether caused by a teammate, captain, or significant other. Consequently, great coaching knowledge is of little value if a parent or team members are not on the same page.

Prematch Entourage Communication

Successful coaches and perceptive parents know that nonverbal communication is the single most powerful form of communication. People don't need to say anything for their stress, nervousness, and anxiety to be felt and adopted by others.

Before matches, players are trying to enter into their competitive state of mind. In this situation, I've found that players receive 20 percent of communication from the words of the coach or parent, 30 percent of communication from the actual volume and tone of the coach's or parent's voice, 25 percent of communication from the coach's or parent's facial expressions and gestures, and 25 percent of communication from the coach's or parent's body language and use of space.

Following are some appropriate match-day topics for both coaches and parents:

- Preparing equipment and adhering to nutrition and hydration requirements
- Using warm-up routines (both primary and secondary strokes)
- Practicing visualization and imagery routines
- Discussing both the player's and opponent's A, B, and C game plans, favorite go-to patterns, stroke strengths and weaknesses, movement issues, and emotional or focus issues
- Listing the top three performance goals to accomplish
- Focusing on the process of endurance and competitive fight
- Referring to match "cheat sheets" when losing
- Suggesting a short run before going onto the court
- Providing positive memories
- Reminding players to simply try their best to execute the correct shot (the shot that the moment demands) rather than worry about the outcome
- Reminding players to smile and laugh and enjoy the day

Here are some inappropriate match-day topics that coaches and parents must avoid:

- Discussing the need for a perfect performance
- Explaining why today's match is the most important of the player's career
- Describing the consequences of the outcome, such as the player's spot in the team's lineup, the team's position in the overall league rankings, or the individual's position in the overall rankings
- Detailing how much time or money has been spent on the player's career
- Listing the successes of opponents, including all the players they have beaten, their past high rankings, their current seeding, or the events they have won
- Giving last-minute technical advice such as revealing a flaw and giving tips for improvement (moments before a match is not the time nor platform for this type of guidance)

In addition, coaches and parents should not allow the player to socialize with other tournament players or parents before a match. Keep in mind that competitive tennis at the higher levels is a brutal, individual sport. Unfortunately, other so-called friends or tennis parents may sabotage the player with the exact discussions that a coach is desperately trying to avoid. Also, socializing pulls competitors away from their routines and rituals. As stated earlier in this chapter, a transformation should take place before each match. Players cannot transform from a normal person into a warrior if they are hanging out with peers.

Postmatch Entourage Communication

After a match finishes, coaches and parents should always consider the player's frustration tolerance and maturity level and should wait an appropriate amount of time before discussing the match. A few minutes after a player suffers a heartbreaking loss is no time for performance analysis. That wound is too fresh and needs time to heal. Once a player is ready for constructive conversation—regardless of the score line—the coach should consistently replace "Did you win?" with "Did you hit your performance goals?" or "Did you execute the correct shots at the right times?"

If coaches or parents are solely fixated on the outcome, they will not be able to convince a player to be performance oriented. Remember, kids pick up every negative word, condescending tone of voice, upset facial expression, and defensive body posture. Therefore, a coach or parent should make a special effort to offer five positive critiques for every one negative criticism.

After each match, the coach or parent should also remind the player to complete a match log and an entry in the daily focus journal.

PATHWAYS TO SUCCESS

A player's career in the open level of competition begins with sectional junior events. Different USTA sections have different naming systems and levels for these events, but all are designed to advance athletes through their own local ranking systems and to prepare the athletes for national competition.

National junior tournaments offer six levels of competition ranging from a super national event (L1) down to the entry-level national event (1 to 5). To assist players in the transition into a higher level of play, several sectional events offer national points. Also, several national events offer ITF (International Tennis Federation) ranking points.

Eligibility requirements, rules, types of draws, and ranking points within a division vary, so the USTA suggests that tennis parents educate themselves on the unique specifications in their area. For example, there are 17 different USTA sections in the United States, and each applies its own set of rules and guidelines. For more detailed information on preparing a junior player's competitive schedule, visit www.usta.com. For those players and tennis parents interested in the national levels of competition, useful information can be found at www.playerdevelopment.usta.com.

ITF tournaments also have their own unique levels and sublevels of competitive tennis. Once again, preparing a tournament traveling schedule requires an understanding of the ITF's grades—A, B, and C (Junior Davis and Federation Cup team play)—and their sublevels, 1 to 5.

International athletes use these tournaments as a stepping stone that enables them to gain exposure (which could earn them a college tennis scholarship) or gain the experience to compete on the professional levels. For more information regarding the ITF junior circuit, visit www.itftennis.com/juniors.

College tennis is another rung on the ladder of competitive tennis and is governed by the ITA (Intercollegiate Tennis Association). College tennis includes various divisions, including three NCAA divisions (I, II, and III), an NAIA (National Association of Intercollegiate Athletics) division, as well as junior college divisions. Each division has its unique subdivisions, known as conferences. The college tennis route is an intelligent choice for players seeking to continue their tennis career while earning a college degree. The goal of many national and ITF juniors is to be offered a college tennis scholarship. For more information regarding college tennis and the ITA, visit www.itatennis.com.

Men's futures level, challengers level, and the ITF women's circuit serve as the gateway into professional tennis. Junior players often have aspirations of competing on the ATP (Association of Tennis Professionals) or WTA (Women's Tennis Association) professional tours. These high-performance athletes try their hand on these minor-league circuits as amateurs before settling into a college tennis career. Athletes occasionally rejoin these circuits after they've earned their college degree.

The men's futures events are governed by the ITF and offer $10,000 to $15,000 in prize money; the challenger circuit is governed by the ATP and offers $37,500 to $150,000 in prize money. The ITF women's circuit is governed by the ITF and offers $10,000 to $100,000 in prize money. For more information regarding the ITF futures pro circuit, visit www.itftennis.com/procircuit. For more information regarding the ATP's challenger circuit, visit www.atpworldtour.com/tournaments/challenger-tour.

ATP and WTA world tours are operated by their own governing body. The ATP tour consists of the international series, the Gold international series, the ATP masters series, and the Grand Slams. The WTA hosts tier 1 through 4 events (1 being the highest level) outside of the Grand Slams. In these events, elite athletes perform at the highest level and compete for millions of dollars, international sponsorship deals, and appearance fees. For more information regarding the ATP professional tour, visit www.atpworldtour.com. For more information regarding the WTA tour, visit www.wtatennis.com.

Table 14.2 lists the paths that a player can take on her road to tennis success, including a short description of each of the levels. All juniors should familiarize themselves

Table 14.2 Pathways to Success

Level	Description
QuickStart	This program aids in the development of motor skills and fundamental stroke production.
Nonsanctioned events	These events act as an introduction to team tennis and basic match play scenarios.
Novice	These events introduce juniors to semiformal tournament experiences.
Satellite	This is where the point-based rankings begin for age-appropriate tournament competition.
Sectional	These events offer both sectional and national ranking points and mark the beginning of a junior's serious competitive years.
Nationals	These events showcase the dominant competitors in each age division.
ITF	These events display the best junior tennis players from across the globe. The ITF junior circuit governs the junior Grand Slams.
College	At this level, players transition their career from the junior level into adult competition. College tennis runs the gamut from the NTRP lower levels all the way up to the elite athletes who are possibly headed into the professional tours.
Futures, challengers, and ITF women's professional tours	These levels are essentially the minor leagues of professional tennis. Amateurs and professionals holding a ranking of 250 or higher compete at the futures level. Athletes ranked 250 or below generally qualify for the challenger circuits. The ladies' minor-league tour is currently known as the ITF tour.
ATP and WTA professional tours	These tours are the platform for full-time touring professionals. The elite players who compete at this level earn their livelihood from prize money as well as sponsorship endorsements.

with each category and should set their goals. Any good road map has a starting point and a destination.

Tournament preparation is a key component for the success of any competitive warrior. Week in and week out, many physically talented players fall short because they aren't able to execute under pressure. Proper tournament preparation brings to light the hidden ingredients that are essential for resiliency under stress. Poise under pressure stems from a player's customized routines and rituals. To the untrained eye, poise and resiliency may look like inherited or natural gifts, but they are actually learned behaviors.

chapter 15

Video Analysis and Match Charting

Seeing is believing. Whether through pictures or data collection, having actual evidence to illustrate a teaching point is invaluable. That's what makes video analysis and match charting such powerful tools for discovering and improving a player's game.

Developing as a tennis player requires growth. From this growth will come success. And one of the best ways for players to achieve growth is to have an invested spectator chart or record some of their matches. Players can fool themselves into believing they play a certain way, but neither the camera nor the numbers ever lie.

VIDEO ANALYSIS

Visual learning is the most common educational style, so it's not surprising that using video analysis—allowing players to see themselves in action—is truly one of the most effective teaching devices. With today's technological advances, producing slow-motion video is as easy as downloading a cell phone app, pointing the phone, and hitting record.

Static Stroke Analysis

Beginners just starting out or seasoned players looking to retool a faulty shot can benefit greatly from static stroke analysis. This elementary version of video analysis requires the camera to be directly behind the player during play, rather than head-on. This positioning is extremely important because it eliminates visual reversal—when players have to reverse their image during playback in order to picture themselves hitting the desired stroke.

Although static stroke analysis is a helpful aid for novices, as players advance they will benefit much more from analyzing video taken of real match conditions.

Flexible Skills Analysis

Videotaping matches can be an eye-opening experience for players. Reviewing the details, preferably with the help of a knowledgeable coach, often dispels the confusion over what players believe they are doing and the reality of their flaws. It illuminates strengths to build on while exposing weaknesses to renovate. Keep in mind that an old motor program (or habit), no matter how imperfect, will feel comfortable to the player. A new swing can feel strange and awkward. But by seeing the difference on video, a player understands that uncomfortable can be right and comfortable is actually wrong.

Watching match play via video uncovers hidden qualities that often go undetected by players. These discoveries separate successful players who continue their progress from their counterparts who become stagnant in their development.

A highly recommended practice is to videotape at least one match per tournament and review the footage after the event. Here are just a few of the things that will be revealed:

- Strengths and weaknesses in stroke production
- Implementation of strategies and tactics
- Proper use of offensive, neutral, and defensive shot selections
- The actual causes of errors
- Dissection of the opponent's game
- Movement, spacing, and fitness
- Emotional control
- Focus control, such as lapses in concentration
- The ability to rise to the occasion at crunch time
- The resilience to endure hardship and have the will to win
- Self-control and self-discipline
- Between-point and changeover rituals
- Good sportsmanship

Flexible skills analysis is also a valuable tool for finding out tendencies of future opponents. Advanced scouting assists greatly in formulating a game plan and offers prematch advantages in the form of mental preparation.

MATCH CHARTING

If videotaping is the visual testimony of performance, charting provides numerical proof. Charting a match provides statistics that can be used to assess performance. Yes, winning is the objective, but the match should also be considered an information-gathering opportunity. Charting quantifies how a player performs under stress in real match conditions.

Self-Charting

The first option in charting matches is self-charting. The ability to do this while playing the actual match is a learned behavior. It may seem overwhelming to tally stats along with all the various mental aspects that go into a match, but dismantling an opponent with similar abilities requires it. A player heading into a first-set tiebreaker who knows the stats for the match—for example, knows that the opponent has committed around 13 unforced errors on the forehand and only 3 on the backhand, and that the opponent has hit every second serve in the ad side to the backhand—has an enormous advantage in the breaker. The well-schooled player can now prepare a winning game plan. The player who says, "I can't think like that and play," is about to bow out and catch an early lunch.

Spectator Charting

An alternative to charting solo is enlisting the help of a savvy spectator—somebody who knows the game. This could be a parent, coach, spouse, friend, playing partner, or even someone willing to do it for a small fee. Before the match begins, the player should decide which of the 10 charts (provided later in this section) are appropriate for the day's information-gathering mission. The observer should review each chart's directions beforehand to prepare for the session. Players often play the same opponents over and over again; in this case, charting both players is recommended. This will provide a strategic base for future clashes. Forward-thinking players may also want to consider charting potential future opponents for later review.

Charting a match begins with identifying certain details. These details are listed in figure 15.1 (a blank version is available for download at www.humankinetics.com/products/all-products/championship-tennis).

Figure 15.1   Match Statistics

Date: _October 15_

Time of day: _8:00 p.m._

Event: _Westchester Open_

Court surface: _Hard_

Opponent: _Tim Holloway_

Ranking: _21_

Style of opponent: _Aggressive baseliner_

Elements and conditions: _Indoors with chilly air temperature and dim lighting._

Additional match notes: _It's Tim once again. I can't get sucked into a slugfest with him, or else it will be a quick evening. This is a good chance to measure my ability to manage my errors while producing them in my opponent._

Over time, charting matches is also an effective way to track overall progress. As a series of common charts are analyzed and compared, quantifiable information is available for judging development. Comparison of match charts will expose reoccurring nightmares—blunders that appear match after match, month after month. This helps keep the focus on the performances rather than on the outcomes of matches. Regardless of wins and losses, elevating first-serve percentage or reducing the average number of unforced errors per set is progress in the player's performance. If a player makes enough improvement in various categories, winning will take care of itself.

Following are 10 statistics that are helpful to track during match play. Blank versions of the accompanying forms are available for download at www.humankinetics.com/products/all-products/championship-tennis.

Between-Point Ritual

Critical mental and emotional solutions are found in between points. The three common phases of between-point rituals are getting over the previous point (commonly done while walking toward the back of the court), planning the patterns for the next point (commonly done while standing approximately 10 feet behind the baseline, quiet and motionless), and revisiting relaxation rituals (for example, taking the same number of bounces before a serve or applying the same footwork before a return). Being proactive instead of reactive is often the difference between winning and losing. In the chart, tally each time the player uses a between-point ritual and each time a ritual is skipped (see table 15.1 for a completed example). A key to spotting between-point rituals is learning to recognize systematic patterns within a consistent length of time.

Table 15.1 Between-Point Ritual

Applying between-point rituals	Skipping rituals
~~HHT~~ ~~HHT~~ ~~HHT~~ ~~HHT~~ ~~HHT~~ ~~HHT~~ ~~HHT~~ ~~HHT~~ ~~HHT~~ ~~HHT~~ ~~HHT~~ ~~HHT~~ ~~HHT~~	~~HHT~~ ~~HHT~~ ~~HHT~~ ~~HHT~~ ~~HHT~~ ~~HHT~~ ~~HHT~~ ~~HHT~~ |||

From *The Tennis Parent's Bible* (www.thetennisparentsbible.com). © Frank Giampaolo.

Court Positioning

Playing inside the baseline is imperative in hitting more offensive shots while giving the opponent less time to recover. In the chart, simply check whether each point is won or lost when the player is playing from behind or inside the baseline (see table 15.2 for a completed example). Often, players feel more comfortable and believe that they are better from behind the baseline. Sometimes, nerves get the best of players, and they unknowingly retreat. However, the sample court-positioning chart exposes that the player consistently wins 39 percent of the total points played from behind the court and 80 percent of the total points played inside the baseline. For this player, making a concerted effort to move forward inside the baseline will clearly assist in winning more matches.

Table 15.2 Court Positioning

POINTS PLAYED BEHIND BASELINE		POINTS PLAYED INSIDE BASELINE	
Won	**Loss**	**Won**	**Loss**
~~HHT~~ ~~HHT~~ ~~HHT~~ ~~HHT~~ ||	~~HHT~~ ~~HHT~~ ~~HHT~~ ~~HHT~~	~~HHT~~ ~~HHT~~ ~~HHT~~ ~~HHT~~ ~~HHT~~ ~~HHT~~ ~~HHT~~	~~HHT~~ ~~HHT~~ ||
	~~HHT~~ ~~HHT~~ ~~HHT~~	~~HHT~~ ~~HHT~~ ~~HHT~~ ~~HHT~~ ~~HHT~~ |||	

From *The Tennis Parent's Bible* (www.thetennisparentsbible.com). © Frank Giampaolo.

Coach's Corner

While I was attending an early-round match of Serena Williams at the Australian Open, Serena's mother, Oracene Price, was constantly screaming to Serena, "GET OUT OF MELBOURNE! GET OUT OF MELBOURNE!" My wife, seated next to me, leaned over and asked, "What is she talking about? Leave the city now?" I responded, "No, it's Oracene's way of telling Serena that she's playing too defensively." Serena was actually playing 10 to 15 feet behind the baseline, on top of the MELBOURNE on-court logo. This is a fine example of court-positioning awareness at the top level of the game.

Shot Selection

Check the appropriate column to identify the shot selection for each stroke that the player hits in each rally (see table 15.3 for a completed example). Total each column and calculate the percentage. (Professionals usually hit 20 percent offense, 60 percent neutral, and 20 percent defense.)

Table 15.3   Shot Selection

Offense	Neutral	Defense
ＨＨ ＨＨ ＨＨ ＨＨ ＨＨ ＨＨ I	ＨＨ ＨＨ ＨＨ ＨＨ ＨＨ ＨＨ ＨＨ ＨＨ IIII	ＨＨ ＨＨ ＨＨ ＨＨ ＨＨ IIII

From *The Tennis Parent's Bible* (www.thetennisparentsbible.com). © Frank Giampaolo.

Depth of Groundstroke

The depth of a shot is a critical factor in competitive tennis. Short balls give opponents more angles to run a player and take away recovery time. Players who consistently hit short don't win many high-level matches. In the chart, tally each time the player hits the ball inside the opponent's service box and each time he hits with more depth (see table 15.4 for a completed example).

Table 15.4   Depth of Groundstroke

Inside the service box	Outside the service box
ＨＨ ＨＨ ＨＨ ＨＨ ＨＨ ＨＨ ＨＨ ＨＨ ＨＨ ＨＨ ＨＨ ＨＨ ＨＨ IIII	ＨＨ ＨＨ

From *The Tennis Parent's Bible* (www.thetennisparentsbible.com). © Frank Giampaolo.

Length of Point

Controlling matches begins with controlling points. Understanding a player's preferred shot tolerance level will assist in devising appropriate strategies and tactics. Record the number of points on which the player hits three balls or less versus four balls or more before the point ends (see table 15.5 for a completed example).

Table 15.5   Length of Point

Three or less	Four or more
‖‖‖ ‖‖‖ ‖‖‖ ‖‖‖ ‖‖‖ ‖‖‖ ‖‖‖ ‖‖‖ ‖‖‖ ‖‖‖ ‖‖‖ ‖‖‖ ‖‖‖ ‖‖‖ ‖ ‖	‖‖‖ ‖ ‖ ‖

From *The Tennis Parent's Bible* (www.thetennisparentsbible.com). © Frank Giampaolo.

Cause of Error

Detecting the actual cause of the error is the first step in the correction process. For each error in the match, place a tally mark under the appropriate reason listed (see table 15.6 for a completed example). Use sound judgment in deciding on the probable reason for the mistake.

Table 15.6   Cause of Error

Poor stroke production	Poor shot selection	Poor movement or spacing	Poor rituals, focus, or emotional control
‖‖‖ ‖‖‖ ‖‖‖ ‖‖‖ ‖‖‖ ‖‖‖ ‖‖‖ ‖‖‖	‖‖‖ ‖‖‖ ‖‖‖ ‖‖‖ ‖ ‖	‖‖‖ ‖ ‖ ‖ ‖	‖‖‖ ‖‖‖ ‖‖‖ ‖‖‖ ‖‖‖ ‖‖‖

From *The Tennis Parent's Bible* (www.thetennisparentsbible.com). © Frank Giampaolo.

Error Placement

Check the appropriate column to identify the location of each of the player's errors (see table 15.7 for a completed example). These include both forced and unforced errors. It is common that 70 percent of errors fall into the net. Remember, tennis is a "lifting" game, and the enemy is not the opponent; it's the net.

Table 15.7   Error Placement

Net	Long	Wide
‖‖‖ ‖‖‖ ‖‖‖ ‖‖‖ ‖‖‖ ‖‖‖ ‖‖‖ ‖‖‖ ‖‖‖ ‖‖‖ ‖‖‖ ‖‖‖ ‖‖‖ ‖‖‖	‖‖‖ ‖‖‖ ‖‖‖ ‖‖‖ ‖	‖‖‖ ‖‖‖ ‖‖‖ ‖ ‖ ‖ ‖

From *The Tennis Parent's Bible* (www.thetennisparentsbible.com). © Frank Giampaolo.

Unforced Errors Versus Winners

For each game, put a tally mark next to the stroke that causes an error or a winner (see table 15.8 for a completed example). Fill out one chart per set.

Table 15.8   Unforced Errors Versus Winners

Game	1	2	3	4	5	6	7	8	9	10	11	12	Tiebreak
UNFORCED ERRORS														
Forehand	/				/								
Backhand		//	/			/			/	/			
Serve	/						/						
Volley			/										
Overhead				/									
WINNERS														
Forehand	//		//		/				/	//			
Backhand							/						
Serve					/								
Volley								/					
Overhead		/				/							

From *The Tennis Parent's Bible* (www.thetennisparentsbible.com). © Frank Giampaolo.

Serving Percentage

Use tally marks in the corresponding boxes to determine serving percentages (see table 15.9 for a completed example). Is a player reaching a first-serve percentage of 65? Does the player have a winning ratio of 70 percent? Is the serve consistently directed to the opponent's weaker side? Is the player comfortably holding serve? The answers to these questions will help improve a player's game.

Table 15.9   Serving Percentage

FIRST SERVE IN		SECOND SERVE IN		SERVE LOCATION		SERVICE GAMES	
Win	**Loss**	**Win**	**Loss**	**Forehand**	**Backhand**	**Win**	**Loss**
‖‖‖‖ ‖‖‖‖ ‖‖‖‖ ‖	‖‖‖‖ ‖‖‖‖ ‖	‖‖‖‖ ‖‖	‖‖‖‖ ‖‖‖‖ ‖‖‖‖	‖‖‖‖ ‖‖‖‖ ‖‖‖‖ ‖‖‖‖ ‖	‖‖‖‖ ‖‖‖‖ ‖‖‖‖ ‖‖‖‖ ‖‖‖‖	‖‖‖‖ ‖	‖‖‖‖

From *The Tennis Parent's Bible* (www.thetennisparentsbible.com). © Frank Giampaolo.

Mega Points

In tight matches, the outcome is often decided by a few points. The player who spots and manages the game points will come out on top. In a tightly contested two-set match, there are usually 50 to 60 mega points. Record how the player does in these critical situations (see table 15.10 for a completed example).

Table 15.10   Mega Points

Won	Lost
‖‖‖‖ ‖‖‖‖ ‖‖‖‖ ‖‖‖‖ ‖‖‖‖ ‖‖	‖‖‖‖ ‖‖‖‖ ‖‖‖‖ ‖‖‖

From *The Tennis Parent's Bible* (www.thetennisparentsbible.com). © Frank Giampaolo.

While charting match play, it is often wise to dig a little deeper. Keep in mind that often, the cause of a player's error is found in the shot deployed before the error. For example, John hits a weak backhand that lands inside the opponent's short-ball range. The opponent dispenses an offensive blow to John's forehand corner. John gets to the shot, but his return misses a foot wide. John's forehand may have delivered the error, but it was his short backhand that caused the error.

In addition, remember that the style of the opponent greatly affects charting. Retrievers, for example, thrive on allowing opponents to self-destruct and provide many opportunities for them to do so. While competing against this kind of player, expect to see a rise in the unforced error total. On the other hand, opponents who are flashy but inconsistent make mistakes so quickly that they don't give their opponents much of a chance to commit errors. When playing against this kind of opponent, expect to have fewer total unforced errors.

Match charting and video analysis are powerful tools for discovering strengths and weaknesses. Use both to complete the developmental plan you've honed while reading this book, and results will immediately follow.

Index

Note: The italicized *f* and *t* following page numbers refer to figures and tables, respectively.

About the Authors

Frank Giampaolo is a veteran author whose acclaimed book, *The Tennis Parent's Bible* (www. thetennisparentsbible.com), is being used by ITF leaders, academy directors, parents, and coaches worldwide. Giampaolo's innovative approach has earned him numerous honors, including being named the 2001 USPTA Southern California Tennis Director of the Year and being voted a top teaching professional in consecutive years by *Southern California Tennis & Golf* magazine. Giampaolo founded the Mental–Emotional Tennis Workshop in 2002; since then, participants in the program have gone on to win more than 71 U.S. national titles. His students have won ATP and WTA Tour singles and doubles titles. Giampaolo pioneered the Tennis Parents Workshop in 1998 and has conducted seminars throughout the United States, Mexico, Australia, and Canada. Additionally, he hosts a blog site, www.tennisparentsolutions.com.

Frank is a popular international speaker. He has appeared on NBC's *TODAY Show*, Fox Sports, OCN World Team Tennis, Tennis Canada, and Tennis Australia. His instructional articles have appeared in *Tennis View* magazine, USPTA Coaching Publications, The Active Network, Parenting Aces, Tennis One, Tennis Australia, and Tennis New Zealand. He currently runs workshops at his high-performance training facility in Southern California.

Jon Levey has been working in sport media since 1998. From 2000 to 2009 he was a senior editor at *Tennis* magazine; five of those years were dedicated to handling all copy for the instruction section. Jon has edited hundreds of instructional articles with top coaches and former players such as Nick Bollettieri, Paul Annacone, Brad Gilbert, Nick Saviano, Stan Smith, and Tracy Austin. Jon also served as coauthor with Chris Evert on her chapter in the ESPN book *Fathers & Daughters & Sports* (2010).

Levey lives Greenwich, Connecticut.

You'll find other outstanding tennis resources at

www.HumanKinetics.com/tennis

In the U.S. call 1-800-747-4457

Australia 08 8372 0999 • Canada 1-800-465-7301
Europe +44 (0) 113 255 5665 • New Zealand 0800 222 062

HUMAN KINETICS
The Premier Publisher for Sports & Fitness
P.O. Box 5076 • Champaign, IL 61825-5076 USA

eBook
available at
HumanKinetics.com